Imagination/Space:

Essays and Talks on Fiction,
Feminism, Technology, and Politics

Imagination/Space:
Essays and Talks on Fiction,
Feminism, Technology, and Politics

by Gwyneth Jones

AQUEDUCT PRESS | SEATTLE

Aqueduct Press
PO Box 95787
Seattle WA 99145-2787
www.aqueductpress.com

Imagination/Space

First Edition: November 2009
ISBN: 978-1-933500-32-4

Library of Congress Control Number: 2009938753
9 8 7 6 5 4 3 2 1

Cover painting: "The Curie Family Investigate the Crab Nebula"
© Jennifer Mondfrans

Cover and Book Design by Kathryn Wilham
Printed in the USA by Thomson-Shore Inc.

Contents

What Is Science Fiction?

Originally presented at the Finncon Science Fiction Researchers meeting, July 2004.

First, a little bit of background. I've been writing science fiction for more than twenty years, and writing juvenile (teenage? children's?) fantasy and horror fiction for longer than that: but when I started out as a serious writer (this is hindsight, I mean, this is where I now see that I started out), I was an undergraduate at University and I wrote modern fairytales. This came about because I used to lay Tarot for my friends, but I was far too lazy to study the cards, and anyway, I quickly realized that like all fortune-tellers I was not reading the cards, I was reading the person in front of me... So, I dispensed with the cards, and I told my friends stories of destiny unfolding, with fantasy elements but set in the modern world, that somehow reflected (in my opinion) the personality and the situation I thought I saw... [Eventually, a *long* time later, the ones I liked best were published in the collection *Seven Tales and a Fable*; but that's another story...] My course at University was called The History of Ideas. I didn't do a stroke of work, but I read some interesting books, and in my way I did find the course fascinating (the period was seventeenth-century Europe: Descartes, Spinoza, Galileo et al., plus modern texts like *The Structure of Scientific Revolutions*). And it all went into the work that really engaged me. My fairytales were suffused with historical theory and seventeenth-century situations: the collision of scientific method and industrial civilization with the traditional world view, economic constraints on the feudal marriage-system, social effects of prolonged warfare. Meanwhile the only essays I ever handed in were more like weird stories, dramas, dialogues... I didn't even know that I was keen on history and the roots of things when I signed up; I just picked History because what I really wanted to do was out of reach. I'd have been amazed, and so would my tutors I'm sure, if anyone had told me then that my choice of degree course would influence my whole life. But it did.

So, that's where this session is coming from. I still, always, want to get back *ad fontes* as Erasmus advised, to see why things are the way they are; and that's why my topic today is sweeping and yet pedantic, just like a history book. What is Science Fiction? Where does it come from? I'm going to talk about some of the answers to those questions that have resonance for me, and I hope this will suggest some more generally applicable insights.

Roots

To some people it's obvious that science fiction "comes from" the pulp magazines and cheap paperbacks of the nineteen-twenties in the USA: part mass entertainment, part deliberate propaganda. To others it's equally obvious that science fiction is an offshoot of the European Gothic novel: that in fact the whole genre is descended from Mary Shelley's *Frankenstein*. Another line of descent that's often mentioned is Travel Writing, the "letters home" of official and semi-official emissaries and agents, exploring alien lands, and that makes sense too. There's also something the French call a *roman d'eclat*: a popular form that predates the cheap pulps, the sensational novel that gives its highly-colored plot an air of verisimilitude, of "fact," by incorporating non-narrative text into the fiction: newspaper reports, police interview transcriptions, advertisements, letters, court statements.

I'm going to set aside the technophile pulps for the moment. So, we have the Gothic novel of the eighteenth and nineteenth centuries, which was basically an adventure story for the middle and lower-middle classes, predominantly an Anglo-Saxon phenomenon, usually set somewhere exotic, like Italy, featuring a plot that flirts with the supernatural without ever quite making the leap. I see the Gothic novel as a determined effort on the part of writers and readers (remembering that both writers and readers are *consumers* of the paraliterature; we writers imagine what we enjoy imagining and then try to get the market to place a value on our fantasies) to reclaim for adults the spookiness and the thrills of traditional horror stories (sometimes known as fairytales), and make them contemporary. Gothic thrills—headless monks, evil banditti, innocent young women spirited off and condemned to die imprisoned in sinister convents—may also have represented an escape from censorship: permission, under license, to admit that death, disease, and other dirty secrets had not been banished from the Industrial Revolution world of progress and reform and "rational, scientific explanations."

Travel writing, on the other hand, isn't supposed to be fiction. The official or semi-official agent of the State (or maybe agent of a great merchant house) is supposed to be collecting reliable information, for trade or diplomacy or aggression. The traveler who "reports back" affirms the value of his (or her) own culture by using its standards as a measure of civilization: like the emissaries of the Emperor of China, two thousand years ago, "reporting back" from Afghanistan the astonishing fact that there were cities outside the Middle Kingdom, intelligent extraterrestrials, even, who lived in streets of houses, exactly like human beings…! Needless to say, just as the wandering storyteller of the oral tradition drew a larger audience by making the news "nouvelles" he (or she) presented more colorful, literate travelers would often be tempted to exaggerate or to recount as fact what they knew had been told to them as fable or malign invention. You can get some very interesting and weird aliens into your report, if you listen to what enemies say about each other. Demons, amazons, people with heads growing out of their chests. (See Herodotus…)

Gothic novels *rescued* some degree of thrilling supernatural dread from the encroaching tide of reason: travel writing developed the tools of world-building, cultural relativism, and tall tales, so they were ready to hand for the Utopian writers (like Thomas More, for instance, in sixteenth-century England) who wanted to describe "another country, where they do things differently"—for satirical or political reasons. The *roman d'eclat*—for which I'd take as my type, following the great French critic of fantastic literature, Jean Marigny, Bram Stoker's *Dracula*, published in 1897—is a further advance toward science fiction, a big step beyond *Frankenstein*. Predictably, getting closer to sf doesn't mean an advance in literary merit. *Dracula* is popular, mass-market fiction, but here we have a gothic novel that's fully engaged with the supernatural and at the same time with *la vie moderne*, in Baudelaire's sense. Stoker's characters, including the monster, are plunged into contemporary public life, in the crowd, in the city, and in the streets. The fireside story is told through the media of steam and telegraph-driven, globe-trotting Late-Victorian society (with an opening straight from the Victorian Rough Guide to Transylvania). The sensational drama, instead of being recounted by an omniscient observer of private events, has become literally "news," and storytelling has caught up with itself, has made a leap in scale and addresses the global village.

The Sublime

So much for genealogy. You could also look at the growth of the mass audience, with a newly-leisured and literate urban proletariat, or at the lucky invention of cheap, poor-quality wood-pulp paper. At last! After four hundred years of those annoying consumer durables, books with built-in obsolescence! But although it's interesting to trace the family tree of paraliterature, this approach only tells you how the tools developed; it doesn't tell you much about the ideas that put the tools to use. Did science fiction start happening *after* all these components were in place? I don't think so. In fact, I think there's very good reason to place the birth of science fiction in the Romantic period of European arts-history: but not exclusively in that one novel by Mary Shelley. There's a concept, an aesthetic concept called "the sublime," defined here by Edmund Burke, which I find very illuminating.

> WHATEVER is fitted in any sort to excite the ideas of pain and danger, that is to say, whatever is in any sort terrible, or is conversant about terrible objects, or operates in a manner analogous to terror, is a source of the *sublime;* that is, it is productive of the strongest emotion which the mind is capable of feeling. I say the strongest emotion, because I am satisfied the ideas of pain are much more powerful than those which enter on the part of pleasure. Without all doubt, the torments which we may be made to suffer are much greater in their effect on the body and mind, than any pleasure which the most learned voluptuary could suggest, or than the liveliest imagination, and the most sound and exquisitely sensible body, could enjoy. Nay,

I am in great doubt whether any man could be found, who would earn a life of the most perfect satisfaction, at the price of ending it in the torments, which justice inflicted in a few hours on the late unfortunate regicide in France. But as pain is stronger in its operation than pleasure, so death is in general a much more affecting idea than pain; because there are very few pains, however exquisite, which are not preferred to death: nay, what generally makes pain itself, if I may say so, more painful, is, that it is considered as an emissary of this king of terrors. When danger or pain press too nearly, they are incapable of giving any delight, and are simply terrible; but at certain distances, and with certain modifications, they may be, and they are, delightful, as we every day experience.

The full text of Burke's "A Philosophical Inquiry into the Origin of Our Ideas of The Sublime and Beautiful" is available on line here: http://www.bartleby.com/24/2/

This idea of "the sublime"—a kind of beauty so huge in scale it's completely divorced from moral or sensual sweetness — was extremely popular around the turn of the nineteenth century. You can see this as a fashion-revolt against the artificial formal perfection of the previous generation, or a reaction to the chaos of the French Revolution, or a by-product of the fact that leisured, educated Anglo-Saxons were getting out more and actually *seeing* great big snowy mountains and ghastly huge caverns… You can see the idea of "the sublime"—which doesn't necessarily deny the existence of God, but chooses to confront the universe *without* the comfort of religion—as dating back to antiquity, or to Petrarch's famous venture onto Mont Ventoux (which was often quoted, when I was an undergraduate, as the first expression of the modern mind). But something different, maybe even something new, happened when the idea of the sublime met the scientific revolutions of the Romantic period. Here's another quotation:

> …and over these
> The jagged alligator and the might
> Of earth-convulsing behemoth, which once
> Were monarch beasts, and on the slimy shores,

And weed-overgrown continents of the earth
Increased and multiplied like summer worms
On an abandoned corpse, til the blue globe
Wrapped deluge round it like a cloak, and they
Yelled, gasped and were abolished; or some God
Whose throne was in a comet, passed and cried
"Be not!" And like my words, they were no more…

—Shelley, from *Prometheus Unbound*

That's from Percy Shelley's *Prometheus Unbound,* a revolutionary narrative all about Man (and Woman too, as I'm sure the poet would have agreed) breaking free from the tyranny of outworn patriarchal creeds and restraints. But the illustrations Shelley chooses for this mighty theme are taken from the thrilling and disturbing scientific discoveries of his time, specifically, here, the fossil discoveries made by people like the extraordinary Mary Anning on the south coast of England: the dinosaur bones that were opening up, as never before in Anglo-Saxon culture, the vistas of geological time. These days, when we hear a news item that adds or subtracts a few billion years from the age of the universe (the cosmologists and astrophysicists do that, occasionally, don't they), it does not raise a shudder. It's hard to get hold of what geological time meant to people who were convinced the world had been made specially for Adam and that the whole thing was around seven and a half thousand years old (give or take a week). It's hard to grasp the shock of that inhuman leap in scale…but Shelley tries. With a special-effects budget that restricts him to words and meter, he does his best to create some huge, gosh-wow George Lucas special effects. This is the feeling that we call "sense of wonder" in modern sf. I've never found that expression adequate; it sounds like a child meeting a Christmas tree; it sounds far too harmless. But sublime, yes. Now that's what it's about.

Unfortunately for Percy Shelley, epic poetry was about to go out of style, whereas the novel was to remain popular, so it was Mary's Frankenstein and his reanimated patchwork corpse who survived to reach Hollywood and the real mass market. If it had been the other way round, who knows, maybe he'd be getting called the Founding Father of hard science fiction… But encounters with the sublime, although there will always be room for more waltzing spaceships and exploding Death Stars, can sometimes be insidiously intimate. The most disturbing, thrilling discoveries of our day are not happening on the scale of geological time or galactic space (those vastnesses now seem empty of threat). They are happening in neuroscience, where the staggering technology of the digital age is enabling us to investigate our own consciousness: the place where the picture we have of the universe really lives, the self that thinks and feels. And for those still trying to believe that human beings are the Crown of Creation, it's not good news…

> The tent was bigger than it had seemed from the outside. She looked into the booths around the inner walls and was disappointed to find that most of the things you could try involved getting hooked up to computers. Fiorinda liked playing fantasy games, but on the whole information technology had passed her by. Her childhood in the cold house had left her convinced that she could never catch up. A few people were examining a coffin sized cigar-shaped cylinder on a giant swivel arrangement.
>
> 'What's this?' she asked the Zen Selfer who seemed to be in charge.
>
> 'It's a centrifuge,' said the young man briskly. 'You get in there. We subject your body to stresses equivalent to several gravities. You lose consciousness.'
>
> 'Is that fun?'
>
> 'Well, it's interesting, because on the way out you will have a Near Death Experience. Anyone can have a Near Death Experience. There doesn't have to be a pathological reason. As the blood leaves your brain you get the tunnel vision, you see the bright light, you feel you're floating, you seem to be outside your body. You reach a beautiful place, you may feel you are being judged, you'll meet the people you love most, you won't want to come back. The whole thing. It's simply what G-LOC does to the Cephalic Nervous System. Want to have a go?'
>
> 'Um.'

'We give you a medical check first.'

'What's it about, though?'

'It's about consciousness. That's what all our stuff's about. You can get your brain imaged in action, you can get hooked up and see your own 40 hertz oscillations. You can see a real time simulation of the information-loading in the hydrophobic protein sacs of the neuronic cytoskeleton; or you can try the blindsight experiment. Over there, you can get the two halves of your brain virtually dissociated and experience being two people: try to contact your right-brain self. Or you could do the collapsed wave-function experiment—'

'Thanks for explaining everything. I think I'll just—'

'Most people,' said the young man, 'do the reductionist things first. Then they listen to Olwen. That's also somewhere to start. There's a workshop beginning now.'

In the centre of the tent there was a low, circular wooden staging. A woman in a yellow sari and a crimson blouse was walking about on this stage in front of a projection screen, fussing with her laser pointer and checking over her props: an amaryllis lily in a tall glass vase, a cage of white rats on a table, graduated plastic models of animal brains; a detailed plastic human brain that came apart. That must be Olwen Devi, the Zen Self guru. Fiorinda moved inward, as ready to listen to a lecture on the science of consciousness as she was to do anything. She sat on the grass, which here around the stage was uncovered, and remarkably green.

Olwen Devi led the group, which had grown to about fifty people, through some relaxation exercises, designed to be performed by a close-ranked, seated audience. She talked about the extraordinary range of things we do, in which intentionality does not play the part we imagine: courtship, friendship, decision-making, learning, ambition; then about the animals that do things we would call human. Ant farmers, bird artists, altruistic vampire bats, duplicitous monkeys. 'It seems we must either award self-awareness to the ants,' said Olwen Devi, 'or accept that hominids may have practiced agriculture, and buried their dead with ceremony, before they reached the threshold that we have crossed—the state of *being conscious of being conscious*. Think of this. When you decide to perform an action (reach out your hand) the neuro-muscular preparation for that movement has already begun: around 350 milliseconds *before* the onset of volition. We act first, then we decide to act. We 'think' first, then we know we are thinking. This can be shown by experiment. Perhaps our self awareness is merely an observer, after the fact.'

Someone raised a hand. 'But couldn't that reversal mean, guruji, that self-consciousness is a quantum effect, and not controlled by the time's arrow illusion?'

'It could be.'

Many of the students, or punters, had adopted the lotus posture. Fiorinda knelt, sitting back on her heels, her thoughts reverting to the hard lesson that *Rufus wasn't here*, that he wasn't going to turn up and she might as well leave. Part of her still didn't believe it. She was irrationally convinced that staying on would somehow make him appear.

'It could be that consciousness, the experience of being conscious, puts us in touch with a plenum, the sum of all states, where the arrow's direction is lost. Erwin Schrodinger once said, if we cannot find ourselves in our world picture—meaning that image of the world which is the work we do in our brains—it is because the sentient self *is itself* the world picture.'

What's all this to me? wondered Fio.

—The Zen Self Tent, *from* "Innocence and Experience,"
Bold As Love, Gwyneth Jones, 37-39

Times change, and also, although I enjoy *Star Wars*' special effects on the big screen, I'm not a huge fan as a writer... But I think I'm still trying to do the same as Shelley (which is something different from the moral fable of Mary's *Frankenstein*). This is the twenty-first century, where the street finds its own uses for the technology, and William Gibson's children are *never* going to be impressed by the infinite spaces between the stars. It's important for my contemporary style that I use the workshop, lab-science jargon rather than poetic language; and it's important that the shock and awe encounter with the sublime is given a disrespectful reception (as the Zen Self techie reels off the details that destroy the possibility of human free will and self-conscious action, "Oh" says Fiorinda). But I'm still reacting, aesthetically, to the cutting edge of knowledge and responding to the naked, elemental beauty of a universe that keeps on making human beings feel smaller, and smaller, and smaller...but, paradoxically, can't diminish us. Maybe we don't have the control we thought we had, but we're still the ones doing the talking!

The Grotesque (Strangeness Is Real)

The Romantic poets and painters and composer-performer rock stars like Beethoven, Chopin, and Liszt were inspired by turbulent political times, whether or not they approved of the Rights of Man or of violent revolutions; and they enjoyed—especially the late-comers—an unprecedented economic independence as artists. Maybe Shelley's image of those antediluvian monsters replicating "like summer worms in an abandoned corpse" just comes from a punkish desire to shock, which he could exercise with impunity. It could equally be a reference to the Napoleonic decades of permanent warfare, or even to sights from his own travels.

The thrilling period of discoveries and upheavals was followed (as we've noted) by a century of explosive economic growth. For paraliterature of all kinds, this meant a huge new audience, in cities and towns; but the explosive growth of spiritual independence that Shelley dreamed of proved much more elusive. For Franz Kafka, son of a domineering Jewish shopkeeper in a dependent state of the mighty Austro-Hungarian empire, there was certainly no escape from patriarchal tyranny.

As Gregor Samsa awoke one morning from uneasy dreams he found himself transformed in his bed into a gigantic insect. He was lying on his hard, as it were armor-plated, back, and when he lifted his head a little he could see his domelike brown belly divided into stiff arched segments on top of which the bed quilt could hardly stay in place and was about to slide off completely. His numerous legs, which were pitifully thin compared to the rest of his bulk, waved helplessly before his eyes. What has happened to me? he thought. It was no dream. His room, a regular human bedroom, only rather too small, lay quiet within its four familiar walls. Above the table on which a collection of cloth samples was unpacked and spread out—Samsa was a traveling salesman—hung the picture, which he had recently cut out of an illustrated magazine and put into a pretty gilt frame. It showed a lady, with a fur hat on and a fur stole, sitting upright and holding out to the spectator a huge fur muff into which the whole of her forearm had vanished! Gregor's eyes turned next to the window, and the overcast sky—one could hear raindrops beating on the window gutter—made him quite melancholy. What about sleeping a little longer and forgetting all this nonsense, he thought, but it could not be done, for he was accustomed to sleep on his right side and in his present condition he could not turn himself over. However violently he forced himself toward his right side he always rolled onto his back again. He tried it at least a hundred times, shutting his eyes to keep from seeing his struggling legs, and only desisted when he began to feel in his side a faint dull ache he had never felt before...

—Franz Kafka, "The Metamorphosis"

That's the opening of a very famous novella called "The Metamorphosis," written in 1915 (around twenty years after *Dracula*, and in the first year of the Great War, just to keep track...), though not published until after Kafka's death. As some of you will know, first he wakes up a cockroach, and then things really start to go downhill... Why has Gregor become a cockroach? Well, maybe it's Freudian—sexual—to do with that domineering father. Maybe it's political commentary, maybe it's something to do with encroaching sickness: maybe "becoming an insect" was Kafka's code for "becoming a writer"—a distasteful, inescapable transformation that alienates friends and family. Maybe it's about the mean and narrow laws of bourgeois society that turn human beings into vermin. Take your choice. What I see is not Kafka's intention, which remains mysterious and multifaceted, but a technique. A positive, totally non-whimsical use of the fantastic, completely *unlike* the European literature called "the Fantastic," which aims to leave the reader in a state of troubling uncertainty. And equally unlike the "Magical Realism" of the Americas, where passages of whimsical, impossible imagery highlight the characters' emotional states, temporarily interrupting the mimesis. Gregor wakes up a cockroach, and *this is no dream*. (I have to say, I'd have advised against the assertion "it was no dream," if Franz had been in my class. Although it's perfectly in character for Gregor, it could be taken as a sign of weakness. We're supposed to avoid that kind of pathetic plea for reader-acceptance, these days.) No matter why the cockroach turned up, Kafka has realized he can skip the middle term (no figure of speech, no explanation that this is a paranoid delusion, or a spell, or a genetic experiment gone wrong). He can apply the rules of mimesis to the unreal, seamlessly, and confront the reader with something utterly *strange*.

The grotesque is an aesthetic category that's been around—like the sublime—for a long time: the term itself dates from the Renaissance, when the gentry were fond of scattering weird statuary around the grottos (*grotteschi*) in their elaborate gardens. It had another flowering (so to speak) in Europe between the two great wars: the Europe of fascism and (I'm not trying to make a connection) the development of some fearsome atomic physics. It adds something to the world-picture of science fiction that the gosh-wow special effects leave out of the account. Nothing is real. Solid objects are illusion, time and space can be distorted or wiped out... It seems the more we get to know about this universe, the more we find that it is not only vast and pitiless, it is also irreducibly bizarre, and wickedly unstable as a nightmare. Here's another ugly awakening, from *Castles Made of Sand*.

> Next thing Fiorinda knew, she was in bed and Sage was fuck-ing her. A moment at the wellspring, the wingspan sweep of his shoulders, his taper waist, the beautiful muscles of his bum... but no. *This is not Sage*. She was in the nightmare, the worst nightmare. She fought out of it and lay there shuddering. No

one to call, no comfort. The evening wouldn't come back to her. Damn. I must've got drunk. She couldn't remember what she'd said to Fergal, or what he'd said; the whole conversation was gone. Fuck. I'm an idiot. Something moved heavily beside her in the dark. A body turning over, a disgusting waft of carrion breath. Oh, shit, thought Fiorinda. *Shit!* What the fuck possessed me—?

Fergal put the bedside light on and there he was, propped on one elbow, his coarse-grained face and aging, geezer's body, rusty mat of hair around his nipples, slackened flesh over middle-aged muscle, red tan stops at the throat and the rest is cheesy-white. Then he laughed, and all thought of dealing with this daft, embarrassing situation ended.

For a moment Sage was there: a perfect simulacrum, except for the malevolence.

Fiorinda shot out of bed and grabbed her kimono.

'*Who are you?*'

Sage was gone. Fergal sat up, legs over the side of the bed. He had an erection, but his sea-green eyes were blank, bewildered. He looked like an old man in hospital. 'I'm dead.'

'*What?*'

'Oh Jaysus, I'm dead, can't someone kill me?'

'Of course I won't kill you. I don't kill people. What the fuck's going on?'

'Augh! This can't be right. Why the bluidy hell can't someone do something?'

His eyes came into focus. For a moment someone she had never met before was staring at her, out of such naked fathomless fear and agony it caught her breath—

The entryphone light on the wall by the bed was winking.

Fergal leaned towards it and listened. 'Aye,' he said, 'come up.'

She ran into the living-room. This is going to be bad, I'm an id-iot, *why* am I here alone? Because we are wild and free, citizens of Utopia. Because I'm supposed to be safe, Brixton is my… The door opened. Three big, Celtic-style barmy army types came in. Oh yes, she thought, I remember. Fergal took over. One of the men grabbed her. She didn't struggle or scream. If I'm to die, I'd die before I could be reached. If not, I don't want this public, not until I *think*. The other two started going through the room.

'What are you looking for?' she asked, calmly.

'Something they can use,' said Fergal Kearney, coming out of the bedroom, and she noticed that the brogue had gone out of his voice. He was dressed. He sat at the back of the big open room, turning a chair to face the scene that Fiorinda and the three men made: very relaxed, one leg crossed over the other. She didn't understand, and then she did, because one of the barmies had found Elsie.

Poor Elsie, she's not half as tough as she makes out. She was scared out of her mind, so cowed she didn't even spit until the men began to hurt her. Then she spat and clawed and bit and yowled and struggled, but it didn't do her any good. Fiorinda yelled, 'STOP IT!' and 'LEAVE HER ALONE YOU BAS-TARDS! WHAT DO YOU WANT?' But they weren't going to stop, whatever Fiorinda surrendered. This wasn't that kind of torture. There was only one way to stop what was happening.

The agonised little body went limp.

The two men put Elsie down on the rug, tried her eyes and shook her a bit.

'The cat's dead, Rufus,' said one of them, doubtfully.

Fergal laughed. (No. That's not Fergal Kearney. It never was.) A rumble of soft thunder. A body that belies its occupant. Behind him on the wall Mr Preston and Mr Pender were taking sherry, in a clear, cool, dispassionate light… She was conscious of the grip on her arms as something that was happening far away, but acutely, immediately conscious of each breath she took. The sound of air taken in, the expansion of her lungs. The cat's little mad presence trotting around the flat, insistent lap-seeking missile. She loves Ax best. She loves him with all her tiny heart. But Sage and I, we can be useful occasionally. We know where the food is, we'll watch when she shows off.

'What do you want?'

'I want you.'

She stared at him, fighting her thoughts into order, fighting terror and bewilderment: seeing the long masquerade, stunned and yet not surprised. The first time I met Fergal Kearney, I felt sick to death… *But Fergal saved Ax's life!* Oh, he didn't want Ax dead. That would have been too easy and too quick, he wanted to *destroy* Ax. That's what this has been about. He's not going to kill me either. He doesn't have to rape me, he can take me any time, he just did it. No, he's not going to kill me. He wants more than that.

The smile that Fergal's face was wearing sat uneasily in the facial muscles of a difficult, diffident loser of a dead artist. 'This is nothing,' he said. 'This is just so you know where we are at. If you're wise, you'll tell no one. Think about your options.'

—From "The Night Belongs To Fiorinda" *Castles Made of Sand*, Gwyneth Jones, 321-324

I don't know what Kafka "meant" by "Metamorphosis." I can unpack a couple of layers of my own meaning. The dead man walking, who has been taken over by Fiorinda's monster of a father, to be used as his instrument of torture, is a political comment. This is a modern fairytale about a time of social and scientific revolution, and Rufus O'Niall, Fiorinda's father, represents the eternal patriarchal tyranny, the big callous agencies of power, who use "dead men" with no will of their own—brutalized soldiers, deluded paramilitaries, armed opposition groups, gun-crazy street-gangs—to control and punish any opposition to their plans... I could go further and say Fiorinda's impotence is my own.

The dead man walking, however, is also a real person. I found him in a report on consciousness by a writer called John McCrone, who describes the case of a man who had both his hippocampi burned out by disease. These two little organs, buried deep in your brain, are somehow crucial for the formation and retention of memory. The man without them lived in a perpetual moment, and yet, although he no longer seemed able to perceive duration, he was convinced he was dead and would say, in lucid flashes, just as I report here "I'm dead, won't somebody kill me..." It seems we don't need God or judgment. Eternal torment, neuroscience style, is something that can just *happen*... That's a very frightening thought. And yet (I don't know whether Franz Kafka felt this too, but I sort of suspect he did), I find some kind of saving grace in contemplating the ugly, unmanageable reality of strangeness. By my reckoning, writers who use the fantastic as decoration or metaphor, and regard mimesis as the true record, are missing the point. They're out of touch: I'm the one who's writing about the real world. I may be crazy, with my weird visions of other planets and nightmare creatures; but I'm no crazier than God.

A Literature of Ideas (Progress Is Real?)

Prometheus was the Titan who stole fire from heaven (in Greek myth), representing us; and he was sentenced to be chained to a rock having his liver torn out, forever. *Prometheus Unbound*, generally held to be Shelley's masterpiece, is a four-act verse drama about the perfectibility of the human race. In the last act, Man, freed from the yoke of tyranny (and Woman too, of course, but I said that didn't I...) immediately sets about building an ideal society. Prometheus, as the scholars among you will know, is Greek for *the one who looks forward*. He could be the patron saint of Science Fiction, but the last quote I've brought along isn't fictional (well, not in the conventional sense: it's an extract from a political speech).

> I have a dream that one day this nation will rise up and live out the true meaning of its creed— "We hold these truths to be self evident, that all men are created equal."

I have a dream that one day on the red hills of Georgia the sons of former slaves and the sons of former slaveowners will be able to sit down together at the table of brotherhood.

I have a dream that one day even the state of Mississippi, a desert state sweltering with the heat of injustice and oppression, will be transformed into an oasis of freedom and justice.

I have a dream that my four little children will one day live in a nation where they will not be judged by the color of their skin but by the content of their character.

I have a dream today.

> Martin Luther King, "I Have a Dream" Speech
> August 28, 1963, Lincoln Memorial, Washington DC

I didn't bring a fictional quote, because in this category I don't think the fiction has anything to add. From out and proud Utopians like Kim Stanley Robinson (the Mars Trilogy, *The Years of Rice and Salt*) to writers and editors (like the notorious John W. Campbell or Isaac Asimov) with a distinctly patriarchal and tyrannous vision of the ideal state, science fiction can only repeat the real world manifestos on "Progress" toward the ideal state—with varying optimism and pessimism, sincerity or cynicism. Personally (although I was born in a socialist Utopia, all built on borrowed US money, hahaha) I think it's an extremely slippery, slightly repellent concept: it happens, obviously; it isn't a straightforward progression, obviously…small steps forward, giant leaps backward, major problems of scaling. But that's by the way. "Progress" isn't really the issue, it's the manifesto itself.

Science fiction is often called a literature of ideas, but it would be more accurate to say science fiction writers tend to be idealists. Note that this doesn't mean the ideals or ideas have to be intelligent, or humane, or "good" by any standards. It certainly doesn't mean the genre is dominated by great thinkers of the twenty-first century. But the most hack-written science-free spaceship fantasy has a tincture of commitment to something other than the here and now, something other than any individual's personal drama. In space opera, galactic empires are won at the price of billions of wasted lives. In science fiction novels, characters live and die in the shadow of some great idea or purpose, whether it's in the lab or on the barricades or on the bridge of the Starship Enterprise. Their emotional fulfillment—love, pleasure, status—always comes second: the big idea always takes precedence. Just pause a moment to think about what this means and how contrary such a state of mind is to the zeitgeist of our disillusioned, appetite driven times; where *idealist* (with or without any reference to Plato) is about the dirtiest word left.

Is it a good thing or a bad thing, intrinsically, to feel that life, every-day happiness, is something that happens in the background, while the great adventure sweeps you away? I'm not sure, but, contrary to popular opinion, I don't think it's entirely bad, and I do think that it can make life sweeter. Maybe (as a result of historical accident or genetic predisposition or both) it's the way I'd like to live myself, and that's why I keep on writing in this strange style.

Romantics

The only brief I had for this session was that I was to talk to you about something that would interest science fiction researchers. I don't know if I've managed to do that, but I'm sure you must have noticed the intriguing way I brought along three texts that aren't science fiction at all. I suppose I did this partly because I often find myself acting as an ambassador, presenting "science fiction" to teenager or adults who feel that sf is a strange, alien, inexplicable growth on the body of popular literature, so I got into the habit of looking for links, looking for proof of continuity. There usually is continuity in the History of Ideas. Romantic poets did it; politicians do it; bleak Bohemian satirists did it. What could be more normal than that? I often manage to persuade them—as I've persuaded myself—that science fiction was not invented by William Gibson, nor by John W. Campbell, nor by H.G. Wells. It has a history of at least two hundred years, which can be traced back not to a single maverick novel, but to a major aesthetic movement in literature, music, art, and poetry, which flowered, curiously enough, in times rather like our own: when science was leaping forward, the ideals of the Enlightenment and Progress had fallen catastrophically from grace, and all Europe was in a ferment of change.

You Can Read It Like a Detective Story: Understanding Genre Fiction

Paul Bleton. *Ça Se Lit Comme Un Roman Policier,* Québec, Éditions Nota bene, coll. «Études culturelles», 1999

First published in Paradoxa, ed. David Willingham, Vol. 5,
1999-2000, 397-403.

Comment peut-on lire des histoires pareilles? How can you read that
kind of stuff? It's strange but true, as a reader of genre fiction (and particularly as a reader of science fiction and fantasy) one does encounter
active hostility to the activity. This hasn't happened to me often, perhaps
because I'm certainly not M. Bleton's dedicated *lecteur seriel*, but more of
an occasional dabbler; yet I do meet that reaction of outrage, and it always startles me. The antagonism of devoted genre readers (fans) to high-
culture, mainstream literature is, at first glance, more understandable. It's
the resentment of the underdog, the low in status. But why on earth does
the reading of debased literature by people with poor taste arouse ire, instead of pity or tolerance, among the learned? You'd think they'd be glad
we were reading anything at all. What is the threat, the challenge, that
fuels such aggression? This collection of essays, *Ça Se Lit Comme Un Roman Policier,* has some answers to suggest. But primarily, Paul Bleton sets
out to investigate the "genre of reading" involved in reading genre fiction,
to examine its competences and to establish an identity for this genre-of-
reading as an activity valid in itself, essentially distinct from, rather than
inferior to, more socially and intellectually acceptable forms.

It has to be admitted, however, that *belles lettres* bigots will find much
in Paul Bleton's analysis that confirms their worst suspicions. The reading
of genre fiction as essentially *serial* fiction, which is central to Bleton's
thesis, necessarily involves concentration on that part of the book we can
collectively refer to as the *paratext*—the repetition of trainspotter details:

the intense recognition of an eponymous hero in twenty-five different tranches of his adventurous career; the allegiance to an imprint, an editor, a style of cover art, a pseudonym and its variations. From the "book least like a book possible," the serial story in newsprint, to the modern *culture bédéistique*, the serial (genre) reader stands accused of using fiction like a drug, or like a hot water bottle, or like a prostitute—for comfort or for (adult) relaxation rather than for edification; of being interested in absolutely anything about the book except the quality of the prose. If this is the accusation, *Ça Se Lit* doesn't really attempt to mount a convincing defense. The overlap between different essays (chapters), making for repeated iteration of the paratext details, exaggerates the effect, but I felt this to be a real difficulty. To an extent, *Ça Se Lit* confirms everything you ever feared about genre reading, about its pernicious non-prose, about its ruthless anti-art libidinal aims.

But what are the specific characteristics of this type of reading? Genre reading is a consumer activity, which developed as part of the nineteenth-century industrialization of leisure. Paul Bleton covers the ground on this angle—reminding us, for instance, that *pulp* fiction is a term with a concrete meaning, involving the innovation of cheap, wood-pulp paper that made mass-market fiction economically viable. He stresses that genre fiction makes a commercial contract with the reader, where certain goods are promised and must be delivered, and obeys the law of the mass market—make as many as you can and make them as near to identical as you can, while yet convincing the consumers to buy more and more of these well-nigh identical products. Hence the eponymous hero, the strongly identified imprint and cover design, the endless sequels: all the factors signaling or promising exactly the same thing over and over and over again. On the other hand, the project of reading a genre fiction *is serial*. It does not dwell on the pleasing arrangement of words in a sentence. It follows a succession of "things in a line" (or events in a plot) in a single-minded drive from A to B, from mystery to solution, driving *un sillon à travers le texte*, to paraphrase Barthes. It is this ideal, above all, that drives a wedge between the serial reader as reader and the serious reader of literature. The serial reader judges the book not on individual merits, after the fact, but on its conformity with a previously established model. He or she respects the skill of the writer only in so far as this skill (or art) remains invisible. The words have to be there, but they must be "transparent," they must not attract or (heaven forbid) *require* attention. Only the story is important. These attitudes—the formula is valued above the example, the cover art above the art of words—combine to form a shocking assault, however naïve, on conventional literary values.

And yet, Paul Bleton argues, this genre of reading is not deficient, in its own terms of reference. Genres of genre fiction (sf, fantasy, crime fiction, romance, etc.) have each their appropriate, albeit unfrocked establishment, with conventions of criticism, conferences and journals, shibboleths and sacred cows. Not only are there traditionally trained academics (such as M. Bleton) who specialize in the genres, there are also fan authors, fan experts, fan critics, self-taught and contemptuous of normal academic standards, but likely to startle the academic bystander with their narrow yet deep erudition. Paul Bleton recounts a conversation (at a *bédé* convention, naturally!) in which two sf fans with differing loyalties discuss the relationship between an obscure, decades-old paraliterature text (*Les Fleurs Pouvantes*) and a modern, psychothriller imprint of the same name. But is this depth of knowledge anything more than mere trainspotting? Is there a difference between the fact-filled fan of science fiction and the *idiot savant* who mechanically stores away endless lists of train numbers for no reason at all beyond the mindless pleasure of seeing the list grow and filling in the gaps?

The answer to this question brings us to one of the central propositions of *Ça se Lit*: the "encyclopedia of reference" that is developed by the habitual genre reader. While consciously (or mechanically) pursuing the non-literary hobby of reading every single Hercule Poirot novel and story, or searching the secondhand bookshops for that infinitely desirable missing volume to complete his (or her) collection of Patrick Moore's early juvenile sf stories, the genre reader is unconsciously amassing a store of effective knowledge. The very fact that these stories are in many ways well-nigh indistinguishable from each other means that this information can be acquired, and subsequently accessed, on an effortless, intuitive level. Bleton gives the example of the romantic heroine, who grows pale and goes off her food, whereupon of course the experienced genre reader knows she is in love. I consider this rather too mild and hackneyed, a cliché so clichéd it hardly deserves the name. But if our heroine is not seen around in the daytime, avoids mirrors, and has a strong aversion to garlic, I think any normal genre reader would speedily spot what was going on. While quite unconscious of any intellectual effort, the genre reader may become a virtuoso at the art of *knowing what is going on* in a story. A scrap of ostensibly innocent dialogue can unveil horror, a single incident or circumstance can pinpoint the outcome from chapter one. No amount of authorial hand-waving can prevent the virtuoso romance or thriller reader from recognizing instantly which girl is going to get the guy or which characters are going to survive and which succumb to the serial killer. Anyone who decries this fiction as "formulaic" has missed the point. The genre reader reads the story (again) not to find out what happens, but to find out how it happens this time. Like the audience of classic Greek drama (or so I was taught, long ago), or the Commedia del' Arte audience in renaissance Italy, readers are assumed to know "what's going on" before the show starts, and though for many the skills involved may remain unconscious, "knowing what is going on" does not necessarily compromise a genuinely sophisticated appreciation.

The furrow driven through the text of *Ça se Lit* takes as its starting point the fighting fantasy "novel" in which *vous etes l'heros*—and compares this most stripped-down of genre fiction experiences with a current scholarly definition of genre fiction (Daniel Couégnas, *Introduction à la paralittérature*), teasing out the misconceptions of the academic view. Skipping from one numbered paragraph to another, moving a hundred pages forward or twenty backwards according to one's guess at the outcome of an episode, clearly involves something different from mere bland simplification of the reading experience. Reading is being used not *deficiently* here, but as a means to a non-literary end. With the proviso that I have never known an adult, not even the most trainspotteresque, to take fighting fantasy seriously, this juvenile sub-genre of the adventure story certainly demonstrates the ludic, technoscientific element in genre fiction at its most extreme. This same theme of the book as game or puzzle emerges again after the conventional "mainstream" identity of genre fiction has been critically analyzed. Serial reading is straight-line reading, but the line may turn back on itself, self-referentially and knowingly, until that straight line becomes a paranoid, convoluted labyrinth. The expert genre writer knows about that "encyclopedia of reference" and can play on (and with) the reader's expertise. A "polar" or *roman policier* can be a version of *Hamlet* in modern dress: Shakespearean characters and puns hinting at the outcome of the police procedural. A step further still (to continue Bleton's argument into my own experience), and the detailed conventions of the genre can be invoked, according to critic John Clute, to give an anti-genre message*s*—as in the science fiction of seventies feminist Joanna Russ, who has absolutely no intention of telling a tale of technophile, patriarchal romance. A step beyond polemic, and the game of reference and allusion can become an absurd obsession in itself. I particularly enjoyed, as a genre writer with obsessive tendencies, Bleton's description of the novel *Le Mytheux*, by an inveterate pair of *polar* game-players, Henri Viard and Bernard Zacharias, which is, as I understood the anecdote, laden with skillful references to an obscure play by Alfred de Musset (a secret content they then felt obliged to reveal in the text, so that it would not blush entirely unseen by the police-novel reading public… Oh, I have been that writer!). But strangely enough, this reading of the book (by writer and by reader) as a contest of wits and skill, brings us in full circle, to something like the ideal, receptive passivity of the classic *bon lecteur*. At its most baroque development, the richness of a genre text of this teasing kind, the sheer multiplicity of references, achieves a surface of complete naturalism, realism, with just the occasional *clin d'oeil* to alert the attentive reader to the nature of the game.

However rich, genre reading is never pure art. It remains a transaction, both commercial and libidinal. By citing pornographic and erotic fiction, Bleton uncovers the shameless, positive desire that lies behind that traditional negative euphemism "escapist." The genre reader is not so much fleeing reality as rushing toward pleasure: sexual gratification, cathartic emotion, the adrenalin thrill of danger. The classic adventure-hero story aims to deliver, quite frankly, triggers to hormonal release buried deep in the psyche, and the serial reading experience promises the ideal delight of a pleasure always reliable, always repeatable. In this sense an outright pornographic novel (moments of intensity, Bleton suggests, strung out on a thread of improbable incidents) bears the same relation to more decorous genre fiction as the *vous etes l'heros* in the case of fiction-as-game. The thread of incident may be more carefully crafted; the pleasure principle remains the same. It is this frankly libidinal purpose that links genre fiction, as Bleton argues, not to the past, to an oral tradition of storytelling, but to the *culture médiatique* of the present day. Rejecting the received wisdom that genre fiction is a poor descendent of the oral tradition, a kind of living fossil, he sees it as part of an ongoing proliferation into the niches of the mass-market, a lawless hybridization between text and tv, movies, *bédé* (of course), computer games, any possible medium of the future.

I found it fascinating to read a book about genre fiction seen from the point of view of a different culture, and also from the point of view of a different genre. As Paul Bleton points out, *paralittérature* is never singular and yet always particular; for many romance readers, detective fiction remains a closed book, and so on. But it is possible and fascinating to compare the gestalt of one "encyclopedia of reference" with another. The title *Ça se lit comme un roman policier* refers to a novel that can be read as a detective story, that follows the line from mystery, through investigation, to solution, from Umberto Eco's *The Name of the Rose* to Agatha Christie's *Ten Little Niggers*, and by extension, to any novel that can be read as a thriller or an adrenalin-charged adventure—*la littérature a faire peur*. A similar treatment of the theme from the point of view of science fiction might have considered the constructed world and the "encyclopedia of reference" itself more central—as in the old adage that non-science fiction readers cannot read sf because they don't have the right encyclopedia stored in memory. Equally fascinating were the generous glimpses of actual genre fictions. I am now filled with longing to read *Je Suis un Roman Noir*, or *Au Bois Dormant*, the remix of Chateaubriand's *René* with an anti-romantic twist ending, and not least the pseudonymous Lovecraft story with the enchanting title "I Wore the Brassiere of Doom." I know where to find it now, but alas I haven't yet run a copy down.

If there were weaknesses in the book, aside from the perhaps inevitable repetition of the paratext material, as an inexpert second-language reader I am not the one to point them out. However, the whole chapter on character relied, I felt, too exclusively on examples taken from extremely antiquated texts and lacked a discussion of the intense interest of the genre reader in the *soap-opera* element of any story. The most successful sf or spy story (look at the sales figures) is not the ludic, technoscientific or philosophic narrative; it's the everyday story of star-faring folk having tiffs and love-affairs; it's the espionage tale with the gourmet and shopping guide included...

But the weaknesses are few, while the depth of exposition cannot adequately be conveyed in a review. The only question that remains, a question that nags all the way through the essays, is: *if this is genre fiction, and the approach of the genre reader to fiction, what is left for those others?* Is there really such a thing as "non-serial" fiction? Or is there only (as we may have suspected all along) a shift in gestalt, a choice of genres of reading?

The Icons of Science Fiction

First published in The Cambridge Guide To Science Fiction, eds Farah Mendlesohn and Edward James, Cambridge, CUP, November 2000.

Science fiction stories have the same diversity, and the same range, as any other fiction. A science fiction novel may be a political satire, an examination of social or gender roles, a speculative work of popular science, a picaresque account of imaginary travels, a coming-of-age story, a thriller, a romance—or it may combine any number of themes. The feature that unites every kind of science fiction, and marks its difference, is the construction—in some sense—of a world other than our own. This world of the book may be literally another planet (or even another universe); or it may be a "future world" in which technological, social, or political conditions have changed in some dramatic way. But whatever new conditions or circumstances apply—alien invasion, Martian colonies, a permanent cure for the ageing process—the writer has to use some means to signal the changes, and the reader has to be able to understand the significance of these signals. Thus, the reading of a science fiction story is always an active process of translation (Jones 1999, 6): What kind of world is being described here? What are we being told about the characters, the politics, the social conditions of the imagined world, through the medium of these bizarre artifacts, landscapes, relationships, industries, and customs? The icons of science fiction are the signs that announce the genre, which warn the reader that this is a different world, and at the same time constitute the difference.

More than in any other fiction, in sf the medium is the message. The imaginary setting is a major character in the story, and this fictional surface is held together by the highly foregrounded description of unreal objects, customs, kinships, fashions that can be identified and decoded by the reader. The word "icon" is derived from the Greek *eikon*—it means an image; but the term came into English usage via Byzantine art, where an "ikon" is, specifically, a stylized representation of Christ or one of the Saints. Similarly, a science fiction icon will represent something supernatural (or at least otherworldly) and artistically conventional (in that certain features are mandatory), yet clearly belonging to the public domain. Just as Mary Shelley's Doctor Frankenstein constructed the monster rather than "invented" him, it is probably fruitless to trace any of the icons of sf back to a single, original author. Vampires existed (widely) in folklore before Bram Stoker's Dracula, and mechanical men were imagined before the word robot was first used in the sense that is now so familiar. Equally, since icons are culturally determined and to some degree each individual sf book or story is a culture, each book or story will have its own variant iconography (a differently designed robot, an idiosyncratic form of faster-than-light drive) to match the writer's particular intention. However, it is possible to identify, or to suggest, a core repertoire of these salient images, and to examine their meaning—meaning that is available and relevant not only to sf readers, but to any consumer of twenty-first century folklore.

Rockets, spaceships, space habitats, virtual environments

The rocket, with its upward thrusting phallic shape and dramatic flight, is an inevitable symbol of energy and escape, but a rocket is a weapon (first deployed on the battlefield in mediaeval China) as well as an innocent, spectacular firework. Though it was the science-fictional dream of interplanetary travel that inspired Tsiolkovski, the seminal theorist of modern rocketry, theory became practical application only in the development of the German V-2 super-weapon. This ambivalent identity has been a vital feature of the rocket's career, in the real world and in science fiction. Thomas Pynchon's *Gravity's Rainbow*, the American postwar novel that is a text of central significance to modern sf, weaves the story of this deadly icon, in the closing phases of the Second World War, into a rich and complex myth of origins: the rocket as both the climactic achievement and the embodied death wish of modern civilization. As the innocent adventurer, Tyrone Slothrop, pursues his quest for the ultimate device, we find the combination of hero-tale, technical specification, and mystical speculation, which is the great romance of classic science fiction; but we also find modern (i.e., post 1984) sf's insistence on conspiracy theory, seductive gadgets, brand-names; and sf's love-affair with ever more potent weaponry.

A rocket with a human payload is the ultimate image of *Gravity's Rainbow* (Pynchon 1975, 758-760), and in the real world it is still impractical to launch anything into space except by sitting it on top of a giant V-2 stuffed with explosives and, so to speak, lighting the blue touch paper. In science fiction, however, the rocket as a symbol of escape to the stars has long been superseded. These days, planetary launches are rare in space-faring sf; the whole struggle to leave earth has usually been elided into the distant or recent past. (Stephen Baxter's *Voyage*, with its highly technical yet emotionally charged account of a first crewed flight to Mars [1996], is a very interesting exception.) The finned, phallic cone has been replaced by the spaceship—a much more commodious vessel. Designed not for experimental parabolas but for exploration, for freight and passenger transport, and long-term occupation, the spaceship (whether it carries colonists or invaders, or hides monsters in its secret depths) is an alternative, contained world in itself.

Post-war science fiction writers, grasping the barren prospects of our solar system and the immensity of the journey to any more hopeful land-fall, quickly realized that traveling to the stars (even at the most fantastic speeds) would be a matter of years, or even many generations. Alexei Panshin's *Rite of Passage* (1968) is a rewarding example of the complete starship novel, in which social engineering, town planning, and education schemes have equal status with the adventure story. Panshin's characters leave the ship for their initiation into the terrors of the unknown, but the assumption that danger lies in the abyss *outside* the spaceship's metal shell can be reversed to great effect. The nightmare scenario of the monster within can invoke an exquisite sense of vulnerability, as in Ridley Scott's 1979 movie *Alien*—foreshadowed as early as 1958 in the seminal movie *It: The Thing From Beyond Space* (screenplay, Jerome Bixby).

In Bruce Sterling's space opera *Schismatrix* (1984), terror is a proof of social sophistication. Members of an elite social group remind each other, through a dangerous initiation ceremony, of the truth about what lies outside the space station, which their community prefers to forget:

"we remember the cold…" But in spite of that most celebrated of science fiction images—the fragile giant jewels, drifting in immense darkness, against a backdrop of pinprick diamonds—from the Kubrik film *2001*, the fictional spaceship is usually a place of refuge, security, stability. In C. J. Cherryh's Merchanter series the great ships that ply between habitable planets have a baroque, feudal culture of their own, like privateers on the Spanish Main—the crew members loyal only to their officers and fellows, stripped by the vast, time-distorting distances of any ties to the planet-bound. Space "stations," hubs where ships like these are serviced and exchange goods, personnel, information, become multilayered cities, with exotic markets, zoning laws, class divisions, slums, and parkland. Voyages may be so endless (as in Gene Wolfe's Urth of the Long Sun series) that all notion of a destination is lost, and the ship's inhabitants remember their original purpose only in myth. Stories closer (notionally) to the foreseeable future reflect the military origins of real-world space flight. The Starship Enterprise may be read as "a US navy nuclear submarine, cruising aimlessly around the Pacific, dispensing the morality of the Age of Liberalism at a vaguely dove-ish period in the Cold War" (Jones 1999, 6); and there are many variants on this naval, expeditionary theme. Even more realistically, the space habitat may become a giant shopping mall, which might as well be parked in the suburbs rather than voyaging through outer space. The ship can be a huge living organism, like Moya the Leviathan in the tv series *Farscape*, or a hollowed-out asteroid, as in my own novel *White Queen*. Whatever shape the vessel takes, it will be the locus for a drama of human relationships, an examination of ideas of conflict and dependence, recalling the mediaeval image of the "Ship of Fools." In the end the spaceship, forging its lonely way through a vast, inimical ocean, must always become an image of the human world itself—a vulnerable, yet demanding, closed environment, contradicting the rocket's promise of escape from our origins. The idea of escape from the human condition, by means of applied technology, has transmuted into a different form.

Can the virtual-environment be an icon? Access to the virtual world has as yet no fixed, visual image attached, either in reality or in fiction. The nearest equivalent to the universally recognized finned cone, or the sleek gleaming shape of the Starship, is the rather disgusting body-bag or vat of slime (as depicted in the definitive cyber-movie *Matrix*) in which the cybernaut must be immersed for a full, sensurround virtual experience. In Pat Cadigan's intuitively satisfying (but equally disgusting) variant, people remove their eyeballs so that they can be plugged-in to the virtual via their optic nerves (Cadigan 1987, 4). Other authors have found a modem-jack inserted into a hole in the back of the skull sufficient. In *Permutation City*, Greg Egan's powerful treatment of virtual space as a colony-world in political revolt, the cybernauts download their whole human personalities into the software avatars they have adopted in the world behind the screens, abandoning the "real world" and their "real bodies." In my 1997 novel *Phoenix Café* I reversed the transaction and had the virtual environments of my futuristic videogames prepared in the form of eye-drops loaded with molecular code. Your mind doesn't enter the virtual world, the virtual world enters your mind and becomes an optional overlay on the everyday scene (which is possibly the sf idea closest to market-reality). Whatever mediation we choose, the persistence of the physical body, the "meat" (Gibson 1985, 12) that is left behind when we enter the seamless digital-fantasy world, remains—linking this new concept to the ancient sf image of the super-potent but absurdly vulnerable disembodied brain. The debate will continue, as inner-space becomes—in sf as in the real world—something like the supplanter of the romance of galactic exploration and empire. But whatever kind of vessel we choose, what companions do we have with us, on this science-fictional voyage?

Robots and androids (and gynoids); cyborgs and aliens

A robot (from the Czech *robota*) is a worker. In Karel Čapek's play *R.U.R.* (1920), from which this name derives, mechanical men are created as workers but become so competent that they supplant their masters. Perhaps the most visually definitive robot was Robby, the metal-box-bodied, goggle-eyed good servant in the 1956 film *Forbidden Planet*; but it was Isaac Asimov, in a series of story collections published between 1950 and 1977, who developed the familiar sf concept (*I Robot*, 1950; *The Rest of the Robots*, 1964; *The Bicentennial Man*, 1977). The Three Laws of Robotics, the unbreakable code of ethics written into an Asimov robot's "positronic brain" have been so successful in fiction that they are worth quoting in full:

1. A robot may not injure a human being or through inaction allow a human being to come to harm.

2. A robot must obey the orders given to it by a human being, except where such orders would conflict with the first law.

3. A robot must protect its own existence as long as such protection does not conflict with the first or second laws...

While real-world robotic devices proliferate and the question of "machine intelligence" (intelligent washing machines?) becomes blurred for us, Asimov's image of the machine as the *good servant* has proved to have an abiding charm, and the Three Laws have passed into received sf scripture. In *Divine Endurance*, my first sf novel, Cho, a "metagenetic gynoid," the perfect intelligent machine, becomes the unwitting nemesis of a remnant humanity by following Asimov's laws to the letter; and the grandmaster's message—our machines are innocent but they may still destroy us—forms the basis of a tragic love story. In Asimov's scenario the fact that the Three Laws are there to protect the humans from their mentally and physically superior creations was always clear. Robotic *virtue*, however, was the preferred image in Liberal sf, becoming a theological romance in the legendary story by Catholic sf writer Anthony Boucher, "The Quest for St Aquin" (1951)—where a flawed and doubting priest is brought back to grace through the faith of his sentient mechanical steed. It took a renegade, anti-technophile sf writer, P. K. Dick, to write with pity and conviction of the revolt of the "replicants," in *Do Androids Dream of Electric Sheep*, now most famous as the inspiration of the Ridley Scott film *Bladerunner.*

The conviction that the perfected "intelligent machine" will have a human or quasi-human form, which now has support from the neuroscience of robotics, raises ethical questions. In sf, sentient facsimile humans are often read as a futuristic underclass and if female, a sexual underclass, defined and devalued by their artificiality. I "coined" the term gynoid in *Divine Endurance,* since calling a sentient AI in female human form an android sounded ridiculous to me. Post *Divine Endurance* fictional "gynoids" have always been sex-objects, sometimes docile, sometimes malign. Philip K Dick's replicants, or "andys" have an absurdly shortened lifespan and can be terminated without censure. In Melissa Scott's *Dreamships* (1992) a software-entity with a human personality, and more than human intelligence, can be legally executed like a rebellious slave. What is the ontological status of a genetically-engineered biological human being, mass-manufactured to order? Or of a being born human, who has elected to exchange some or all of her body parts for hardware, or to morph into a non-human body more suited to some alien environment? In the real world, medical technology has already created cyborgs—human beings entirely dependent on machine parts inserted into their bodies. *In vitro* fertilization techniques have blurred the line between children who are created "naturally" and children made to order, while the full humanity (or otherwise) of possible cloned human babies is a matter of debate. In science fiction these situations have been examined and re-examined, and the sf readers' skill of active translation has allowed readers and writers to construe the apparently bizarre dilemmas of post-humanity as familiar moral questions—of social dominance, race, and ethnicity; so that asking "Does a cloned baby have a soul?" is as meaningless (and obviously distasteful) as asking the same about the child of a chattel-slave in the nineteenth-century US.

It may be already inevitable that the human race will fragment into the genetically rich and the genetically poor, or the biologically natural versus the bio-mechanically enhanced (a future history intensely documented in Nancy Kress's Beggars in Spain series of novels, and the 1997 movie *GATTACA*). It may be inevitable that "Machine Intelligence", will become recognized as equal or superior to our own. It is by no means inevitable that the final transformation of the "other beings" icon—the intelligent extraterrestrial—will ever cross over from fiction and twilight-zone delusion into fact. The career of "aliens" in sf has reflected (as all science fiction concepts must) changes and developments in the real world. In the late nineteenth and early twentieth century there was sober, Darwinian speculation about life and ecology on other planets, with the sensational corrective of H.G. Wells' *The War of the Worlds* (1898). Aliens are competitors, and therefore our deadly enemies. In the chastened, exhausted years after WWII, and even more so in the sixties, decade of the Vietnam debacle and the Civil Rights Movement, peace was the message, and aliens could be pitied, admired, or defended—though remaining monstrous invaders in the movies, because battle provides better spectacle than trade missions. More recently, colorful (but conveniently humanoid) sf aliens—sometimes known as "demons" in tv sci-fi and fantasy shows—have implicitly taken on a range of topical, dramatically useful roles: immigrants, ethnic minorities, underprivileged guest-workers, wily diplomatic opponents. But the sincere beliefs of UFOlogists and the hopes of SETI (The Search for Extraterrestrial Intelligence) notwithstanding, the scientific exploration of space has discovered no accredited evidence of any neighbors, only a puzzling blank where they "ought to be." Greg Egan, one of sf's uncompromising and poetic realists, gives the sorry picture of our prospects in his novel *Schild's Ladder*—where a young boy of the very far future, instead of having a spaceship land in his garden, finds a tiny patch of slime-mould that *might* be of genuine alien origin and trembles in awe.

> When the lamplight finally returned the rainbow sheen he'd glimpsed from inside the building it was unmistakable, an irregular gleaming patch of some filmy substance...Tchicaya approached and touched it with his fingertip. The substance was slightly sticky, and the film clung to his finger for a fraction of a millimeter as he pulled away... (Egan 2002, 70)

Not exactly a spectacular find—but this colonized, terraformed planet will now have to be evacuated and become a nature reserve, because alien life, throughout the galactic empire, is so incredibly rare... As the great silence out there continues unbroken, actual "aliens" may have to go the way of Martian canals and Venusian swamps, banished from our imagination. But the prospect of posthuman speciation moves in to fill the vacated niche with an array of humanoid grotesques, and the far distant future will still provide a locus for stories of competition and conflict between widely divergent former colonies of earth. As long as there are other people around (especially if they look a little strange), the image of otherness provided by the term "aliens" will survive, to fascinate and instruct us.

Animals, Vegetables, and Minerals

In the hierarchy of sf plausibility, technophile extrapolation from the here-and-now takes precedence. Martians who build (or once built, long ago) canals, like jungle-infested swamps on Venus, were dismissed by the arrival of improved information about the conditions on our neighbor planets. Equally, the status of a fully imagined and constructed alien ecology—somewhere, out there, far beyond our present reach—has been at times dubious. Isn't this kind of make-believe just fantasy, a kind of Narnia in sf clothing? But while the concept of an alien *person* allows us to discuss social, political, and psychological permutations of human otherness, the alien planet (or universe!) or artifact, is equally vital. It is perhaps science fiction's greatest aesthetic gift, and the concept that brings us closest to experiencing the romance of real-world scientific endeavor. It is important that the sense of wonder invoked at coming face to face with the workings of the cosmos should be freed as far as possible from economic and political constraints, and it's no accident that some of the most beloved images of sf are enshrined in narratives of pure encounter. Arthur C. Clarke's *Rendezvous with Rama* (1973) is perhaps the most famous of these; where the fifty-kilometer-long alien artifact, or space probe, paying our system a glancing visit, remains almost entirely mysterious. In less ascetic versions of the same narrative, vanished aliens become intelligible, as in Frederick Pohl's remarkable *Gateway* (1979) and its sequels; or else it turns out that the archaeology of Elder-alien life (as in Jack McDavitt's *The Engines of God*, or Alastair Reynold's *Revelation Space*) contains information that's urgently vital to all concerned. From these encounter-points, the obligatory thriller plot descends into the banal: the center of these stories is a vastness, an inhuman majesty that cannot be reduced to human terms.

Real-world space exploration provides a convincing template for deep-space encounters: science fiction is at its least fictional here. The practice and theory of Alien-archaeology can be extrapolated, with little alteration, from the conditions in Egypt or Iraq a hundred years ago. The most admired of *living* imagined worlds is still probably Frank Herbert's *Dune* (1965). The desert planet Arrakis is supposedly a crucial supplier of a precious drug for a huge far-future, galaxy-spanning human polity;

but it was the arid terrain and its extraordinary wildlife that caught the reader's imagination, more than the fantasy power-politics of the plot. Roger Zelazny's *Lord of Light* (1967), belonging to the same period, i.e., science fiction's Age of Liberalism, draws admiringly on Hindu mythology and the culture of India in the same way that Herbert uses Islam and the desert Arabs; and Zelazny writes even more evocatively, though with less narrative strength.

> Near the city of Alundil there was a rich grove of blue-barked
> trees, having purple foliage like feathers. It was famous for its
> beauty and the shrinelike peace of its shade.
> (Zelazny 1969, 96)

Reading those words as a sixth former in Manchester around 1970, I was instantly entranced… Generations of sf readers have been introduced, sometimes without knowing it, to the fabulous diversity of their own planet by the alchemy of science fiction. As our world becomes more and more crowded and ignorance is dispelled by the Information Revolution and the popularity of long-haul travel, science fiction's imagineers have become self-conscious about these borrowings (Jones, 1977). Today you are likely to find an author openly declaring that the invented planet has been terraformed and reconstructed on purpose, as a theme-park devoted to ethnic identity and cultural nostalgia (for example, in Orson Scott Card's later works in the Ender series, John Barnes's *A Million Open Doors,* or Nalo Hopkinson's *Midnight Robber).* Thus we can have a twentieth-century Caribbean-flavored *quartier* of the human Diaspora, just a dimension veil or two away (so to speak) from a recreation of "Mediaeval France." But the most thrilling of imagined worlds are those that combine a high level of intuitive satisfaction as "real" ecologies, with an equally high degree of authorial *meaning*—a purpose in the work, other than faux-verisimilitude. Frank Herbert's *Dune* succeeds because the story of the desert planet is a story about scarcity and the kind of human culture that scarcity produces; Herbert was, at the time, involved in the environmental science of the sixties. Sheri Tepper's *Grass* (1979), an imagined-ecology novel of the same caliber, uses the sf device of a whole planet without habitat diversity to create a stunning pampas world. Here the meaning of the story is found in an ensemble of native animals with a remarkably coherent, thrilling, and fearsome metamorphic life cycle.

The denizens of *Grass* pass from an entirely animal larval stage, through a phase of callous, destructive, and aggressive sentience, and struggle to reach a final multidimensional imago almost beyond human comprehension. The close juxtaposition of a callous, destructive, and aggressive culture of human expansion (humans are colonists of the pampas planet) points the same moral as Arthur C. Clarke's *Childhood's End*—the perennial admonition and promise of the genre. If science fiction were an education scheme, the report card for the human race would always read *Could Do Better*. But the sf audience will go on coming back for more, as long as the stubbornly aspirational message is wrapped in such an envelope of wonder, delight, and playful invention.

Mad Scientists and Damsels in Distress

It is often said that science fiction is a genre devoid of convincing characterization. Whether or not they have the skill, science fiction writers don't have the time or space for studied character development because they are bound to foreground the imagined world, the action-adventure, and the gadgets. There may be exceptions to this rule, but it is true that sf relies, like the other popular fiction genres, on a set of stock figures, recognizable and emblematic as the characters of pantomime or the *Commedia del' Arte*. There are countless hero-tales in science fiction and many futuristic or alternate-history permutations of the basic romance of the young male adventurer. However, although plenty of sf heroes happen to be scientists, they usually, like Indiana Jones, display their sterling qualities outside their professional discipline. Gregory Benford's *Timescape*, one of sf's few serious treatments of time travel, provides a rare exception, but this (like most real-life science) is an ensemble piece. Perhaps, ironically, the Faustian nature of scientific heroism is a difficult topic for the genre. Faust, the seeker after knowledge who challenges God and is destroyed when he makes a pact with the devil, is not the ideal central figure for a fiction designed to promote and celebrate Man's God-like dominion over the material world. The measured, exalted insanity of Mary Shelley's Doctor Frankenstein, with his horrific project of creating life out of a collection of dismembered body parts, is the exception rather than the rule. A notable and wonderfully crazed example can be found in Greg Bear's *Blood Music*, the early masterpiece of a writer who has become one of the genre's most respected apologists. Vergil Ulam, geek *par excellence*, has been ordered to destroy his colonies of intelligent lymphocytes (white blood cells engineered to possess self-awareness and naturally supplied with a Darwinian drive to increase, multiply, and take over the world). He just can't do it.

> He held the syringe before his eyes for several minutes, know-ing he was contemplating something rash. *Until now,* he ad-dressed his creations mentally, *You've had it real easy… No severe test, no stress, no need to use what I gave you.*

> So what was he going to do? Put them to work in their natural environment? By injecting them into his body, he could smug-gle them out of Genotron… (Bear 1985, 24)

Of course, Vergil commits this folly, and cataclysmic mayhem ensues.

In Ursula le Guin's *The Dispossessed*, Shevek, an Einstein-like figure, provides a deeply thoughtful version of this story: the scientist viewed as a brilliant creative artist, forced by circumstance to confront the human meaning of his "pure research." When Shevek chooses unilaterally, and in wartime, to make an extraordinary, momentous technology available to all humanity, the parallel with our own world is clear—but to many of the voices in *The Dispossessed*, Shevek appears as dangerously insane as Vergil Ulam. What should Shevek have done? Should he have buried his discovery (analog of nuclear fission)? Scientists of genius will find them-selves in the service of the powerful: how far are they responsible for the havoc their work can cause in ruthless hands? It's clear that to both Le Guin and Bear, the "mad scientist" is not a bogeyman or a cartoon figure. He's a fully satisfying fictional character, but he also represents an idea, a discussion about the nature of responsibility, a topic for debate.

Feminism and Gender issues are not the business of this article, but in an examination of sf's icons it seems appropriate to re-consider that cliché of genre cover art, the diaphanously clad exotic damsel (or, equally, the bronze-breasted spacewoman dominatrix) who will, alleg-edly, represent the only female role available in the story. It is true that there is an unavoidable subtext in the science fiction adventure. Hero-tales generally involve the hero being rewarded after his trials, by gaining access—in some sense—to the desirable female: when he's slain the monster the prince must get his princess as well as half the kingdom. The male reader always expected a taste of that reward from the original pulps and was rarely disappointed. But cover art often belies content, and though feminism finds much to contend with in sf, the classic writers were often—according to their lights—positive and generous toward women. The scientist at the heart of Asimov's *I Robot* stories is a female character. She is presented in essentialist terms, as a frustrated mother to her machine-babies; but she's there.

One of the most striking developments in modern sf has been the emergence of the female-hero icon, who appears (like Joss Whedon's Buffy the Vampire Slayer, or Eidos's Lara Croft) to have captured the hearts of a generation of younger male writers. Clearly these potent young women characters have been appropriated by the male imagination, seen not as rivals but as permissive alter-egos (Clover 1992)—tough and tooled-up and yet "feminine"—emotionally soft, sexually desirable. Intriguingly, the female-hero of Alastair Reynolds's recent novel, *Revelation Space*, depicted in print as a bony, uncompromising, shaven-headed action-figure, appears on his website, with authorial approval, with a much enhanced cuteness quotient. Androgynous, child-like, culturally deracinated, lost in a hard-edged, grey-scale machine-made world in which she is only tangential to the vast scheme of things; maybe Ilia Volyova, masculine on the outside, feminine on the inside, is a suitable candidate for the iconic sf human being of our new century.

Traditions and Challenges

In the twenty-first century, the traditions of science fiction are under dual attack. The supernatural, sacred status of the genre's icons is being rapidly eroded by the advance of applied technology. Rockets and space stations may remain marginal to most people's lives, but Cyborgs, virtual environments, hand-held global communicators (their eerie resemblance to the Star Trek version owing more to ergonomics than sf prescience) have passed into the mundane. At the same time, the most *visual* of print-fiction genres is challenged by developments in the entertainment media of film, tv, and videogames. Gone are the days when the B movies could not hope to provide the kind of spectacular special effects, eye-kicks, and entrancing false-realities that could be created by the reader's and the writer's inner eye. But an icon is meaning as well as spectacle, and there is a logic to the icons of sf that will always recall the reader of these signs to the printed page, to verbal rather than visual argument. These images of the future and of human desire deserve to be revisited in their original forms. They may not be technically accurate drawings (the encroachment of reality generally reveals the absurdity of the science of science fiction), but they occupy a strange and very specific borderland. They are not drawn from nature or invoked from the notional freedom of "fantasy": they are the reasoned hybrids of imagination and the machine.

Works Cited

Asimov, Issac. *I The Bicentennial Man*. London: Gollancz, 1977.

——. *The Rest of the Robots*. London: D. Dobson, 1964.

——. *Robot*. Garden City, NY: Doubleday, 1950.

Bear, Greg. *Blood Music* (Legend edition). London: Arrow Books, 1985.

Boucher, Anthony. "The Quest for St Aquin." In *The Complete Short Science Fiction and Fantasy of Anthony Boucher*. Ed. James A. Mann. Framingham, MA: NESFA Press, 1999.

Cadigan, Pat. *Mindplayers*. New York: Bantam, 1987.

Cherryh, C J. *Devil In The Belt*. Aspect (Warner Books), 2000.

——. *Downbelow Station*. New York Daw, 2001 (1981).

——. *Merchanter's Luck*. New York Daw, 1982.

——. *Rimrunners*. New York: Warner Books, 1990.

Le Guin, Ursula. *The Dispossessed: An Ambiguous Utopia*. New York: Harper & Row, 1974.

Panshin, Alexei. *Rite of Passage*. New York: Fairwood Press, 2007. (Ace, 1968.)

Reynolds, Alastair. *Revelation Space*. London: VGSF, 2000.

Tepper, Sheri. *Grass*. New York: Doubleday, 1989.

Clover, Carol J. *Men, Women, and Chainsaws: Gender in the Modern Horror Film.* Princeton, NJ: Princeton University Press, 1992.

Egan, Greg. *Schild's Ladder.* London: Gollancz, 2002.

Gibson, William. *Neuromancer* (Panther edition) London: Grafton Books, 1985.

Jones, Gwyneth. *Deconstructing the Starships.* Liverpool: Liverpool University Press, 1999.

———. "Metempsychosis of the Machine: Science Fiction in the Halls of Karma," *Science Fiction Studies,* 24, 1, 1997.

Pynchon, Thomas. *Gravity's Rainbow.* (Picador edition) London: Pan Books, 1975.

Scott, Melissa. *Dreamships.* New York: Tor, 1992.

Zelazny, Roger. *Lord of Light.* New York: Avon Books, 1969.

Postscript to the Fairytale

A Review of *The Two of Them* by Joanna Russ; Foreword by Sarah Lefanu (Middletown, Connecticut: Wesleyan University Press, 2005).

A shorter version of this review appeared in *The New York Review of Science Fiction* No. 203, Vol. 17, July 2005.

The Poet Vanishes

Science fiction writers who favor the vast laboratory of the multiple worlds hypothesis like to drop sly hints. In Joanna Russ's *The Two of Them*, Irene Waskiewicz, whom we have met as a girl in a familiar-seeming USA of the fifties, makes reference to a famous, long-dead, woman poet called Laura Dickinson. Don't bother googling her, it's Emily, slightly shifted; Emily differently named in a version of modern earth just a little astray from ours. It's not very surprising that Dickinson should turn up: *The Two of Them* is ostensibly a novel about women poets, and about greatness. There is an additional meaning here, however, which may be entirely lost on twenty-first century readers—even those readers, women and men both, who regard themselves as "feminist." What Russ is saying, in one of those momentary, almost subliminal flashcards of hers, is that in her view Emily Dickinson, the US poet of genius, never existed, not in any of the worlds; she never wrote a line.

Puzzled? Try this: we cannot know what Emily Dickinson would have been like, as a person or as an artist, if she had lived as a free human being. The poetry that we have was produced by someone whose gift had to grow like something crushed under a stone, whose mind was broken and bound from her earliest childhood, like the feet of a little Chinese girl, to satisfy a perverse ideal of feminine beauty. We have an unreliable record, a found object that we admire for our own culturally bound reasons. The tightly-controlled, exquisitely confined beauties of her verse may be traits that Emily herself would have rejected joyfully if she'd had the freedoms we have now. I can well sympathize with the people who find that academic relativism (rife in the seventies) makes their heads spin. What can we ever know? What record can we ever trust? But as a flashcard, as a speculation, as something to add to the sum of what we think about Emily Dickinson, maybe it works...

Modern feminism, the radical feminism of the seventies of the last century, was born out of anger and desire. The desire was to be treated as a model of the human, like a man, rather than as an inferior knock-off version. The anger was aroused by the myriad injustices, on every scale—public, social, and domestic—that leapt into view when women, often already involved in the fight for Civil Rights or the Anti-War Movement, experienced the awakening known as raised consciousness, in the idiom of radical politics, about their own condition. Anger and desire informed the science fiction feminism, born in the radical sixties, that reached its maturity in the sf of the seventies, when James Tiptree Jr, Ursula K. Le Guin, Joanna Russ, Marge Piercy, Suzy Charnas, and many others were stirring up the public. Women in fandom, fan writers and professional writers, created a community and provided a primary readership for explicitly, trenchantly feminist novels that were also powerful sf, some of which have become classics.

But the desire to be free, like a man, swiftly and naturally generated an opposite need to valorize the feminine. Women in sf and fantasy began turning away from the rebarbative aspects of radical feminism, retreating to more comfortable fictions about the power of women, the secret, innate superiority of the traditional female world. The rewriting of classic fairytales flourished at this time. It was a two-pronged attack, on the one hand a righteous, somewhat naïve vandalism, aimed at saving children from the indoctrination of Sleeping Beauty and Snow White, on the other a re-discovery and reclamation of the earthy, sexual, and often savage hearthside tales of the deep past. But as the mission to escape from the wispy role-model of Disney's Cinderella became a mission to "rescue" the tough, resourceful heroine of the original folklore, sf feminism quietly, almost silently, morphed into celebration of the alpha female. The old tales are uncompromising. They have no hope in the revolution. They are not about changing the world, they are about making the best of a bad deal. Before taking issue with *The Two of Them*, which is, in structure, a kind of postscript to the whole Cinderella story of twentieth century womanhood, it's worth looking at what happens in the classic, beloved tale of rags to riches, in political terms.

So Cinderella managed the household for her stepmother and sisters, didn't get upset at her father's defection, kept the hearth clean, did her duty without complaint, and thereby gained the patronage of a powerful older woman. She shed her working clothes and went to the ball, as glittery and as helpless-looking at the rest of the high-caste marriageable maidens, because she was in charge and she knew how to make it to the top. But what was the prize this feisty, "real" Cinderella had won at the end of the tale? The keys to the finest gilded cage in all the land and the happy knowledge that from now on other little servant girls (probably economic migrants, from somewhere down south) would be sleeping among the cinders, wearing the rags, and doing her dirty work... What does Cinderella do, when she realizes she's become the poster girl for the world that tried to crush her? Does she feel humiliated? Does she care about those other girls? What happens to the fairytale, if she does care? The message of that "Laura Dickinson" flashcard, if we choose to accept it, is difficult, painful, and disturbing. It's not pleasant to see yourself as something that grew under a stone. But women who have learned to feel successful and empowered *as women*, in the twenty-first century, and girls who aspire to become alpha females in a world where gender is still the single most important factor controlling any human being's fate, have entirely missed the point of Joanna Russ's feminism.

Wise Girls

Irene Waskiewicz makes her first appearance in *The Two of Them* as a sci-fi cut-out doll ("Here they are. They are entirely in black, with belted tabards over something like long underwear, that makes them look like the cards in Alice..." [1]) We learn that she's an agent of Trans-Temp, an organization serving some far-future government, on a mission with her male partner to a "pseudo-Islamic" nation ensconced inside a hollowed-out asteroid. The story really begins, however, when we meet

Irene in flashback, in the suburbs of the fifties-USA: an angry, distinctly aggressive young woman, wistfully attracted by her father's taciturn leisure, depressed by her mother's housewifely fate, making precociously cold-hearted sexual experiments. There are hints that Rose Waskiewicz, like Joanna Russ's own mother, is a Squashed Woman, "guilty at being intelligent, guilty at having been to graduate school, guilty at being competent at anything…" (ix, Sarah Lefanu's Introduction to *The Two of Them*). She's remarkably tolerant of her angry daughter, but she clearly assumes Irene will have to accept the same defeat. When the mysterious Ernst Neumann turns up, a visitor from Rose's past, Irene soon figures out that there's something clandestine going on. The set-up suggests the underground of US radical politics (Rose is letting her address be used as a mail-drop; the Squashed Woman may once have been a revolutionary); but as Irene discovers—when, desperate at her limited choices, the teenager throws in her lot with this attractive older man—the truth is much stranger. She is swept out of her own time and place in the universe. She learns that there are many, many versions of the future, the present, and the past, and that the parallel worlds are not shadows, popping in and out of existence as quantum superposition collapses. They are real places. It is possible to travel between them, tweaking history, adjusting cultures. She will become a trans-temporal agent, one of the elite, working for a super-power whose hegemony spans time, space, and probability. It's implied, though never stated, that recruiting talented young women from oppressive situations may be part of Ernst's job.

Flash-forward again: Ernst and the grown-up Irene on, or rather in, Ka'abah. Their mission remains vague, but they are splendidly realized: ornery, difficult, attractive people (sexy, too), natural outsiders locked in an intense alliance, the two of them against the world. The age difference has not divided them, they're true—though not easy—soul mates. Their elliptical private dialogue is like the secret language of two lonely children, the sheer strangeness of their lives with TransTemp is illuminated by reflections—Polish Irene and Jewish Ernst—on the immigrant experience. Their secret agent skills, when described, are satisfyingly concrete (Irene's logic-based feats of computer deception, parsed when computer use was still in its infancy, read just fine, even now). They have been welcomed into the household of 'Alee Shems-er-Nehar, where Irene, of course, is mistaken for a man, and where they meet the irrepressible and talented twelve-year-old Zubeydeh, who wants to be a poet (her family is sure she'll grow out of this absurd notion). Irene and Ernst have been mentor and pupil. They are now, ostensibly, equal partners. They find the fussy, tinkling, over-decorated, miniature home of their host irksome; they are both, literally, "too big" for this little world inside a stone. Irene especially is repelled by the helpless, cosseted life of their host's wife, on permanent medication for her nerves, whose greeting cry "have you bought anything?" sums up her entire life. But Irene's prepared to tolerate the local customs, freely chosen by this artificial society, until Zubeydeh discovers the existence of "Aunt Dunya" — a mad woman who once wanted to be a poet. "Aunt Dunya" was supposed to be dead. Instead she is being kept in a filthy cell, a secret shame in the heart of 'Alee Shems-er-Nehar's house. Zubeydeh is distraught. The mad woman is not reclaimable, but her fate shocks Irene into action. She decides that she and Ernst must rescue Zubeydeh. He agrees without demur, and they quickly achieve this: all it takes is a little intimidation and a forged visa.

Seventies science fiction feminism was a co-operative venture. Fan writers, professional writers, critics were bouncing ideas around, reading each other's stories, sharing their discussions with like-minded men (notably, in the legendary *Khatru* Symposium from which a certain James Tiptree Jr was ejected as a sexist male). It illuminates the background and explains some of the wrinkles in *The Two of Them*, when we know that the novel began as a response to a story called "For the Sake of Grace" (1969) by another feminist, Suzette Haden Elgin. In Elgin's "Islamic-style" world, prowess in poetry is the only path left open to women who want to achieve greatness, and it is made as difficult and threatening as possible. "For the Sake of Grace," in its turn, pays homage to the classic proto-feminist story "The Yellow Wallpaper" by Charlotte Perkins Gilman (1892), a chilling description of exactly how a talented woman goes mad when she's locked up to "cure" her of her talent as a writer. In Elgin's original story the young girl, Zubeydeh, knows of the fate of her Aunt Dunya, who failed the crucial exam and was condemned to life in solitary confinement, but she still persists in her ambition; in Russ's version it's the girl's discovery of the mad woman, the living skeleton in the family closet, that precipitates crisis. But where the earlier stories, so far separated in time, remain in the same, relatively comfortable orthodox feminist space, the Joanna Russ novel abandons righteous indignation. She insists that we recognize that talented, forceful women, as long as they will play the game, have never really had much of a problem. Cinderella shall go to the ball! The project of kidnapping Zubeydeh so that she can become a successful poet is treated with irony in *The Two of Them*: "Zubeydeh will marry a millionaire. She'll make his life wretched. She'll keep a salon and write. And wear her native costume. And be famous…" (100). Here the oppressive family isn't simply wicked, and the society isn't strictly alien. The women of Ka'abah are hopelessly complicit, in many different ways, in their own oppression; and it's Irene, the successful, liberated woman, who is changed.

The story behind the fiction, the story of a generation, always starts the same way: I was a girl-child in the fifties. I was attracted to the alien culture (indubitably alien!) of a set of books with rockets on the spines. Maybe I was influenced, though I didn't really know it, by my mother's memories of the halcyon days of World War, when women's work was needed outside the home and she had a life. Maybe I felt her unease, though she never talked about it, at being socially engineered back into the kitchen and the negligée. (Maybe I called this "not wanting to be like my mother.") The books were exciting and adventurous, and there were plenty of tomboy girl characters. I didn't know they were there for decoration, I thought it meant the genre had a place for me! So I ran away with Science Fiction, to start a new life. And here I am, still happy to be dressed in long underwear, with my raygun, but sorely disillusioned about those tomboys… And then the story divides. The unregenerate tomboys keep their rayguns, the alpha female fans create a female, womb-friendly space within sf; but aren't they both playing by the rules of the boys' club? *The Two of Them* examines this dilemma, with illustrations. The hollow-asteroid world of Ka'abah is a meticulously imagined space-technology construct; it's also packed with this freight of meaning. Russ's pseudo-Islamics live inside a black stone, which is called after the sacred black stone (Ka'aba) of Mecca. Just as the male-oriented religion of Islam circles around that ancient symbol of the Mother Goddess, every man's mind in the asteroid circles around the idea of treasured women. Like Islam, Ka'abah perceives itself as a woman-loving culture, and Russ seems prepared to go along with that. Male Ka'abahites are portrayed with affection, especially the hapless 'Alee Shems-er-Nehar: bullied by his clever little daughter, bewildered by his wife's problems. Even the discovery of the "failed" woman in her filthy cell is not a crude unmasking of evil. It's the miserable revelation of a good-willed family's failure to cope with dysfunction. The damage done to the talented girl-child is limited. Zubeydeh makes her tearful farewells to the family where she was truly loved. The girl's mother, Zumurrud, supporting her husband in his distress, even seems about to begin a happier life. Any reader at this point may find herself, or himself, thinking, these Ka'abahites aren't so bad, they're really just folks, just ordinary people....

Then, on the voyage home, disaster strikes. Irene realizes that rescuing one child is not enough. The horrible, woman-smothering culture of K'abah must be dismantled. She knows that the superpower she works for is actively supporting the regime (that's what the mission was about), but she needs to know more. She'll have to get into the secret files of the Trans-Temp Agency itself, to find out just what is going on. Of course she tells Ernst everything. His response is disquieting. He doesn't see a large-scale problem with Ka'abah. It seems he's only interested in rare, highly gifted females, the ones who do not deserve the natural subordination of their sex. (In the language of radical politics, he turns out to be a "fellow-traveler," when Irene, all these years, thought he was all the way.) The discussion goes rapidly downhill, and Irene behaves just like a girl. Broken-hearted rather than threatened, she goes off to cry over her loss, and she blames herself: she sees he didn't necessarily mean to deceive. Ernst, meanwhile, takes drastic measures. Next thing Irene knows, her TransTemp identities have been wiped from the ship's computers. Her partner has rendered her a non-person. Faced with this unequivocal hostility, our heroine pulls herself together, tricks the computer, and is about to escape with a new identity, taking Zubeydeh along. Ernst intervenes. They fight, she ends up shooting him dead. The shooting of Ernst caused consternation in science fiction criticism, in those heady days when sf's feminists were movers and shakers. It's probably what people are most likely to recall about *The Two of Them*... Oh yes, that's the feminist rant where the heroine shoots the hero, for no good reason except that he's offended her extremist views... The highly respected liberal critic, John Clute was prompted by this incident above all others to an incandescent denunciation of Joanna Russ as a writer bent on destroying science fiction:

> …you think I'm telling you X; well I wouldn't tell you X if my life depended on it. In fact my life depends on my not allowing you to get away with hearing X from my lips. Your willingness to suspend disbelief so as to luxuriate in the telling of X is tantamount to complicity with the invidious systemic viola-tion of women in this world, whose roots are homologous with the engendering impulses behind traditional genre fiction, or X, baby.…

(John Clute, review in *Foundation*, n.15, Jan 1979, 103-5)

"The gentlemen," as Zubeydeh would say, "always think the la-dies have gone mad…" (*The Two of Them*, 122)

In a review of Sarah Lefanu's *In the Chinks of the World Machine*, in the same journal some years later, I affected bemusement. (I wasn't really bemused.) But I had a right to protest. Social and political analysis isn't a contradiction of the genre, it's one of the things the genre was invented for. Arguably, the purpose of US science fiction, in its original, didactic form, was to provide a forum for technophile, right-wing ideas. Is it for-bidden to discuss any other shade of politics? When was this decided? Isn't wounded fury, directed against an impressive science fiction, by a writer the same critic acknowledges as working at the top of the sf field, a little disquieting, a little extreme? Readers of the present generation might be puzzled as to why an eminent male critic was even engaging with a blatantly feminist novel. Surely those books are only meant for girls? Ah, it was different then, for a while. (See Jeanne Gomoll, "Open Letter to Joanna Russ" on what happened to the "lost" decade.)

Returning to the novel in the twenty-first century, two things strike me about the notorious incident. First, Irene is not the aggressor. Far from it. It is Ernst who turns on his partner of many years, who is also his lover, without negotiation, and betrays her. It's not as if Irene had sprung her feminist views on him out of the blue. He knows how she feels. They have conspired together to rescue Zubeydeh… Second, the duel with Ernst is hardly an atrocity. It's a standard issue thriller plot de-velopment. The CIA agent, on a routine mission, spots connections she wasn't supposed to notice, pointing to a conspiracy that may go all the way to the top. She shares her suspicions with her partner, the only colleague she can trust. Unfortunately, it turns out he's one of the bad guys. He betrays himself by trying to destroy her, this leads to a confrontation. Tragically, the good guy ends up being forced to shoot her buddy. This is pure Bourne Identity territory, pure Hollywood. In short, though the killer is a woman and the issue is women's rights, Joanna Russ could have got away with murder, even in 1978—except for her own determination to call Irene's act a transgression. It's the narrative that directs us to see Irene's shame and distress, *not* Ernst's abuse of power. It's the writer herself who finds the death of Ernst so shocking that it shatters the storytelling illusion.

> It occurs to me that she only stunned him, that soon he'll get up... I've contemplated giving Ernst stomach flu and letting the other two run while he's retching, but I don't think so...
> (136)

Why was it so hard to write that Irene killed Ernst? Why was killing Ernst such a violent act that it threw our feisty alpha female Cinderella right out of her fairytale? Look through the veil of fantasy (which should be easier for the general reader these days, our lives are so full of narratives, from "reality tv" to music videos, that scratch and jump between fantasy and realism), and the explanation becomes obvious. The story of Irene and Ernst is the story of a gifted young woman of the mid-twentieth century. She was rescued from her housewifely fate by a charismatic older man. Maybe he was her post-grad supervisor, her boss, her mentor in the artsworld; maybe he was all those things and also her loving husband. Gradually she realizes that she will always be his junior. He sees her as an exceptionally gifted pet whom he has rescued from the inherent inferiority of her sex. There comes a point (maybe circa 1975, heyday of women's escape stories in mainstream fiction, when Marilyn French wrote *The Women's Room*) when she knows that much as she loves him, much as she appreciates their intelligent conversations, he's a closet patriarch, and he's keeping her in the doll's house with him. Worse, her daughter is going to be brought up in the doll's house and never have a chance of self-realization. She has to leave him, and it feels like murder. She has to abandon him, and—as Joanna Russ makes clear, by characterizing Ernst so sympathetically, by letting him tell his own version of the story alongside Irene's—this is not a triumph. This is a tragedy. The tragedy of such a divorce is not only emotional. In the real world, for the fifties girl, it usually meant a devastating loss of income and status. In the science fiction world, of course, Irene is on the run. She's lost, at a stroke, her job, her home, her world, her identity. Her only recourse is to make her escape from the whole TransTemp universe, and drop back into the timeline where she was born, with the rescued Zubeydeh. She's a nothing, a nobody now: but she holds the secret of the true revolution. Whatever she makes of her life will be her own.

Radical Science Fiction

In telling the painful feminist awakening as sf Russ risks letting readers down with a bump when Irene steps from the inter-dimensional space ferry (on which she's sneaked a ride, before anyone knows Ernst is dead) to the side of the highway somewhere near Albuquerque: a divorced thirty-year-old with a young daughter and not a lot of money; Cinderella busted right back down to the scullery. A reviewer on Amazon.com (a thoughtful review and he could be right) complains there are thousands of words left out at this juncture, pages and pages that should have led us persuasively back to Irene's original world and kept the doubling of the narrative intact. But that was the seventies, experiments were made: and that's Joanna Russ. She doesn't do dilution, every word's a wanted word—and the brutal disjoint is no doubt intentional.

These days, I'm better able to understand how a liberal male critic, convinced that women in sf were a well-served special interest group with nothing to complain about, could have felt so betrayed and indeed bewildered by *The Two of Them*. Nothing says a liberal sf critic has to be an authority on the radical politics of his era. And yet there are clear signals, not the least of them the title itself, telling us that this isn't meant as an attack on the male-dominated themes of science fiction or on men. Far from it. There are two victims of patriarchy, of global capitalism, in *The Two of Them*. They are both revolutionaries, living in a secret dimension, alongside normal life; they are both dedicated to making the world a better place. Only one of them gets out alive, because only one of them succeeds in making—or rather, in completing—the imaginative leap that's called raised consciousness. There's a point in *The Two of Them* (aside from Joanna Russ's guilty musings) where it seems as if Ernst is going to survive. Irene stops seeing him as all-important and begins to transfer her allegiance to Zubeydeh, to the project of nurturing that young life. One could see this as a Cinderella variant in which Ernst has played the role of the fairy godmother. He provided Irene with the means to escape, now he can just step aside while she finds fulfillment with her true love. Separatism was very much a live issue in the seventies... There's another point, when Zubeydeh is pestering and bullying a hapless, dirty little boy, on the starship out of Ka'abah, where we can see an even-handed suggestion of the nasty way men and boys might be treated in a woman-dominated world. But Ernst cannot be discarded so easily, and the little boy doesn't work out, he is a pentimento. The issue that we must engage with, as feminist Cinderellas, is the problem of adult men, men of good will, our brothers in the struggle. As the alchemy of science fiction allows Ka'abah, a cunningly exotic dystopia full of mirrors, to be gradually unmasked as a jaded look at Joanna Russ's own US, twentieth-century culture (neurotic housewives, popping pills and obsessed with shopping, the Ka'abah "psychology" of femininity, echoing US self-help texts on how to be a successful wife and mother), the thrilling TransTemp recruiting agent, Ernst, is able, by the same magic, to represent not only the whole superbly powerful, technologically advanced, world-ruling culture of patriarchy, but also, paradoxically, a hero of the revolution, a lost lover, a vital ally fallen by the wayside. *The Two of Them* ends on a poetic, elegiac note. Irene has a dream, but it has none of the ringing triumph of Martin Luther King's. She sees Zubeydeh, a grown woman, looking down from a rocky promontory into a valley of dry bones.

> Irene knows that they are in the centermost vacancy of someone's mind, they have found their way at last into the most secret place of Ka'abah...here all is still, and in the grey, colorless half-light Irene can see that the floor of the valley is thickly covered with bones. Innumerable skeletons are spread from wall to wall and piled up immeasurably into the half-grey, half-lost rocky ceiling, so far from any open love or light... bones intermingled with bones, heaps of bones, choking the

dry watercourse and stretching back between the valley walls, a
dry silent carpeting as far as the eye can see. (149)

Ka'abah is our world, and the bones are the bones of crushed and
silenced women, who have remained crushed, remained silent even if
they have become outwardly successful, sexually aggressive, staggeringly
rich. The lucky few will still be crushed, still be silent, in their inmost nature, until the whole world changes. This vision, in which hope is a bare
whisper, is as true to the global statistics today as it was in 1978. Many
women, over most of the world, are worse off than they were thirty years
ago. Writing poetry can get you killed, by your outraged husband, in
some bigoted Islamic societies. Poetry competitions aren't much of an issue where girls don't get access to basic education, or even access to food
and water, until after the males have been served. Overwhelmingly, in
our brutal times, women's hard-won rights are being stripped from them,
and even in the rich USA they may be casualties of the galloping divide
between rich and poor, just as they are the casualties of war, famine, rape.
I could go on, but I won't, I know it's boring.

But not all the bones in that valley are women's bones.

The Spirit of the Beehive

It is relatively easy today, perhaps it has always been relatively easy,
for a talented middle-class woman to aspire, work hard, and become an
alpha female, subordinate to the alpha males but pretty close to the top
of the heap. It's not inconceivable for a potential alpha female to set the
tainted privileges aside and live as "nothing and nobody," in solidarity
with the millions of servant girls still sleeping in the cinders. (Though I
have to say, Irene's conviction that ordinary people are "nothing and nobody" might be a poor place to start.) It's much more difficult to find an
answer to the problem of Ernst, that dead body of the New Man. Why
did Ernst have to die? Why couldn't he make the same leap of imagination that Irene has made? He loves at least one woman, he hates injustice, why couldn't he throw in his lot with Irene and trust her, the way
she trusted him, years ago? Joanna Russ, a lesbian feminist, has made it
clear that she considers Ernst's death pivotal. His death is not a personal
tragedy, a loss "Irene" has to accept on the way to self-realization. It is the

collapse of the project of equality... And yet Russ doesn't seem to know the answer to that question. In all radical movements (compare the Civil Rights Movement in the USA, the Anti-Apartheid movement in South Africa, even the distant ancestral voices of the French Revolution) there comes a time when the oppressed can no longer be led by the privileged. The white or middle class or aristocratic activists must either bow out or be engulfed in the Terror of the proletariat unleashed. This has to happen (so the story goes) because freedom cannot not be bestowed. It must be taken, with ugly violence; and the only way the man of goodwill can serve the revolution without betraying his ideals is by dying on the barricades... The male fellow-traveler cannot be a leader of feminism; therefore, he has to quit. Is this Ernst's answer, is this why he took the bullet? In the mysterious postscript to *The Motorcycle Diaries* (Ernesto Ché Guevara's record of an early voyage around Latin America), the twenty-four-year-old Guevara describes a meeting between himself and a veteran Latin American Communist, a meeting that inhabits the same dreamlike space as Joanna Russ's valley of the dry bones. The old soldier foretells, with eerie precision, Ché's own death and the meaning of it:

> I also know—and this won't alter the course of history or your personal view of me—that you will die with a clenched fist and a tense jaw, the epitome of hatred and struggle, because you are not a symbol (some inanimate example) but a genuine member of the society to be destroyed; the spirit of the beehive speaks through your mouth and motivates your actions. You are as useful as I am, but you are not aware of how useful your contribution is to the society that sacrifices you...

(Ernesto Ché Guevara, *The Motorcycle Diaries: Notes on a Latin American Journey*, London: Harper Perennial, 2004,164)

The revolution can only be instigated by men of goodwill, who are doomed to become savages in the savage struggle, because they embody the corrupt society they are trying to destroy... This gloomy self-analysis, so cruelly accurate in the case of the gentle young doctor, so perfectly encapsulates Ernst Neumann's position in *The Two of Them* it's hard to believe the reference isn't intentional.

Joanna Russ was writing at a time when the whole USA was stirred and shaken by unimaginable defeat and passionate hope and tragically—as it seemed to her, as she tells here—men in radical politics simply could not see the feminizing (or rather the de-masculinizing) of global culture as a worthwhile project. They believed that the revolution MUST be masculine, a work of war, although they knew it was doomed by the path of violence. I don't know about you, dear reader, but from where we are now, it looks like a hell of a missed opportunity. In the twenty-first century, in science fiction and fantasy as in the real world, feminism is a small, more or less contented niche-market, as incomprehensible to the mainstream as any other special interest group, and somewhat more repellent; while women of ambition explore the baroque opportunities of alpha female, emphatically NOT feminist, roads to power. And the world goes on the same: right now falling into a very brutal phase of its endless reiterations. In *The Two of Them*, Joanna Russ places the blame for the failure of the equality project firmly on Ernst's shoulders. I'm not so sure about that, but it's worth discussion. I'm certainly sure that women of goodwill can't win a single battle if their lovers, colleagues, friends betray them. Will the New Man, our brother in the struggle, ever bring himself to change, to lay down his own tainted privileges? This is the real question that *The Two of Them* poses, and it's as relevant today as it ever was. What will it take to wrest the stone tablets of the law from Ernest's grip, before he caves in? What will men of goodwill have to lose, in order to become human?

Works Cited

Russ, Joanna. *The Two of Them*. Foreword by Sarah Lefanu. Middletown, Connecticut: Wesleyan University Press. 2005.

Elgin, Suzette Halden. 1969 "For The Sake Of Grace." *Magazine of Fantasy and Science Fiction*.

Gilman, Charlotte Perkins, *The Yellow Wallpaper*. Boston, MA: Small & Maynard, 1899. (Text and commentary by the author available online here: http://www.library.csi.cuny.edu/dept/history/lavender/wallpaper.html.

Lefanu, Sarah. *In the Chinks of the World Machine*. London: The Women's Press, 1988. Review published in Gwyneth Jones, 1999. *Deconstructing the Starships*. Liverpool: Liverpool University Press.

Guevara, Ernesto Ché. *The Motorcycle Diaries: Notes on a Latin American Journey* London: Harper Perennial, 1993. (Reprinted, 2003.)

Gomoll, Jeanne. "An Open Letter To Joanna Russ," *Fanthology* 87. Reprinted from *Sixshooter*; http://www.geocities.com/Athens/8720/letter.htm.

Shora Revisited: Three Blog Posts on SF Feminism in a Time of War

1. Shora

If I were invited to name myself, by the raft people, I would be Gwyneth the Greedy.

And then I would have to spend the rest of my life learning to be satisfied, not abstemious but *satisfied* (no greed like an anorexic's): now there's a challenge.

Rereading *A Door into Ocean* (finally!) has caused me—more than any other of the re-reading I've been doing—to review my own career as a writer and critic of feminist sf. When it came out in the UK, on the Women's Press's daring attempt at establishing an sf imprint, I admired this book greatly as first-class science fiction. But I didn't like the way it went, politically. I felt, and I still feel, that separating out a package of all the virtues and identifying the non-violent, nurturing, creative, life-enhancing society of the future as female-dominated is a dangerous tactic. Not only are you making sure you preach to the converted, by providing a helpful label for the rest, that says in big letters Don't Bother, This Is Not For You…. You're also traducing what to me was, and is, one of the basic tenets of feminism. The society of the future, non-violent, creative, life-enhancing, will not be female-dominated or male-dominated. It will be beyond gender. It will be human.

If you don't know the story, it's about a water world (actually a moon) inhabited by a race of exclusively female human beings who have adapted to aquatic life with the aid of superb, subtly high-tech life science skills. They reproduce by lab-assisted parthenogenesis, they have colonies of oxygen-storing bacteria in their skin (which turns them purple), they "farm" their world sustainably and humanely, they have learned long ago to check their population growth so that it never exceeds a balance with nature. Etc, etc. Their ancient culture is clearly descended, complete with beloved rituals like sit-down strikes, from the unimaginably distant past of Earth, the 1960s, USA, non-violent wing of the Civil Rights and Anti-War movements. Their big, patriarchal neighbor planet tries to take over, forcing them into "free trade," raping the oceans, plundering the ocean bed minerals, and so on. The women resist, non-violently, by all the means their culture provides, and no matter what the bad bosses and their minions do, they won't stop resisting. Nor will they pick up a weapon. It gets nasty, and it gets heartrending. It gets very close to home, maybe more so *now*, in the twenty-first century.

Joan Slonczewski makes you care for her characters, makes you believe they have plenty of other things they'd rather be doing, before she starts having them torched, beaten, blown up, poisoned, etc. The violence is very real, and it just goes on, and on... And this, I recall, was and still is one of the problems for feminist sf, or indeed for any woman who takes on the natural topics of sf (war, invasion, political intrigue) and tries to write *well*. The punters want violent fantasy; they don't want it real. They want the torture scenes to be fun and the bit where the revolutionary hero blows up the bad guys (hey, we all want to be on the side of the angels) to be a riotous firework display...

Women writers are really good at doing what science fiction purports to do, but science fiction is really doing something else. "What we have here is a failure to communicate" as the man with no eyes said (*Cool Hand Luke*; Stuart Rosenberg, 1967): a comedy of fatal misunderstanding, truly funny if you like black humor (luckily I do).

Anyway, where was I? The feminism in my sf. The books I wrote in the eighties and nineties were all about that black humor. I was doing serious work, for my own personal consolation, on investigating the causes of the battle of the sexes. I was also (for nearly all the time I was writing the Aleutian Trilogy) working on the Amnesty International UK Women's Action Committee, which meant I was finding out more than I ever wanted to know about who does what to whom. Yes, it's the men who rape women and children and then have them stoned to death for the crime of having been raped. Yes, for sure, it's the men who go to war, and the women and children who die. More than 90%—if you want a bullshit statistic—of the casualties of so-called modern war are civilians. That means nearly all; and nearly all of them are women and children. But the men's womenfolk are urging them on, and it has always been so, the world over. The mothers-in-law are burning their son's wives to death. The mothers are holding their eight-year-old girl children down, screaming, for the clitoridectomy.

A lot of this inconvenient truth got into the Aleutian books, and I think it was clear that I shared the viewpoint of my "alien" Aleutians. Women are weaker and men are stronger, but the underdogs are treacherous, self-interested, and vindictive as all hell, whenever they get the chance. There's no fair way to apportion blame, no way to make peace; this is just going to have to burn itself out. A plague upon both your houses. We've had enough, we're leaving.

The nineties saw the rise of sf feminism for a larger group, if not for the masses: a rationale and a canon of texts for men and women who wanted to see themselves as "feminists" but who at heart remained ordinary sf punters. They didn't want the violence to be real or the truths to be inconvenient. They wanted feel-good science fiction, as before, just with women in the starring roles and essentially feminine values celebrated. I found this development exasperating, and yet, I respect it: can't blame 'em for being only human. It was what I'd just been writing about, in a bake-sale teacup. Women are just like men! Women want what men want! A bigger piece of pie.

Meanwhile, my personal investigation kept coming up against the wall, the real problem. Speaking bitterness in a society that oppresses women but doesn't know it (such as the sf community, as addressed by "seventies feminism") is brave, but it's easy. Celebrating the feminine—the womb above the penis, motherhood, lesbian starship captains, sexy cyberbabes—is easy, too. Though if you miss out the rip-roaring adventure fantasy you won't catch many punters, and if you don't, it's hard to see how the story differs from any old sf (where the feminine has always been celebrated; ask Robert Heinlein). It's all easy, as long as *la lutte continue*. The wall is when economically liberated women—readers and writers—have to face the fact that when patriarchy goes, we all go.

No one is born a woman. No one is born a man. You can have an evil patriarchy that is secretly an evil matriarchy (which is too damn close to the situation in our world right now, in my opinion). You can have a corrupt liberation, informed by the "Spirit of the Beehive," as Guevara says (cf Joanna Russ's chilling, prescient, *The Two of Them*). You can have a matriarchy that secretly, shamefully oppresses men and denies it and lies about it with every breath (cf *The Gate to Women's Country*, *Divine Endurance*, etc.). You can't have the goals of feminism if you want to keep the Great Divide. And we, we in the editorial and every other sense: everyone, including myself, we do not want to lose the Great Divide. Some greater force, some Invisible Hand—Evolution, Market Forces, the Logic of History, one of those kind of things—is going to have to take that final step and let the other shoe drop. This was the lesson I faced, personally, in the late nineties. I wrote about it in a book eventually called *Life*. Which was intended to be, and indeed remains, my "so long and thanks for all the fish."

It certainly didn't seem like it at the time, but looking back, those were hopeful days.

Anyway, where was I? *A Door into Ocean*. What happens in the end? Well, if you are reading this you won't mind a spoiler. They get rescued. The women get rescued by a male scientist, who's been sent to spy on them and steal their science. They turn him, not by preaching, just by doing what they do. He admires their brilliant lab work and their kindness. He watches them doing the sit-down strikes and getting dragged off by the police, doing it again and getting napalmed by the troops and still going back for more. And he crosses over. He convinces the bosses that the women have a secret weapon. Plus, they probably have the covert backing of the Great Emperor of All.

You could say it's a cop out, why couldn't the women rescue themselves? But they did. Conversion by example is the only victory that those NVDA-types will consider (don't know if she still is, but Joan Slonczewski was a Quaker at the time); so you have to respect that. I just wish someone would rescue Aung San Suu Ki. And I hope someone's around to rescue Arundhati Roy, when she gets herself in real trouble. More later...

2. Shora Revisited

> There was madness in any direction, at any hour... You could
> strike sparks anywhere. There was a fantastic universal sense that
> whatever we were doing, was *right*, and we were winning...

I was too young, the wrong sex, and arguably living in the wrong
country for Hunter S. Thompson's revolution—but I know the feeling he
describes, in a reflective moment during *Fear and Loathing in Las Vegas*.
The elegiac mood when you look back, just a few years later and you
can almost *see* the high water mark, where mad conviction reached its
peak, where the wave (though you didn't know it) was about to break and
roll back...

My high water mark was the mid-nineties. At that time I was working on Amnesty International UK Women's Action Committee. There
was the International Conference on Population and Development in
Cairo (1994), and then the Fourth World Conference on Women in
Beijing (1995); it was exciting to be on the fringes of these huge events.
AI (not the most women-friendly of organizations, oddly enough) was
struggling with the concept of extending its mandate to include *domestic*
human rights, as opposed to the public and State mediated kind. If we
campaign against torture, why not against Female Genital Mutilation?
Isn't a nation state that condones this "traditional practice" to be held
accountable for the misery of their female citizens? If unjust imprison-
ment is an issue when the State does it, what about the millions on millions of people routinely imprisoned without trial in their family homes:
starved, assaulted, raped, abused, denied access to education, to freedom
of expression, to freedom of movement, to medical care, to entry to the
professions? Most of the worst offenders are signatories to the relevant
UN Human Rights Treaties. Most of them, bizarre as it may seem, have
written constitutions, committing them to equal rights for women. What
they're doing—or not doing—is flagrantly illegal.

Let's tell them so!

Many supporters (and this was in the UK, may I say) took a dim
view of women's issues. Many AI apparatchiks swiftly realized the appalling *scale* of the problem, once you decide that women in the Developing
World have human rights, and doubted if Amnesty was capable of taking

the job on. But the moral arguments were strong, and the "feminists" (though you had to be wary of using that term) prevailed.

At a loss for their usual excuses, since the Cold War was over, World Leaders were looking at problems of human welfare. The future looked very alarming: fossil fuels would give out, our miraculous food supplies would fail, hordes of refugees were advancing on the rich countries of the north, wars would soon be fought over water. The problem was population, and bizarrely enough there was a feminist answer (if you don't like the traditional resorts of WAR FAMINE PESTILENCE etc.). Empower the women. *Of course* the World Leaders were going to mangle whatever came out of Cairo and Beijing, but Women's Liberation had reached the top of the inbox; it was getting an interview for the huge job it had always known it could do. Thrilling.

It was very much the *Door into Ocean* scenario. All the *humane* human beings—the good guys, charity workers, aid organizations, human rights defenders—were lined up on the Change and Reform side (by no means all of them women). All the big guns were on the other, defending Business as Usual and Traditional Practices (by no means all of them were men). Naturally, as I'm not a deranged male gonzo journalist, I was at least as scared as I was elated.

"Seventies feminist" sf rarely mentioned the plight of women in the Developing World. Traditional cultures, with all their constraints and prohibitions, were seen as womanly and had to be respected. But the narrative of *exposure* (where the awful price of patriarchy's magnificent escape from nature, aka industrial capitalism, suddenly comes due) was familiar, and the exegesis not very encouraging. It was *de rigueur* at least to suggest that the battle of the sexes—forced out into the open both by scarcity and by women's sudden decision to resist—would become a shooting war. Monique Wittig, Suzy McKee Charnas, Joanna Russ, Marge Piercy, et al.: unlike Joan Slonczewski, they all believed in violence.

When I came to write the Aleutian Trilogy in the mid-nineties, my Gender Wars were even worse, I'm afraid. The violence was on a global scale, not tucked away in some small region of the USA (it's amazing how little one *noticed* that there was no world outside the USA, first time of meeting those texts). It was pretty ugly: I'd had Bosnia and Rwanda to instruct me. Plus it was no longer really possible to have faith in Armed

Struggle. I believed in the ungovernable, outraged anger of men against liberated women, and I could believe that our Secret Rulers would put weapons in their hands: I didn't believe that the good guys could come shining through, untouched, uncorrupted. Savage acts of terrorism were perpetrated by twenty-second century opposition groups still bearing names like CAFOD, OXFAM, and SAVE THE CHILDREN. The gentle can't always hang on until some vital bad guy has a conversion experience. Priests and doctors will pick up guns, if they're made desperate enough by hope denied. Even though they know that the moment they do so, the revolution is doomed.

Maybe it was fear of reprisal, or anger-fatigue; maybe it was manipulation from on high (probably all three); but in the academic world sexual politics was showing a strong drift away from terms like "Women's Studies" or "Feminism" toward the less confrontational "Gender Studies." (There was money in it! You got more funding if you agreed to drop the words "Women" and "Feminism" from course titles.) You can read the pitfalls and the virtues of this peaceable, inclusive approach in the sometimes disconcerting career of the Tiptree Award—defined from the start as an award for works about gender, *not* as a feminist prize. "Gender Studies" is a useful concept, defining both masculinity and femininity as constructed and equally open to analysis. Studying *gender itself* can reinforce the conviction, already strong in the feminist sf community, that there is something ineluctably important about *being female* and behaving in what society says is a female way. It also handily uncouples the study area, or fiction of choice, from that hidden holocaust. But it's fascinating, nonetheless.

The research I'd done for the Aleutian Trilogy and then for *Life* had led me to the conclusion that biological gender is as fake as race. To the eye it looks like a duality, or a handful of variants (Black, White, Asian…). Look any closer: look into the cells, the chromosomes, the neurons, and you see as many different mosaics as there are individuals. The same view was expressed in Raphael Carter's terrific "Congenital Agenesis of Gender Ideation" that won the Tiptree Award for 1998. But Carter's fictional science paper left the roots of gender untouched: and wisely so. They go down *such* a long way, once you start digging. It's frightening in an existential way. What would happen to us, with or without a shooting war, if something so vital, so intricately wound into our being (gay, lesbian, trannie, inter or straight, feminist or womanist, nobody escapes) were taken away???

And yet, if we can't let go of gender, what the hell is going to become of us? The other strand in *Life*, the basic science bit, concerns the alternative, collaborative, and co-operative model of evolution and speciation, which was on the table in the works of Lynn Margulis et al., when I was writing. As an undergraduate, Anna Senoz, my fictional scientist, becomes convinced there's something wrong with Modern Darwinism, something missing from the isolated, selfish gene model of DNA inheritance. Of course she's right, and of course (since she's in a feminist sf novel) she makes a discovery that amounts to clinching evidence for the collaborative and co-operative model. But will she manage to get a hearing in time? Will Anna's scientific revolution, shocking as Copernicus's revelation, Galileo's assertions, change the world before Stupid Darwinism destroys modern civilization?

The Structure of Scientific Revolutions strand (I didn't make it up, it's really happening, right now) which I had found in the careers of Lynn Margulis, Evelyn Fox Keller, Barbara McClintock—the story of The Science That Men Don't See—didn't attract much attention; in fact I can't remember that anyone noticed it. Once you've been nailed as a feminist, it never crosses anyone's mind you might have something to say about science. Only it's not as simple as that, is it? What we have to say *about science* has often, just as it was in *A Door into Ocean*, already been labeled feminist. Evolution as a collaboration, species developing through co-operation instead of conflict, porous boundaries, genes in constant communication and negotiation... How *girly* is all that?

(Actually it's not very girly. Girls, biologically female or otherwise, are hellishly competitive, on an individual by individual basis. But you know what I mean.)

Anyway, by the end of the century I'd pretty much given up trying to get *Life* published. I was enjoying myself with a near-future-fantasy starring a valiant young twenty-first century woman who is aware of feminism, cynical about feminism, and sarcastically resigned to "playing the girl" in a gang of three Indie musicians out to save England from meltdown. After *years* of noting the startling number of male sf writers, from Robert Heinlein to Alastair Reynolds who favored "liberated" female protagonists, and how readily these male-ordered spacebabes were accepted by the audience, the penny had finally dropped, and I was having particular fun with Fiorinda's two adorable boyfriends. And a big thank you here to the blogger (who shall remain anonymous, in case she'd prefer to be) who was the first and only person to mention (ahem) the word *Slash*...

No, seriously, I felt I was following in the footsteps of Maureen McHugh's *China Mountain Zhang*, of Suzy McKee Charnas with her *Vampire Tapestry*: experimenting, intellectually, with the romance of the masculine. It's a feminist issue. If we don't love men (whether or not we want them for sexual partners), if we don't invent heart-warming heroes, or at least male characters we'd like to meet, why the devil should the men listen to us? It was about this time—rather late, because *Queen City Jazz* had come out in 1994—that I ran into Kathleen Ann Goonan and liked what I found. Although *Queen City Jazz* is a gender-bending update of Mary Shelley's *Frankenstein*, I'd still agree with the people who say Goonan writes as if gender doesn't matter. Yet her books are clearly written by a feminist thinker. Cool, challenging, cutting-edge science. Plenty of sci-fi special effects, humane values, wise insights, and the shock of a truly weird posthuman future. Nice!

The Vatican and the Mullahs slung a wrecking ball through the resolutions on Reproductive Rights that came out of Cairo. Beijing fared no better. I was still writing letters (it's what we do) for AIUK, though I'd quit the committee work; so I knew that Women's Human Rights was proving a tough nut to crack. And yet, in ways, I was not unhopeful. I could look back on that high water mark and think, *maybe it's just as well we gave up the confrontation*. Once the weapons are out, everybody loses... Inch by inch, argument by argument, one step forward, two steps back, the lives of women and girls in the Developing World *were* changing. And the liberated women of the Developed World, clinging to their spike heels and their jeweled thongs—irritating as they might seem, those sexy domestic goddesses and investment bankers—were demanding what might well be called feminist (wash your mouth!) rights, with the courage of their growing wealth and power.

"You can suppress the truth as often as you like," says one of the characters in *Life*. "If that's all it is, abstract truth, because who cares? Nobody cares. You can't suppress the facts, because, well, there they are, all over the place—"

I was putting my faith (ironic, huh?) in that good old Invisible Hand. What activism couldn't achieve alone, because we speak with the Spirit of the Beehive, as Ché said, economic clout and sheer *numbers* would accomplish. I was interested to see what would happen about gender. Would the growing *presence* of gay, lesbian, transgendered, and other variants in our society reach a natural limit? Or would it go on growing, until the variants outstripped male/female duality? Time would tell. Not a problem.

I just hoped the Crisis would hold off—remember that Crisis we were all waiting for, at the turn of the century? For a global culture of equality between the sexes to get firmly established we needed parliamentary government, democratic elections, freedom of speech, freedom of association, freedom of the press, rule of law; and I was afraid those luxuries would vanish along with cheap food and mass air travel, once the monstrous pressures of Climate Change (aka population, population, population) took hold. It's not for nothing that the radical feminist and the out-and-proud socialist go down in the first hail of bullets in *Bold As Love*. But I'm a science fiction writer, so I don't believe in the spectacular extreme events that litter the genre. Those things never happen in real life.

3. In War Time

We're always most shocked by the things that shouldn't have taken us by surprise.

I remember waking up in the night after the World Trade Towers attack, that hellish ritual marriage of true minds (I don't remember if I was asleep, but I remember the feeling of being jolted awake) realizing the consequences for *me*, for my personal space. The world had just taken a huge, lurching leap to the right. Every problem that ought to be at the top of the global agenda had been toppled. The whole fragile edifice of women's human rights, *anybody*'s human rights, had been blasted to its knees and was about to collapse into a heap of dust and rubble. As for a civilized, gradualist, winding down of the Battle of the Sexes: forget it, Gwyneth, not a chance, that's over.

Six years on, there's good news and bad news. Connections have been made, that were not in place before. Oxfam has declared that the control of small arms is a vital part of feeding the hungry. Domestic human rights (women's rights) are established campaign issues for Amnesty International, and Irene Khan, a Bangladeshi woman from a "quite conservative" Islamic family, the new Secretary General of Amnesty International, says she intends to keep things that way. But how much can the NGOs do? Amnesty's campaign against rape as a weapon of war has earned more publicity for itself, by annoying the Catholic Church, than it can ever hope to gain for the situation in Darfur. The NGOs were built for the past, for a world where certain truths were held self-evident, and where the notional good guys at least kept up appearances. The moral degradation of the War Against Terror defeats the AI agenda utterly (though it won't stop them trying, nor me).

I still write the letters—to Heads of State, to Attorneys General, to Governors of Prisons. I express my concern for incommunicado detainees. I appeal for them to be given access to lawyers, to medical treatment, to their families. I urge that they be released immediately unless they are to be charged with a recognizable criminal offence. I'm supposed to quote the Universal Declaration of Human Rights, I'm supposed tell these authorities that torture is outlawed by all civilized nations and arbitrary detention is forbidden by International Law. Sometimes I have difficulty making my fingers hit the keys.

More good news and bad news. The digital communications revolution has really taken off, a miraculous tool for political discussion. The bad news, as those of us who've been here for a while are well aware, is that the Internet's a lawless place, and where there is no law, the gangsters rule. If you enjoy sharing your conviction that women should be stoned to death for adultery, you can do it on a website now: nobody will stop you, there are plenty to choose from, and the users are from all walks of life. If you'd like to watch the real-time video, eagerly collected on mobile phones, of the stoning of Du'a Khalil Aswad (a young Kurdish woman "executed" for associating with a Muslim, in April 2007 in Iraq), I bet you can still find it. Try CNN. I think of these things, and I remember what my mother said about the Nazi Holocaust. *It was the bureaucracy...* It was the production line techniques from *modern, forties industry*, brought into service for sorting and processing the shorn hair, the gold teeth, the skin and bones and fat and flesh of the Jews, Gypsies, and the rest. I look at the perversion of civilization, and it terrifies me.

Postscript. What's This Got to Do with Feminist Sf?

Everything, as it turns out. You could say 9/11 was a psychological Pearl Harbor for me. Like the average, well-intentioned US citizen, circa 1940, I had known that dreadful things were happening in the world. But I'd been clinging to the idea (while the territory I thought I could defend got smaller and smaller) that since the war was alien to me, my life and beliefs would not be engulfed.

Co-incidentally (except I'm not sure it's a coincidence), Kathleen Goonan's 2007 novel *In War Times* opens in Washington DC, on the night of December 6, 1941. It's on this night, of all nights, that Sam Dance—a graduate student who's been sort-of drafted into some kind of arcane military research—has ended up in bed with physicist Eliani Hadntz, a Hungarian, maybe a Gypsy, refugee. Eliani tells him what he's already suspected: "We are in a race with the Nazis, to create an atomic bomb." But she's working on a different project herself: some kind of gadget that will interact with human nature. What she envisions is "a vast computational network that is capable of helping us to make changes according to what is truly best for each one of us..." She leaves something with him: a blueprint, a complex secret formula, that will allow him to build his own prototype of her strange device.

Kathleen Goonan is a writer I've been watching since *Light Music* was sent to me for review, a few years ago. She's a woman and a virtuoso of *science* fiction (cf Joan Slonczewski), which is rare. In *Light Music*, and in the earlier *Queen City Jazz*, she does a sterling job of describing, in mind-boggling Greg Egan-style flights, a nanotech future. (Sorry, I had to use a man's name; or you wouldn't have known what I was talking about.) Plus, I felt she was writing the kind of novels I'd been looking for, since I'd reached the conclusion that if feminist sf was to have a future, it had to get beyond "fem-sf."

It's not that feminist analysis in an sf format is out of date. The story is as relevant as ever it was, and the books are still being written. Timmi Duchamp's Marq'ssan Cycle (first written in the eighties, but extensively revised before their C21 publication) is a case in point, Janine Cross's *Touched by Venom* also comes to mind: I haven't read it, but the harsh sexual tone sounds rather like Tiptree (people forget just how *brutal* some of Tiptree's sexual stories were). But it's a niche market, a minority interest: whereas the kind of fem-sf reading that the popular audience will read and buy has become practically indistinguishable from mainstream feminine sf. Stories where "girls get to be guys," either on Space Patrol or with a swashbuckly sword and a feathery hat, will always be popular. Stories celebrating feminine culture, where men are to blame for everything evil and women have been innocent bystanders for all the millennia, are also comfort fare. They're womanly. They offer no challenge to conventional or hyper-conventional "separate development" views on gender roles.

We're not in the seventies any more. Feminists who write genre have to move on, address the realities of a changed world. I'd been thinking that since long before 2001. Actually, once you've done your "sexual politics" novel or two, you should *want* to move on. You want to take what you've learned about the human condition and use it in fiction that has no visible connection with women's lib—except that it's the work of someone who never forgets that dimension.

So, anyway, I was interested to find out where Goonan was going with this. After the climactic opening, *In War Times* develops into a fascinating but fairly conventional science-and-engineering account of WWII, a tribute to Goonan's own father, as she explains in the afterword. Need I tell you that there's a whole lot of jazz? It's a romantic war story, told from the point of view of a single, curiously privileged *male* US soldier, that extends into a family saga covering the following decades. What can I make of that? Well, as observant readers will spot, even before Eliani turns a corner and slips into another dimension, the 1941 of the opening scenes is not *exactly* the same as the one we know. We are in a multiverse story, time seen as a rope of braided possibilities (just like *The Female Man*; in fact "Eliani Hadntz" is a very Russ-like character, the visitor from the future in "The Second Inquisition"). And as you should know, dear reader, in sf that generally means something other than adventure fantasy is going on. A point is being made. Some possibilities may be better, some worse. Compare and contrast. Try to shift the whole braid a little closer to a good place? Could that be it?

What should a feminist do, in war time? In 1914, when the Suffragette Movement in the UK collided with WWI, the Pankhursts had to ask themselves this question. Emmeline Pankhurst and her elder daughter, Christabel, decided they had to drop everything, declare a truce and support the war effort. Christabel's sister Sylvia, lifelong pacifist, felt differently, and went on fighting for the vote (which was finally granted in my country, first installment, in 1918). What should a feminist who writes science fiction do, in the world of the War Against Terror? Sf, *of course*, has also taken that great lurching leap to the right. Hardcore masculine agenda authors are calling themselves liberals now; and no one's going to stop them. The old-style liberals are embattled, fighting a brave fight. Maybe it's time to start rolling those bandages like a good girl. Support the men of good will. Put the feminist agenda, all that human rights and moral high ground *Shora* platform, into mothballs, for the duration—

In Kathleen Goonan's war time, Sam builds himself a "Hadntz device" and becomes some kind of braided-possibilities secret agent. Often the Protean gadget seems no more than a plot device, fixing things so that Sam gets to see all the famous sights: he's first inside the Nazi death camps and visits the slave-labor rocket factories; he flies with the Enola Gay. There are scintillating high-octane solos of sci-fi exposition and a lovely, poignant recurrent theme of ghosting, between one timeline and another. But what's it all about? The terrible events keep rolling by; it seems they all *have to happen*. On the way to where? "Readers new to science fiction," says Douglas Fratz politely, over on Sci-fi.com, "might find it difficult to make sense of the Hadntz device." I'd say sf readers could be equally at a loss. At times I wondered if the gadget was a metaphor for the Bomb itself (a device that *had to happen*, and kept some kind of peace for forty years…). In the end, I think I settled for the Declaration of Human Rights. The gadget that will interact with human nature, that's brought from another dimension by a woman who could not exist in "our" world, is a *morality*: an algorithm for humane civilization.

I think I understand why a twenty-first century feminist and sf virtuoso decided to write about WWII. *Bold As Love* is full of WWII references, too. It's a way of writing about this state of war we're living in, without exploitation. And in my country, it means survival, against all the odds. In Goonan's iconography, I don't know. Maybe it means accepting that *the bad thing has happened*; that you have to deal with it. In either case, it means don't give up. Never give up. Your opponent may make a mistake, sometimes the tables do turn… And that's my message, finally, at the end of this long self-examination. Don't give up. Don't be satisfied with the lovely books where "girls get to be guys." Write the books and seek out the books to read, where the girls get to be *people*, and the boys get to be people too.

Don't celebrate feminine culture. Feminine culture does not need your support. It's a big, strong, greedy animal, with moral values that are neutral at best. It mows down individual women like grass, especially the dissenters. It has been happy to "hold up half the sky" for the most brutal and oppressive regimes the world has known. Celebrate humane civilization instead.

Don't celebrate permanent warfare…

Hm. Does this advice sound boring, dear sisters and brothers? Far too bland for sci-fi? You treasure your rape fantasies, you like a bit of torture? Well, here's *Shora* for you: enjoy. You don't know much about human rights defenders if you think their story is bland or lacking in pain and horror… And get over it. Your junk-food obesity is not pretty, and it's doing harm both to you and to the world.

One last thing—

Good luck.

Sheri S. Tepper: Avenging Angels
and Worlds of Wonder

First published, in slightly different form, in *Fifty Key Figures In Science Fiction*, eds Mark Bould, Andrew M. Butler, Sherryl Vint; Routledge Media Studies, Talyor and Francis Group, Abingdon UK, July 2009.

Sheri S. Tepper came to sf at fifty-three, as a second career. She'd published some poetry and children's stories, but it was only after she retired from her post as Executive Director of Rocky Mountain Planned Parenthood that her extraordinary genre success story began. Her first works were for young adults (The True Game trilogy of trilogies; The Marianne trilogy) and have the character of fantasy, although the True Game series has an sf premise. Her later fantasies include *Beauty* (1991, winner of the 1992 Locus award), an extensive reworking of "The Sleeping Beauty" with a grim contemporary twist. She has written horror and mysteries under pseudonyms (B.J. Oliphant, A.J. Orde, E.E. Horlak) and has continued to include elements of fairytale, folklore, horror, and the supernatural in a number of acclaimed and much loved sf novels.

The Awakeners (1988, initially published as *North Shore* and *South Shore*, 1987) attracted critical attention and announced some of the themes—planetary romance, gender roles, environmental issues, commensal species, the evils of fundamentalist religion—to which she has remained faithful. *The Enigma Score* (1987, 1989; initially published in the US as *After Long Silence*) is another very attractive genre tale, notable for its marvelously strange imagined landscapes; but her reputation was established with *The Gate to Women's Country* (1988). Set on the Northwestern seaboard of the USA, some centuries after a global nuclear war, the novel describes a refuge society where arts, crafts, and scientific knowledge are preserved in walled enclaves of women and children. The majority of men and all male adolescents live in stark garrisons outside. Female prostitution exists, but the only sanctioned sexual relations are at "carnival," a brief period when the warriors are welcomed into the streets. Ostensibly the women are the weak partners in this arrangement, obliged to support the garrisons with their labor and skills and to hand over all male children to their "warrior fathers." The reality—suggested by oblique hints, but concealed until the last pages—is very different. Flashing backwards and forwards in time, we follow the fortunes of Stavia, daughter of a prominent citizen of Women's Country, as she pursues an illicit friendship with Chernon, a duplicitous and finally irredeemable young warrior. Their relationship—the girl deceiving herself, helpless in the throes of sexual attraction, the boy motivated by cold self-interest from the start—mirrors the secret truth. Chernon believes, until the end, that all the power is on his side: but he's wrong. The warriors of Women's Country believe that they dominate the women and that they are the fathers of their "warrior sons." In fact—as Stavia discovers when initiated into the Ruling Council (the "Damned Few")—both the couplings of carnival and all non-sanctioned sexual transactions are barren. Women approved for breeding by the "Damned Few" are artificially inseminated, without their knowledge or consent, with the sperm of specially chosen "servitors"; men with kindly, civilized traits. Meanwhile "wars" between the garrisons are engineered, and controlled to ensure that the most aggressive and vicious of the troops and officers are most likely to die. Scenes from a pseudo-Classical play called *Iphigenia at Ilium,* rehearsed at intervals throughout the novel, point to the moral. A situation that looks like a Greek Tragedy, for the unlucky women who have survived men's wars, is really a black and mordant comedy. The proud warriors are being systematically culled and selectively bred out of existence.

Despite a negative position on both male and female homosexuality and Tepper's insistence on the right of a "wise" elite to control reproductive rights, *Gate* swiftly joined the canon of feminist sf. It shares many motifs with other feminist works—post-catastrophe scarcity conditions; effortful utopia (for feminists, *utopia* always means *hard work*); regenerative female-ordered governance; the vital project of eliminating organized violence from human society; even the psychic powers that some servitor (civilized) males are developing. Tepper's version is unusual in presenting young characters of both sexes as appetite-driven and self-destructive, and in characterizing the fate of the warrior breed as a tragic, guilty secret. Her even-handedness may account for the book's wide appeal, but it is deceptive. Sheri Tepper's views on the problem of gender are draconian and can be merciless.

The Gate to Women's Country, with its narrow scope and single focus, is anomalous in Tepper's work. In *Grass* (1989), the artistic space in which she conducts her vivid experiments made its first developed appearance. On overcrowded earth, a patriarchal religion called "Sanctity"—closely modeled on the Mormon church—rules with an iron fist. Abortion is condemned, contraception forbidden; the brutalized excess population gets shipped out for slave labor on prison planets. Marjorie Westriding, former Olympic dressage and puissance medalist, wronged wife and troubled Old Catholic, struggles to do good in the teeming slums, aware that she's merely salving her own guilt. Meanwhile an apocalyptic plague is spreading through the settled worlds: highly infectious, hideous in its effects, and invariably fatal—except on the planet called Grass. When Marjorie's diplomat husband, Rigo Yrarier, is posted to Grass, with the mission to find out anything he can about the rumored cure, the family (all accomplished riders) soon discover that their briefing was seriously flawed. The "bons," the aristocratic elite among the human settlers, were supposed to be keen fox-hunters, riding to hounds Old English style. In reality, the Hunt on Grass is orgiastic torture, forced upon the enthralled human riders for the malign entertainment of native semi-sentients. In spite of all warnings, Marjorie's obnoxious husband and her rebellious daughter fall under the dreadful spell. But the fearsome Hounds, the terrifying Mounts, and the "foxen" they pursue are bound together in an extraordinary puzzle, part ecological, part mystical, which Marjorie must unravel to save the settled worlds and her own soul—with the help of the demon lover who brings ecstasy and enlightenment, a saintly, aged archaeologist, and the spiritual presence of the Arbai, a vanished Elder Race.

Widely recognized as a major classic, and undoubtedly Sheri Tepper's most splendid achievement, *Grass* is a crowded and spacious canvas in which many genres combine: a painful family saga, a scientific mystery, a creepily effective sci-fi horror tale, and a close-fought, climactic Battle between Good and Evil. Secondary histories, secondary characters are delineated in lively detail, not forgetting El Dio Octavo, Marjorie's courageous, faithful steed (in Tepper novels, animals are often significant characters). Above all there is the planet itself, the haunted paradise, one of the loveliest of sf's imagined worlds—

> Grass! Ruby ridges, blood-colored highlands, wine-shaded glades… Orange highlands burning against the sunsets. Apricot ranges glowing against the dawns. Seed plumes sparkling like sequined stars. Blossom heads like the fragile lace old women take out of trunks to show their grandchildren. (7)

It's an intensely *feminine* brew; yet *Grass* also carries Tepper's most radical feminist message. Here there are no draconian solutions. Instead there's the foxen, imago form of Grass's metamorphic dominant species. Like the chimera figure in The Marianne trilogy, he represents a potent, idealized image of what *the masculine* means, in Tepper's worldview—part beast, part angel, part fellow-traveler, monstrous, irresistible, and indispensable complement. In her dealings with this majestic alien, Marjorie Westriding not only takes on the role of the investigative scientist/hero, she is also the archetype of humanity, encountering otherness. Thus, at the heart of *Grass*, we find the gender problem resolved through a classic sf diptych. On one hand the blundering, exciting, serendipitous struggle to understand a bizarre and deadly alien species. On the other: *Childhood's End*. Marjorie and her foxen lover complete each other. Having achieved union they are ready to move on—through the technologically-mediated transcendence of the Arbai Door—to a higher level of existence.

Grass was followed, in a loose trilogy, by *Raising the Stones* (1990) and *Sideshow* (1992). Marjorie reappears briefly in *Raising the Stones* and again as an angelic troubleshooter in *Sideshow*, but the real link between the novels is the intervention of the Arbai, the vanished Elder Race. Elder Races who leave artifacts of fabulous power behind them are a staple of sf. Here the "Arbai Device" (or "The Hobbs Land Gods")—a (meta) genetically engineered fungus with the power, when buried shallow with a suitable corpse, to render the belief system of a community concrete and effectual—is used to interrogate the phenomenon of religion. What if our gods were living beings, dependent on our worship? What if

God's presence in the world made us good? What if evil creeds brought supernatural demons to life? In *Raising the Stones* the focus is on fathers and sons, the sons of human society in its original, matrilineal state: who re-invent their absent fathers as gods and found abusive belief systems on a myth of fatherhood. No match for *Grass*, this is still a serious work. The homely utopia of Hobbs Land lovingly evokes an ideal Deep West USA, and Sam Girat, anti-hero, is Tepper's most effective human male charac-ter: sympathetic yet recalcitrant, hell-bent on ruining everyone's life, yet full of goodwill. *Sideshow*, a less successful novel, brings the story to its resolution, reprising the motif of Marjorie's personal ascension (through horrors to transcendence) on a hugely magnified scale: taking us to the apocalyptic End of Man.

Later novels explore the same themes, reworking variants on the same motifs, with unflagging invention, energy, and conviction. *Gibbon's Decline and Fall* (1996) tackles gender politics in a much richer form than *The Gate to Women's Country* does, through the fortunes of a group of col-lege roommates—one of whom, the mysterious Sophia, may be the Third Person of the Trinity (Holy Wisdom) incarnate. *Six Moon Dance* (1998) and *Singer from the Sea* (1999) return to dark and intriguing planetary romance. Population and commensal species issues take the foreground in *The Companions* (2003), where the creed of "Firstism" (introduced in *Shadow's End*, 1994) has wiped out almost every living species on earth, and homage is paid to Tepper's beloved dogs. What if we met sentients who perceived and communicated only through smell? In *The Margarets* (2008), balanced between sf and fairytale, Earth's domestic cats get their turn, as whimsical galactic foster-children.

Sheri Tepper has admitted, ruefully, that she sometimes wishes she could get herself a "polem-ectomy" because in her work the polemic gets in the way of the literature. Her anger is a valid sf mode, arguably justi-fied by our present situation, on the brink of environmental catastrophe, but her absolutes can be bewildering and can seem self-defeating. She presents the traditional gender roles as a nest of horrors: yet believes they cannot be changed and insists that homosexuality is unnatural (though not blameworthy). Eugenics may be used to build Utopia, and the masses need not be consulted. There is no escape from a horrific future or from the terrible dance of the conjoined twins (a Tepper image of human sexual relations, later reprised as an image of the human condition: monster and angel, joined at the hip) except through Divine Intervention. Her popularity, despite the uncompromising harshness of her vision, may rest on the fact that readers are never asked to embrace revolutionary change, only to cheer for the good guys. But above and beyond her anger and her conservatism, Tepper is "that rare thing, a born storyteller," with the added value of a sophisticated, rigorous, science-fiction mind. "In the space of a few years, she became one of sf's premier world builders…" says Peter Nicholls, in the Encyclopedia of Science Fiction. She will be read and studied, for this natural talent and her marvelous skill, when the disasters she predicts—we may hope!—have become dangers long averted.

Secondary Reading

Beswick, Norman. "Ideology and Dogma in the 'Ferocious' Sf novels of Sheri S. Tepper," *Foundation* 71:32-44, 1997.

Clute, J. and Nicholls, P. *The New Encyclopedia Of Science Fiction*, London: Orbit Books, 1993.

Reid, R. A. "'Momutes': Momentary Utopias In Tepper's Trilogies," 1999, in M. Batter ed. *The Utopian Fantastic: Selected Essays from the Twentieth International Conference on the Fantastic in the Arts,* London: Praeger, 2004, 101-109.

Tepper, Sheri. *Grass*; London: Harper Collins; 1996. (1989.)

———. *Raising the Stones*. New York: Doubleday, 1990.

———. *Sideshow*. New York: Doubleday, 1992.

———. *After Long Silence*. 1987.
(Published as *The Enigma Score* in the UK.)

———. *The Gate to Women's Country*. New York: Doubleday, 1988.

———. *The Marianne Trilogy*. (omnibus edition) Corgi, 1990.

———. *Beauty*. New York: Doubleday, 1991.

———. *A Plague of Angels*. New York: Bantam/Spectra, 1993.

———. *Shadow's End*. New York: Bantam/Spectra, 1994.

———. *Gibbon's Decline & Fall*. New York: Bantam / Spectra, 1996.

———. *Six Moon Dance*. New York: Eos, 1998.

———. *Singer From The Sea*. New York: Eos, 1999.

———. *The Companions*. New York: Eos, 2003.

———. *The Margarets*. New York: Eos, 2007.

Wild Hearts in Uniform—The Romance of Militarism in Popular Sf

First published in "Fictions" *Studi sulla narativita Anno III 2004*: guest editors Darko Suvin and Salvatore Proietti.

Spartan Boys

"We're willing to consider extenuating circumstances," the officer said. "But I must tell you, it doesn't look good. Kicking him in the groin, kicking him repeatedly in the face and body when he was down—it sounds like you really enjoyed it."

"I didn't," Ender whispered.

"Then why did you do it?"

"He had his gang there," Ender said.

"So? This excuses anything?"

"No."

"Then tell me why you kept on kicking him. You had already won."

"Knocking him down won the first fight, I wanted to win all the next ones too, right then, so they'd leave me alone."

(*Ender's Game*, Orson Scott Card, 19)

This quotation from Orson Scott Card's phenomenally successful 1985 novel *Ender's Game* illustrates a salutary lesson. The science fiction that sells and therefore must be accepted as deeply, truthfully representative of the genre is neither sophisticated futurology—*Ender's Game* has a Cold War scenario, embarrassingly outdated compared to the cyberpunk *Neuromancer,* the William Gibson novel that had swept the board in a similar way the year before—nor the expertly crafted, anti-literary, technophile propaganda of legend. Popular sf is a literature of arousal, of guilty passion and violent emotion, secured by any means necessary, ruthless brutality or compassion, quite indifferently. The stern, meticulously machined and rational exterior, the autistic passion for weaponry and battle-plans, is the outer, defensive shield of militarist sf. *Ender's Game,* undoubtedly a classic of the (sub) genre, reveals the inner nature.

It is my contention that the *popular* militarist science fiction of the Pause (from the end of the Cold War to 9/11, the period when the sf heartland had no iconic external enemy), that is, the science fiction read and admired by the mass audience, has a very different character from that usually associated with the term "militarist sf." Weapons technology and the science of warfare are minimized; the "science" content is, typically, negligible. The drama of the individual's engagement with the military machine of the State is foregrounded and passionately valorized or else milked for pathos to the extent that submission itself becomes a perverse thrill. In support of this position, I will make reference to the amateur reviews posted on Amazon.com: a dubious forum, but a place where I believe the genuine voice of the mass-market reader—the audience whose response defines sf—can be heard.

Later in the novel the fate of the playground bully downed by the six-year-old hero "Ender" Wiggin becomes, or is revealed as, more dramatic. The six-year-old may have actually killed his playmate—just as he executes, in much the same circumstances and following the same reasoning, a thirteen-year-old rival "officer" in the International Force's army of juvenile military geniuses: "The only way to end things completely was to hurt Bonzo enough that his fear was stronger than his hate" (*Ender's Game,* 229-233).

"Ender" (the nickname for an extra child) Wiggin's parents live under a benign totalitarian regime. An entity known as "The International Force" commands the economy and rules the world—a situation that has come about due to a threat from without: the alien "Buggers" with whom "Earth" is waging a generations-long war (the term "Earth" here designating, as always in mass-market best-selling sf, a planet-sized USA, where multiculturalism survives as a signifier for "poor" or "disadvantaged"—

a reasonable extrapolation, any time in the last few decades, one has to admit). The Wiggins have paid a high price to secure the privilege of a third child in their overcrowded world. They are taking part in a genetic experiment designed to produce super-intelligent warriors, the geniuses who will be able to beat the "Buggers." Ender's psychotic older brother Peter has been discarded as too volatile, his conciliatory sister Valentine is "too weak." Ender, the Harry Potter of modern militarist sf, has now passed the final test. He has proved he has the right motivation. He is willing to commit acts of the utmost savagery, but only in the interests of personal security, not for pleasure.

Ender Wiggin believes that the purpose of waging war is to make it so the enemy will go away and never come back. The concept of war as a limited, normal exaggeration of milder negotiations, "diplomacy continued by other means" would go right by him, uncomprehended. The grumblings of long-term co-existence with social or political rivals are unknown to him: there must be no hostiles; hostiles must be annihilated. At six years old he's already the perfect cannon fodder, a Spartan Boy who will break the social-animal taboos we carry and kill without hesitation. But unlike the licensed soldier of the past, who might be bludgeoned into becoming a temporary killing-machine and take no responsibility for his actions, Ender is obliged to believe himself, for his torment, a moral being. He kills, he slaughters, but he agonizes over what he does: he always feels terrible after a murder.

Ender's Game won both the Hugo and the Nebula awards when it was published in novel form in 1985; the original story dates from 1977. It was immediately acclaimed by professional, as well as popular critics— and deservedly so. The plot may be repetitive (Ender annihilates rival: sheds crocodile tears; Ender annihilates rival: sheds crocodile tears...), but the use of video gaming and the prescient description of the internet, manipulated as a tool of world domination by Ender's brother and sister, Peter and Valentine, was remarkable. When I read it in 1985, my chief feeling was astonishment that such an orgiastic description of State hypocrisy and the utter corruption of a child could be rated by so many as great *undemanding entertainment*. But the popular reader is made of tougher stuff. The enduring importance of this book to the sf masses—at a time when Orson Scott Card's work is in eclipse—can be measured in the 2080+ amateur reviews it has collected on Amazon.com.

Notably, actual military operations play a very slight part in the plot. The part played by the "International Force" is soon reduced to a strand of self-loathing asides from Ender's minders—shedding more of those crocodile tears over the things they have to do to nurture a little boy's genocidal paranoia. Strategy and tactics in the long battle against the "Buggers" are nonexistent, as the characters freely admit. For all the difference it makes, the enemy ships and the enemy armies may as well be what they are to Ender: icons on a game screen, a paper-thin pretext. It's clear, throughout, that what matters to Orson Scott Card, and to his readers, are the hot-house passions of Boot Camp (Battle School) and the heartfelt personal crises that Ender endures there.

It can be argued that militarism is the only justified background and motive force for science fiction, at least for "science fiction" as the term is understood by the general public. Space exploration serves military goals; only superpower military budgets are elastic enough to embrace the giant-scale technologies that must form the launch pad of a space-faring future. If other giants, supra-national corporations, become massive enough to support such huge enterprises then they must inevitably take on the military character of "benign totalitarianism": where an army of employees eats the company's food, lives in regimented housing, sends their children to Company School, wears company uniforms, shops with company currency at the company store. It could be said that the future must be military, if it is to be anything like a science fiction future at all. The social mores of a command economy (take your issued clothing, live here, go there, you don't need money, you have assigned housing and a coupon for the cafeteria) are natural to a newly-colonized galactic empire. It's not for nothing that the traditional "enemy" is an insect with a hive-life civilization. We fear most what most horrifies us in ourselves.

Ender's Game was conceived in the seventies and may be compared to the whole body of Vietnam-inspired movie-making and print fiction of those years, particularly Joe Haldeman's classic "Vietnam" science fiction novel, *The Forever War* (1974), in which a superbly realized exposition of time dilation, as a consequence of interstellar travel, serves the further purpose of invoking the alienation of an over-educated conscript, coming home to find the world cruelly changed. *The Forever War*, far superior in critical terms for its science exposition and for its exploration of the shock of the new, is a less popular choice for modern sf readers than *Ender's Game*, snagging only 219 Amazon.com reviews, though equally highly rated by the fans who have discovered it. Like Ender Wiggin, Private William Mandella has been drafted because he is super-intelligent (as one of the amateur reviewers on Amazon.com points out, an amazingly stupid way to choose your cannon fodder); and like Orson Scott Card, Haldeman has no concept, in this novel, of organized violence as part of a sustainable relationship between nations. War is a tragic accident, coming out of nowhere. When the "Buggers" have been destroyed it turns out that the hostilities were meaningless. Ender spends the rest of his career (spanning several sequels) expiating his guilt for the needless slaughter (*Speaker for the Dead*; *Xenocide*; *Children of the Mind*). In Haldeman, at the end of the 1143-year-long war with the "Taureans," it is discovered that "the Forever War" was "begun on false pretences and only continued because the two races were unable to communicate" (232). In some ways, the curiously innocent view of warfare offered by these US writers—from a culture that had sustained a reasonably bloody *civil* war, complete with full media coverage of the issues, not much more than a century before—contrasts favorably with war Old World style, which involves perpetrating horrific brutalities on the people who live next door and will still be your neighbors when the smoke clears and for a thousand years after that. Yet a non-existent enemy is another means of trivializing the alleged subject of the fiction. There can be no political discussion of the flashpoint in either book. It is not possible to examine the kind of grievances or the pressures (climate change? Population dynamics?) that lead the Buggers, the Taureans, and the Humans to collide with each other; it is not possible to ask why alternatives to aggression were not considered or to anatomize the conflict itself. Neither the readers nor the fictional characters are really interested in those issues anyway. Nobody is. The individual soldier's quarrel and love-affair is with the army, not the hostiles. The hostiles are part of what the army did to you, one of the tools the army used to take away your humanity… And yet the army is still the matrix: unavoidable, deeply reassuring. In *The Forever War* the army or the mad military-industrial complex takes on the demonized role of the First World War generals of Western Europe, but the bitterness this invokes is almost perfunctory.

"It's so dirty"—(says Margay, William's girlfriend, when they have been tricked into re-enlisting for a second tour of frontline duty)—

I shrugged "It's so army—." But I had two disturbing feelings:

That all along we knew this was going to happen.

That we were going home. (*The Forever War*, 133)

Though *The Forever War* was written as an *anti*-war novel, and nobody would make that claim for *Ender's Game*, it's not really surprising that the Haldeman has survived in the popular imagination as a war story. To many of its twenty-first century fans the novel seems a terrific sci-fi war story, second only to Heinlein's *Starship Troopers* for its gritty and satisfying realism, marred by inexplicable outbursts of distasteful sex and "liberal" propaganda. (See Amazon.com Aug. 25, 2004; June 25, 2004.) And maybe this assessment is partly justified.

Miltarist sf has a tendency to invoke historical models, including the ancient classics. In the course of the action of *Ender's Game*, Valentine Wiggin will invent a Hawkish internet persona called "Demosthenes," and she and Peter between them will manipulate political opinion on a global scale with huge success. As leaders of the world's Warparty, the US (here rebranded as the International Force) could easily stand in for the Athenian League: alleged democrats at home tempted into tyranny abroad. Equally obviously, Ender Wiggin is the Spartan Boy, trained at military school to behave like a ruthless criminal because ruthless criminals are the cannon fodder required. But to Xenophon, the Polity of the Spartans was a useful and edifying social study, and to Thucydides the Peloponnesian War was a living laboratory in which the nature of human conflict could be studied. The lives lived and hearts broken, the passions aroused and assuaged under the aegis of a military uniform were scarcely their concern. For popular science fiction writers like Card and Haldeman, human interest must be paramount, and the balance is reversed. There is very little discussion. War is simply a hellish yet unavoidable insanity (one might compare *The Forever War* with Joseph Heller's classic satire, the contemporaneous, *Catch 22*). In this hell, the army becomes life itself, something to cling to, and the repository of a (reluctant) soldier's conscience: the *heimat* where he (or she) is innocent.

But the tormented Ender Wiggin and cynical, good-hearted William Mandella are both, in different ways, children of the liberal sixties. They are universal soldiers, deeply aware of the horror of war, adopting wildly divergent strategies to cope with their responsibilities as fantasy action heroes (for whom there is really no escape from a life of violence). Where will these strategies lead them? What new characters and startling traits will sf readers approve, as the sixties recede?

Romantic Aristocrats

> "The really unforgivable acts are committed by calm men in beautiful green silk rooms, who deal death wholesale by the shipload, without lust, or anger, or desire, or any redeeming emotion to excuse them but the cold fear of some pretended future. But the crimes they hope to prevent in that future are imaginary. The ones they commit in the present—they are real."
>
> *Shards of Honor*, Lois McMaster Bujold (1986) 141

Spartan Girls are not rare in militarist sf, but the feminine takeover of popular military sf series in the decade following *Ender*, reveals again the secret appetite for romance and sentiment that characterizes the "militarist" audience. Significant female characters, contrary to received wisdom on this issue, have always been acceptable in science fiction. In contrast to the malign "phallic female" of the thriller genre, a "phallic" empowered female often plays a positive role in action fantasy (for example the "street samurai" Molly in William Gibson's *Neuromancer*). Ender Wiggin's sister Valentine enjoyed the ambiguous privileges of Spartan womanhood. She was tested for warrior prowess equally with her brothers, and though judged too weak for Battle School (or rather, "too moral," a charge rarely leveled at women in Classical times), she retained an active, public role—as "Demosthenes," and as the grieving chorus who charts Ender's destruction. Ironically, the next decade was to see a woman writer leap into prominence with a series decidedly more positive about militarism. The quote above is from the first published volume of Lois McMaster

Bujold's Vorkosigan series, *Shards of Honor* (1986)—a novel which in fact chronicles the romance between her hero's parents. The speaker, Lord Aral Vorkosigan, could be regarded as (private) William Mandella's mutant offspring. He's a career soldier by default, he really had no choice in his avocation, but basically is decent and honorable. The Betans, socialist and liberal-valued enemies of his own planet, feudal Barrayar, call him "the Butcher of Komarr." This is an unjustified slur, though there are things in his past he's not particularly proud of, such as a homosexual romance with the sadist princeling who was his first wife's lover. He has the same cynical affection for the army and feels the same resigned distaste towards the dirty tactics of High Command as Mandella, but this soldier is more deeply complicit: he is of the same caste as the chiefs of staff, an aristocrat of the highest possible rank.

The narrative of *Shards of Honor* is transitional. The heroine, Cordelia Naismith, is an army scientist from peaceful, egalitarian, sexually polymorphous Beta. Her encounter with the Ruritanian feudalism of Barrayar at times resembles a cheap and cheerful version of Ursula Le Guin's *The Dispossessed*, where a scientist from the dirt-poor Utopia of Anarres is confronted by the unprincipled luxury of the homeworld, Urras. But while Shevek sets out as an apostate from Utopia and then finds himself horrified by Urras, Cordelia—when she returns to Beta after her adventures with the saturnine Lord Aral—finds herself disgusted by the regimentation and the interference of the Welfare State. She willingly chooses the life of an aristocrat's consort in Ruritania, abandoning her career and her "liberated" status in exchange for security, a prettier uniform, and the right to have a husband and a devoted bodyguard bearing arms.

The formal rejection of a "Sixties agenda" seems a rite of passage, a signal that moderately conservative US readers, by far the largest group in the sf buying public, need not fear to enter this world. Equally it was a signal to those more liberally inclined: Bujold is not ignorant, she has made an informed choice and can be trusted not to do anything too offensive... Subsequent volumes (from *The Warrior's Apprentice* and still ongoing with *Diplomatic Immunity*, 2002) recount the history of Miles Vorkosigan, Aral and Cordelia's son, crippled from birth because of a terrorist chemical weapon attack while his mother was pregnant. Barred from conventional military success, he pursues an oblique career: first as the "Admiral" of an irregular force of privateers, then as a highly-placed "diplomatic troubleshooter." Attacks on feminism and welfare politics are never aggressive (which is not the case in the other military series), sexual diversity is presented as acceptable, and human gene-modification is endemic. The reader, male or female, can count on the Vorkosigan saga for clear, undemanding prose, mild adventure, witty dialogue, feel-good plots, a modicum of violence (including rather startling levels of torture), and above all the vicarious sense of being a privileged insider: someone who may seem insignificant, but who at any moment may command the people right at the top of the organization.

Bujold's fragile but steely-willed aristocrat hero bears a marked debt to Lord Peter Wimsey, the fragile but redoubtable aristocrat detective invented by the British writer Dorothy Sayers. Miles Vorkosigan's "job" strongly recalls Lord Peter's ill-defined role in pre-war international tensions in Thirties Europe. Her dialogue and narration, well above average for mass market sf, owe something to Sayers, and also to the historical, romantic comedies of another British woman writer, Georgette Heyer—as does the character of Aral Vorkosigan, who is a dead ringer for one of Heyer's sardonic, soft-centered, prize-fighting Corinthians. (The influence is not so strange as it sounds, and not unique to Bujold. Georgette Heyer's comedies, set during the Revolutionary and Napoleonic Wars, have provided other sf writers with a useful template for the social mores of high society in a time of permanent warfare.) In the late eighties and early nineties the success of Bujold's series was a revelation. Terrified by the radical ideas and literary experiments of feminist sf, unconvinced by fantasy dragons, respectful but slightly resentful of Le Guin and Butler (Ursula Le Guin and Octavia Butler, the two US sf novelists of the twentieth century to gain enduring, mainstream literary recognition), the great science fiction public had finally discovered what it wanted from "liberated" women. There had been, there were, women writing challenging science fiction and challenging space opera (Nancy Kress, Carolyn Cherryh, even Gwyneth Jones) without particular reference to their sex. Bujold was best-selling science fiction's feminine voice: graceful, easy-reading romance, good-willed elitism, a touch of brutality, not too much tech, and uniforms with plenty of gold braid.

Lois McMaster Bujold's Barrayan Universe novels (the Barrayan Universe is the human inhabited space-volume in which her stories are set) received no great critical acclaim but won her three Hugos and a Nebula award—a record that reliably signals broadly based popular respect. The Serrano Legacy books, the military sf series created by fantasy writer Elizabeth Moon (best known for her Paksenarrion trilogy, which recounts the career of a female Galahad, with a ruthless degree of borrowing from fantasy gaming, and—at a remove—from Tolkien), may divide the public more along age and gender lines. Where Bujold discarded her female protagonist, choosing instead the unisex device of a physically handicapped, but still powerful, male hero, Elizabeth Moon's primary heroine, Esmay Suiza, seems designed—whether by calculation or by natural inclination—to appeal to the stereotype of a teenage sf reader. Shy, nerdy, with terrible hair, Esmay is the high-school geek who gets the high scores and never has a boyfriend. In other respects, however, the Serrano Legacy is true to the Vorkosigan pattern. Esmay is a born aristocrat, the heiress of a vast estate on the Spanish-American style rural planet of Altiplano (which bears a resemblance to Elizabeth Moon's native South Texas). Like Miles, she has problems with her powerful family's expectations. As a naval officer cadet she comes unexpectedly into her own, single-handedly rescuing a naval space station and its two hundred thousand crew members from the attack of space terrorists known as the Bloodhorde (*Once a Hero*, 1999). David Weber's Honor Harrington series, in many ways the perfect examplar of mass-market science fiction for this period, features, on the contrary, a heroine (or female hero, if you prefer) the typical female teenage sf reader would go far to avoid. Honor is a six-foot-two, martial-arts trained, modestly beautiful Eurasian: a superb yet unassuming dominatrix, who always gets full marks and is always the favorite of any kind of commanding officer. She has to an extent risen through the ranks, but aristocracy flocks around her sufficiently to make her "yeoman" background immaterial. Weber, whose "universe" is loosely based on the era of the Napoleonic Wars with Honor as the naval champion of the Star Kingdom of Manticore (nineteenth century Britain), says he had Horatio Nelson in mind when he invented her (in real life Horatio Nelson was more of a Miles Vorkosigan type: a fragile, pushy blond with an eye for the ladies). He has expressed his intention of taking her, just as Patrick O'Brian's historical version of the story pursued the career of his Jack Aubery, all the way to Admiral. (Interview with Stephen Hunt, July 2002.)

Science fiction writers mirror their own times, and the mass market series are no exception to this rule. Elizabeth Moon's Familias Regnant Universe is a human inhabited space-volume where the planets take on the geographical and cultural characteristics of different parts of the USA. It has been criticized as "implausible" by some of her fans, but few would contest the idea that this view of the world is very common in sf's heartland. David Weber's transposition of the Napoleonic Wars to deep space features a grumbling interplanetary situation with an enemy of Manticore vaguely identified as a failed Communist experiment. But the real venom in the books is reserved, predictably, for interfering liberals from home: the enemy within. More interesting, in terms of the series's female protagonists, is the position on sexual equality in Weber's and Moon's "universes." Although women may rise to high command, Honor in particular seems extremely lonely at the top. There are other female officers and enlisted women, but except for the distant presence of Queen Elizabeth III, the affectionate high-ranking authority figures she deals with are exclusively male. When Honor gets into sexual trouble—an attempted rape, by the worthless scion of a noble house—she knows better than to expect them to take her side (*On Basilisk Station*). Elizabeth Moon's naval cadet heroines, less exalted and less isolated, have very recognizable teen-movie style high school relationships. When not engaged in action-fantasy derring do, Esmay Suiza's adventures may take the form of cat-fights with a shameless spoiled rich girl, rival for the dishy ensign Barin Serrano, while the spoiled-rich girl—aside from assassination attempts—is in danger of being branded as a predatory female or an easy lay, both of these crimes still well known (*Rules of Engagement*). But though Esmay herself is the survivor of childhood rape, an ugly family secret concealed in suppressed memories (*Once a Hero*), Honor Harrington is worse off. Her career is dogged by sexual harassment. In two oddly parallel stories, Weber's *The Honor of the Queen* (1993) and Moon's *Rules of Engagement* (1998), the preoccupation with rape, with the warrior-women's special and unaltered identity as sexual prey, takes over. In *The Honor of the Queen*, Honor, supposedly riding shotgun on a diplomatic mission to the "conservative" planet of Grayson, finds herself exposed, after an unexpected battle reversal (it's the fault of those interfering liberals, of course), as the senior officer who must negotiate with Grayson's leaders, who are polygamists deeply offended by the sight of a woman in uniform. Things get worse when it's revealed that the female crew members of a ship captured by Grayson's breakaway extremists have been kept naked, beaten, and subjected to multiple systematic rape. In Elizabeth Moon's version, the spoiled rich girl, Brun Meager, gets kidnapped by the god-fearing militia of a planet called Nu-Texas, who are appalled at the existence of "liberated" females. She spends long enough as a sexual chattel to bear twin babies—whom she leaves behind without regret when she's rescued since they're boys and thus won't have a bad life. It has to be said, Moon's spoiled brat makes a far better showing in this kind of adversity than Weber's naval officers—by no means the only sign that David Weber hasn't quite got his head around the idea of *actual* sexual equality. But he's hardly alone in that, and though some of his female fans may splutter indignantly or wince resignedly, they will continue reading. They don't want to hear about a radically different world: that's not the object of this exercise.

Elizabeth Moon tends to High School soap-opera but is more savvy on sexual and social politics and something more of a stylist than Weber. David Weber's prose is extremely far from literary, but he dwells at length on technical detail and fantasy engineering specifications. In both cases the battle scenes are so weighted down by the stereotyped political background and the exigencies of series-continuity that there is little suspense and absolutely no fear of an unexpected outcome. Honor/Esmay/Brun/Heris will suffer terrible injustice, will fail the term-test, will be court-martialed; Honor/Esmay/Brun/Heris will be vindicated, will win the battle single-handed, will be cleared of the imputation of cheating... The level of science fiction ideation is negligible: frankly derisory, if one were to compare it with the science in *The Forever War*. As one reader on Amazon.com puts it, "you plough through all the sci-fi stuff, to get to the characters." The appeal of these books is secretly, exclusively in their prepubertal emotion; it's in the moments of sexless affection between Honor and her high-ranking male father-figures, or of sensuous affection with Nimitz, her faithful—male—pet treecat. Perhaps this is the meaning of the "woman in uniform" in military sf. Licensed by her sex, she provides a safe disguise for the infantalizing of adult characters; one of the sub-genre's guilty treats.

In the final scenes of *Shards of Honor*, after Cordelia Naismith and Aral Vorkosigan have left the stage, a medical orderly watches as a post-mortem nurse tends the dead, recovered from a blasted ship after a space battle. He is repulsed to see the nurse stroke and kiss the body of one dead girl-marine and thinks he's come across some kind of twisted ghoul. Then he realizes this is the nurse's daughter, whom she proceeds to dress in the traditional white gown and lace veil she would have worn to be married. The orderly is much moved. *Yes,* he thinks, *the good face pain. But the great—they embrace it!* (*Shards of Honor,* 253) In the conservative so-cieties of popular militarist sf, warrior maidens die on their wedding day. Rape or the threat of rape is a given; sexual torture is often threatened; but for all the romantic entanglements, consensual sex plays a very small part. The soldier-heroines of Moon's, Weber's, and Bujold's work have embraced a tragic destiny, stripped of sexual life by their role in the hive, but they are not alone. The army infantilizes everyone: you can be a hero and cry like a baby, it's okay, you have a license, you're in uniform.

The Great Embrace Pain

> I could guess, though, what the Admiral's visit would do to *Portia's* morale. My lieutenants had heard him disparage how I ran my ship; his stinging rebuke wouldn't help my authority. And what the midshipmen witnessed was hardly a proper ex-ample for their conduct.
>
> The midshipmen! What was I to do about Philip Tyre? I rocked back and forth, dismayed. The Admiral had given me a direct order; I was to have Philip caned.
>
> The order was utterly unjust; I was Captain of *Portia* and in charge of my ship's discipline. Tyre's demerits littered the Log because of Alexi's attitude, not Philip's. The nightmare relations between Tyre, Alexi and myself had just begun to be resolved, and Lord God knew what effect an unwarranted caning would have on the young middy now.
>
> *Challenger's Hope,* David Feintuch (1995) 74

In Elizabeth Moon's Serrano Legacy sequence, the naked economic supremacy created by genetic-enhancement is mentioned in passing. In Bujold's Vorkosigan Saga, a chemical attack can cause irreparable pre-natal damage, but IVF and embryo optimization are *de rigueur* in the higher castes (among both standard humans and the "races" that have abandoned the original body plan). Typically, in popular militarist sf of the Pause, privilege is innate and unquestionable. The government of choice throughout human settled space-volumes is approximately feudal (the Star Kingdom of Manticore calls itself a Parliamentary Democracy, but that's pretty much of a joke). Main characters have the highest rank and connections. Non-commissioned officers, enlisted men, and enlisted women have walk-on parts (as the necessary casualties the genre knows as "shreddies") or survive, contentedly, as devoted servants. In David Feintuch's Seafort Saga (1994-2001) Nick Seafort, for a change, is an anti-hero, whose relationship with military—or naval—authority is as agonized as Ender Wiggin's, but on a more intimate scale. In his en-gaging introduction to "The Seafort Saga" (the article is available online here: http://www.nickseafort.com/index-1024.htm), David Feintuch has explained how, after a childhood immersed in pulp and Golden Age sf, he came to devise his naval saga:

> …what if someone were in charge of a group, but he knew himself to be incompetent and unable to lead? What if those he commanded also knew it, and he was aware they knew?

> How could I set that up? It had to be important. Therefore a situation where lives were at stake. Command structures would be involved, ergo a military setting. The commander couldn't seek help from home base, else the story would collapse, so the characters had to be isolated as a group for a long period. If the commander were free to resign I'd have no story. Therefore, a hierarchical and rigid society bound by oaths of honor.

> The solution was obvious: the British Navy in the Napoleonic era.

Feintuch then goes on to explain how he decided to set his story in the future and strand his incompetent naval officer in the vast spaces between the stars, because that way he won't have to worry about his ignorance of the technical details—an admission well borne out by the

Seafort Saga itself, which boasts some of the least scientific science fiction and the least convincing alien monsters (giant spacefaring goldfish) of modern times. Perhaps more startling, even if you are familiar with the other militarist series of this period, is the complete absence of the phenomenon known in the British idiom as a "stiff upper lip": the ingrained habit of self-control, vital for discipline and sanity for both officers and men while trapped together onboard a small sailing ship for months. But though these books will never win prizes for their prose, their science, or their common sense, the formula—put an incompetent young man in charge of a situation where emotions *must* be constrained, and then don't constrain the emotions—certainly does the job. Repetitive and formulaic as *Ender's Game* itself, the Seafort Saga rolls on, from one dreadful humiliation to the next, with occasional bursts of brilliant action, to the guilty satisfaction of many readers.

Arguably, sf fans who do not read the mass-market series are not sf fans at all, because here is the modern heartland of the genre: these are the pulps. Those critical readers who admit, with a little gentle probing, to following the Seafort Saga place it low in the credibility league, high in the absurdity ratings. Yet paradoxically, the Seafort future is gritty realism compared to Ruritanian Barrayar or to the Star Kingdom of Manticore. Fundamentalist Christianity rules on earth. The oaths of naval service are backed by a merciless patriarchal God and the merciless fathers who keep that "God" in business. A double standard keeps virtuous women in purdah; though the rich make free use of cloning, donor pregnancy, gene-modification. Furlough in the excitement of Upper New York is marred by the nagging presence of the brutalized underclasses down on the street (in *Challenger's Hope*, Seafort finds himself in charge of a shipload of these raging "transpops," on top of his vessel's normal complement of crew and passengers). But the heart of the Nick Seafort story is in the agonies of the wardroom: where young "middys" haze each other with the orgiastic injustice and unremitting cruelty that is reproduced through the whole chain of command. So much caning on the bare buttocks as goes on in these books! So much hysterical weeping! The British Navy in the Napoleonic era was no doubt a brutal and a brutalizing environment, but as an incredulous German amateur reviewer of David Feintuch remarks (Amazon.com: *Challenger's Hope*), "I know of no army where young officers were subject to such treatment and doubt that there were any" (Amazon.com, February 11, 2000). Yet maybe it all makes sense, in the context of that jealous father/God (Nick finds it difficult to distinguish between the two) and the intimate contact He forbids, between one young man and another.

Wounds and emotional injuries are an important factor in the military series novels, though in the Pause fiction, these wounds are rarely received in conventional action. Honor Harrington, on her way to becoming an avatar of Horatio Nelson, must suffer shattering reverses and is also bound to lose an eye and an arm. The loss of the eye, described in gruesome detail in *The Honor of the Queen* is collateral damage incurred when she's fending off an assassination attempt against a local leader, in a conference room (236-238). Miles Vorkosigan, brittle-boned as a result of that terrorist attack before he was born, suffers major medical trauma in almost every episode. Elizabeth Moon's and Weber's girl-officers are raped and beaten. But in these books, all fantasies of wounding, fantasy wounds, openings of the flesh, may be regarded as having cathartic, sexual meaning for both writers and readers: David Feintuch's saga, here as elsewhere, is perhaps simply a little more candid than the convention of the sub-genre usually allows.

Sexuality is a perennial problem for the armed forces, and equally, the armed forces are a magnet for people whose sexuality is a problem—either personally, or according to the mores of their society. The paradox of gay men/gay women in uniform is well-known, as is the dilemma of heterosexual men in uniform who'd prefer not to use local "comfort girls"—a problem Joe Haldeman solved, in his long ago *Forever War*, by introducing compulsory co-ed bunking, or "indiscriminate promiscuity," to the disgust of many of his modern readers. There is also that female sf reader—heterosexual or homosexual—who identifies herself as having "male" abilities, and feels that this puts her in the aristocracy of her sex; but finds herself barred or disadvantaged in the male world of hierarchies and uniforms. To have the armed forces (or the lab or the corporation) turned upside down by political change would solve nothing for her: but in worlds of the imagination, just a little change is harmless.

Sexuality is not the only problem that can be eased by a retreat into the infantilizing world of the military series. Feelings of inferiority, of helplessness, fear of loss, can be hidden in the organized deprivation of these scenarios, like leaves in a forest. Long ago, in the pause between two movements of a European war that engulfed the world, the science fiction "pulps" provided escape for their humble audience of teenagers and daydreaming technophiles. In those days the traits of heroism were imposed from above. Pulp readers were required to daydream that they were exceptional, that they resisted regimentation, that they were brilliant mavericks, whose emotional life was hidden in decent privacy. They would "buck the system" by inventing some peerless gadget and thereby save the world. Traces of that era lingered long. Ender Wiggin is a brilliant maverick (though he was built, like a robot). But in these mass-market fantasies of war without an external enemy the rich-poor (materially rich, poor in every marker of high-culture) of the USA, of the period between around 1985 and 2001, turned their attention to the personal. The utilitarian, aspirational texts of the old science fiction were subverted into a more consoling catharsis. The irony is that these fantasy militarists, readers and writers, found themselves concentrating (as peacetime governments are forced to concentrate, although it irks them terribly...) on the quality of life for the individual: not on the victory of Manticore over Haven, or Barrayar over Beta, or the annihilation of those pesky giant goldfish—but on the personal fulfillment, emotional well-being, health and happiness of Honor and Miles and Esmay and poor old Nick Seafort.

On the Eve

> "Unusually for people in the entertainment milieu, they supported what they called the responsible elements, the factions in Eurydicean politics who had pressed for a strong defence before any threat had been identified..."
>
> *Newton's Wake*, Ken MacLeod (2004) 50

All of this happened a long time ago, in a galaxy far, far away: so long ago that it's easy to forget that for the last decades of the twentieth century both series science fiction and militarist sf were *in eclipse*— unloved by the critics and denigrated by serious sf readers; even those who were at the same time buying and reading the books avidly. Writers as considerable as C. J. Cherryh, whose Merchanter work is too complex and wide-reaching to be listed as militarist, were put in the shade by cyberpunk and its progeny of future noir, and by great projects of intensively researched realist extrapolation, notably the different versions of an imaginary colonized Mars. Series like The Vorkosigan Saga, The Seafort Saga, The Honor Harrington series, and The Serrano Legacy were the popular but embarrassing face of a subgenre in decline: soft-centered, boarding school stories for grown-ups, which had hijacked certain appealing features of liberalism (the female heroes). But by the turn of the century a vacuum at the top end of the US market had lead critical readers to the UK. The new British science fiction, a resurrection of Space Opera, combined the permanent warfare background and the sexless female heroes of the US militarist series, with more spectacular settings, sharper wit, and superior science content. Alastair Reynolds, Ken MacLeod, and the re-discovered Iain M. Banks appeared on the sacred Hugo and Nebula ballots (along with J.K. Rowling). US authors, both established and rising stars (David Brin, Greg Bear, Dan Simmons, Walter Hunt, and others) swiftly followed suit, and the storylines of mass-market sf returned to the heart of the genre.

But what mark has the reappearance of an external enemy made on the *military* fantasies? As I write (in 2009, revising this article for book publication), all the authors I've cited are still active, except for the late David Feintuch. Lois McMaster Bujold, one of the most honored of living science fiction and fantasy writers, won a Hugo and a Nebula award for her fantasy, *Paladin of Souls,* in 2003, and is currently working on a new Vorkosigan novel. Elizabeth Moon, while still pursuing the Serrano Legacy, has had outstanding critical success with *The Speed of Dark* (2002), a story about living with Autism, barely set in the future. Weber, Scott-Card, and Haldeman are still series writers with a military bent; Haldeman in particular is enjoying renewed popularity. But as military sf (Mil-sf) has become more hardcore, popular militarist women writers have become harder to find—though female soldier characters, "tough girls," are as popular as ever.

The genre bestseller lists are dominated as always by media spin-offs, fantasy epics and (currently) a startling number of female-authored sexy horror series. Military and militarist sf (Mil-sf) is still attracting new (male) writers, and developing stronger ties both with wargamers of the classic variety, and the online and videogaming industry (Tony Gonzales, author of the 2008 print-fiction spin-off of the EVE militarist gaming empire, was a fan-writer before this debut). Yet there are signs, ironically, that in this time of war, fewer genre readers are interested. Sf about soldiers seems to be morphing, like a sci-fi military gadget, into a specialized tool—into sf *for* soldiers: institutionalized fiction, a paradoxical escapism for those whose world is defined by military service (or by the gaming simulacra of combat!), and whose comfort is to believe that there is nothing worth knowing outside that bleak perimeter.

Works Cited (UK editions for quotation purposes):

Bujold, Lois McMaster, *Shards of Honor.* New York, Baen, 1986. (London, Simon & Schuster, 1998.)

Card, Orson Scott, *Ender's Game.* New York, Tor, 1985. (London, Arrow Books, Century Hutchinson Ltd, 1986.)

Feintuch, David. *Challenger's Hope* New York. Warner Aspect, 1994. (London, Little, Brown and Company, 1996.)

———. Introduction to *Challenger's Hope*. In *Seafort's Hope* (Guild America edition). New York: Science Fiction Book Club, 1995.

Haldeman, Joe. *The Forever War.* New York, St Martin's Press, 1974. (London, Futura/Macdonald, 1976.)

Moon, Elizabeth. *Rules of Engagement.* New York, Baen 1998. (London, Orbit, 2000.)

Weber, David. *The Honor of the Queen.* New York, Baen, 1994. (London, Simon & Schuster, 2000.)

———. Interviewed: http://www.computercrowsnest.com/sfnews2/02_july/news0702_1.shtml).

Haraway's Cyborgs
[Mostly] at the Movies

A review of Patricia Melzer's Alien Constructions: Science Fiction and Feminist Thought (Austin: University of Texas Press, 2006).

From a review first published in *Science Fiction Film And Television,* eds Mark Bould and Sherryl Vint, Liverpool University Press, Vol. 1, Issue 2, Spring 2008.

It's an old joke. The Lone Ranger and Tonto are riding along, when suddenly a huge war party of hostile Indians comes pouring over the hills. "Looks like we're surrounded, Tonto," says the Ranger. "Who's 'we,' white man?" responds his faithful Native American sidekick. In the closing decades of the twentieth century the cutting-edge avant garde intellectual was equally beleaguered. The future, which he'd been running as his private fief, had turned on him. Artificial Intelligences were about to render him obsolete. Technology had become equal with its creator; he was just a construct among constructs. Second Nature was not only taking over from First Nature, it had corrupted all the records: it now seemed that his uniquely privileged, unified self had *never existed...* He turned to his faithful sidekick, and she said: "Who's 'we,' white man?" It is from this moment, the iconic moment defined in Socialist-Feminist Donna Haraway's *Cyborg Manifesto* (first published as "A Manifesto For Cyborgs: Science Technology and Socialist Feminism in the 1980s," *Socialist Review,* 15, no. 2 1985), that Patricia Melzer launches her study of science fiction and feminist theory—not from the radical, polemical feminist sf novels of the seventies, nor from later academic feminist theory.

The *Cyborg Manifesto*—lyrical and exuberant, often criticized, often out of style, but an enduring work of feminist scripture—argues, with explicit reference to the phenomenon of feminist science fiction, that *women* (already marked as other; *different,* not original; already aware of their impure, hybrid, constructed nature) are ideally situated to grasp the opportunities of a posthuman future and to embrace post-biological concepts of the body and the self. The texts and narratives Melzer analyzes (either feminist or interesting to feminists) are chosen for their relevance to Haraway's Cyborg concept: Octavia Butler's Patternist series and her Xenogenesis trilogy; Melissa Scott's *Shadow Man*; Richard Calder's *Dead Girls*. In film, it's not Ridley Scott's original *Alien* (1979)—situated in and clearly marked by the First-Nature feminist decade—but rather the fourth of the franchise, *Alien Resurrection*, along with *The Matrix* (1999): virtual bodies in a style-victim revolt against the machine.

The late Octavia Butler's "cyborg" strength is in her characters' awareness that their identity is partial, contested, ironic: socially constructed, not given—a state of affairs that science fiction, as Melzer asserts, can make concrete in ways inaccessible to any other medium. The bizarre circumstances and truly extraordinary events that beset Butler's heroines (an aeons-long struggle with an ancient Nubian mind-parasite, desperate and grotesque negotiations with triple-sexed alien "gene-traders") provide the prepared reader with powerful, emotionally charged tools for thinking about the predicament of an embodied mind in a *woman's* body: marked as other, marked as subordinate, marked as (inescapably) sexual, marked by reproductive function. It is more difficult, however, for Melzer to convince us that Butler's compelling, Orwellian bleakness of vision conforms to the Cyborg-optimism of the Manifesto. In *Survivor* and in *Mind of My Mind*, the books of the Patternist series treated here, *becoming post human* (even with superpowers over the minds of others) is far from a joyous affair, and *embracing difference* is a forced choice, reached through tragedy and humiliation. *Xenogenesis: Dawn* is equally stark. The alien Oankali intend to breed with the human remnant (Earth having been devastated by Global Thermonuclear War), and the humans have no say in the matter. Butler's heroine, Lilith Iyapo, hated by her fellow survivors for dealing with the enemy, has only one recourse: to accept the destruction of her culture; to accept the constructed identity (as go-between, as trusted slave) forced upon her, and use it as best she can for her people's survival and her own. Can the subaltern speak? [The reference is to an essay by radical post-colonial scholar Gayatri Chakravorty in *Marxism and the Interpretation of Culture* (Cary Nelson and Lawrence Grossberg eds., Macmillan Education, Basingstoke 1988, 271-313) frequently invoked by Melzer.] In Octavia Butler's case, the answer is yes: but what she has to say is very tough news.

The irresistible desire to draw an upward graph, to depict the development of feminism in science fiction as an unconditioned progress, is visible throughout this study. It tempts Melzer to mask complexities, not least in the section devoted to the technoscience spectacle of sf movies and specifically the *Alien* franchise. There's a lot of feminist history (backlash, cultural change, compromised successes, bruising encounters with US and global politics) between Ridley-Scott's female hero (1979)— Sigourney Weaver fighting for *us*, the movie-going audience, against the amoral, mindless greed of the Company's profit motive, a greed superbly, explicitly embodied by Giger's wondrous monster—and Jean-Pierre Jeunet's darkly lit third sequel, with its graphic novel ambience, and wilfully defective deconstruction of the *Alien* story.

Once more, the Military Industrial Complex is insanely determined to breed Giger aliens, as some kind of crowd control device. Once more, the setting is a very big space ship, full of hiding places and rapidly infested with monsters. Once more, Ellen Ripley must save us (with more melodrama and less fictional finesse)—but this time around she is no longer *one of us*, no longer a believable challenge to the default male hero. She's a comic book character, with a limited repertoire of smart lines and a swaggering costume, endowed with superpowers bestowed on her by fiat and by magic. Her sidekick, the "female android" Annalee Call, is characterized as virtuous and *therefore* weak, her own brand of heroism derided (she was a secret agent with a mission to kill the Ripley clone, thereby wrecking the breeding program). So much for Second Nature as feminism's powerful ally. The final sequence, in which the last alien is vanquished in a ludicrous pastiche of the airlock scene in *Alien*, is a blatant display of Hollywood cynicism. It's only *sci-fi*, who cares if it makes sense?

Yet this fourth Ripley, cloned from a frozen blood sample two hundred years after her heroic demise at the end of *Alien 3* (1992) is a textbook Haraway cyborg—her embodiment compromised by alien DNA, her identity cobbled together from the memories of Ripley's past, preserved—somehow!—by that same technoscientific pollution. Her descent into otherness, her *ironic* humanity—including the famous encounter with a lab full of failed "Ripleys," and later a profoundly strange moment of maternal bonding—is spine-tingling, disorienting, despite all the absurdities. What I'd have liked to have seen, what I missed in Melzer's analysis, is an examination of the revealing *differences* between *Alien 1* and *Alien 4*: between the year of radical feminism and the year of Girl Power. If the Ridley-Scott version was facile and naïve, and the Jeunet version, dirty and dismissive, is more truthful (which I can well believe), then feminism itself is polluted, feminism shares genes (or must *trade* genes, in order to survive) with the profit-motive monster. Now that's an interesting idea.

Ellen Ripley starts her career as the female Everyman and makes her final bow (so far…) as a lesbian tough guy with a heart of gold, romanced into saving the world by her cute, android girlfriend. Jael, the barely-fictional gender-wars assassin of Joanna Russ's *Female Man* (1975) was reborn as Molly Millions, ex-prostitute and "street samurai" of William Gibson's *Neuromancer* trilogy. Ironically, 1985, the year of the *Cyborg Manifesto,* may be noted, in feminist sf circles as the date of the *demise* of a feminist revolution. It's the year when cyberpunk took over, having stripped the stellar women's lib novels of the seventies for parts and buried the remains. At least Gibson allowed his female tough guy dignity and a life independent of the hero. In their highly successful cyberpunk movie *The Matrix* (1999), the Wachowski Brothers are less generous with the consolation prizes. Carrie-Anne Moss, as Trinity, is merely a tomboy pinup in black PVC, whose fighting skills mean nothing beside her love for the Chosen One.

The Matrix, like most cyberpunk fiction, preserves conservative certainties behind a smokescreen of post-modernity. Unsurprisingly, Melzer comes to the conclusion—after some wrestling with the allure of its gleaming surfaces—that the movie has little to offer Feminist Theory, but recognizes with justice its value as spectacle: the miracles of information-based technologies made visible. Sci-fi film effects, logically analogous to the nuanced sleight of hand in words that writers use—to make the impossible believable—are often not as high-tech as they look. Don't peek behind the curtain, how it was done doesn't matter. By making the immersive virtual world *appear* to appear on the big screen—a world where expert denizens can cheat every physical "law" and the final, mystic boundary, between mind and matter, between idea and reality, has become negotiable—this shallow, silly late-twentieth century style-icon opened unsettling new vistas to the mass audience.

Subsequent chapters return to print fiction, and tackle sf's neologisms of gender, through Richard Calder's *Dead Girls,* Melissa Scott's *Shadow Man,* and further reference to Octavia Butler. In Calder's fable— reported by Melzer as overtly misogynist, cryptically racist—a designer virus transforms young girls, at puberty, into sexually voracious, vampiric automata; letting leash a global plague. Again, Melzer finds *anti*-feminist sf surfaces—the eerie fate of the Lilim, the "decadence" of Calder's language—alluring, but comes to the conclusion that only patriarchy is served by this perverse wet dream. More positively, in the planetary romance *Shadow Man,* a drug-induced "plague" has dismantled the gender binary. On most (post) human inhabited worlds five genders and their permutations of attraction are recognized. On ultra-conservative Hara, Warreven's non-binary sexual characteristics are recognized, but must be suppressed. In a narrative directly invoking the struggles, divisions, and emotional dilemmas of GLBT people here and now, Scott leads her characters and her readers to question the validity of *any* limit placed on the varieties of human sexual nature or human desire.

I missed a sense of the complexity of modern feminist history in this study, but what I missed most was a discussion of feminist sf writers' re-imagining of real-world science. "Technoscience" features only in the movie section, where all the *auteurs* are male and big business rules. This is a serious lack. The technoscience in feminist sf (Kathleen Ann Goonan, Joan Slonczewski, and Geoff Ryman are second-generation writers who spring to mind) investigates the project of creating a humane, global, Second Nature civilization; and this Utopian impulse, for readers and for practitioners of feminist sf, is vital to the whole endeavor. Feminist Theory may have become an end in itself, feminism can never be that. Embracing otherness et cetera, is not the project. The project is embracing our old pal the Masked Man: convincing him that those "hostiles," those traits he has so long resisted, are really friends of ours: truths of the human condition, revealed by the new. And then we can join forces and tackle the real monsters together.

Works Cited

Haraway, Donna. "The Cyborg Manifesto," in *Simians Cyborgs and Women*. London: Free Association Books, 1991.

Butler, Octavia. *Survivor*. New York: Doubleday, 1978.

———. *Mind Of My Mind*. New York: Avon, 1978.

———. *Xenogenesis: Dawn*. New York: Warner Books, 1987.

Calder, Richard. *Dead Girls, Dead Boys, Dead Things*. New York: St Martin's Griffin, 1998.

Scott, Melissa. *Shadow Man*. New York: Tor, 1995.

Gibson, William. *Neuromancer*. New York: Ace, 1984.

Movies

Jeunet, Jean-Paul, *Alien Resurrection*. 1997.

Wachowski, Andy, and Wachowski, Larry, *The Matrix*. 1999.

Fantasy Girls

A review of *Fantasy Girls: Gender in the New Universe of Science Fiction and Fantasy Television*

First published in *Foundation: the International Review of Science Fiction*, No.84, Spring 2002.

Elyce Rae Helford, editor (Rowman & Littlefield, 2000)

Whose head is on the coin? It would be naive to expect the mass-market entertainment business to be offering any challenges to the Ideological State Apparatus of the day. However fantastically empowered, however liberated and successful the American Fantasy Girls (and women) on our tv screens appear, they are never going to escape from the constraints of our society. They're working for Caesar, same as the rest of us, using Caesar's tainted currency and making the compromises that have to be made in order to get by. This collection of essays is an elaboration of that statement: discovering over and over again that the fantasy babes of the nineties (and at the dawn of the twenty-first century) are still, beneath all the hype, as secondary, as submissive, and as desperate for male attention as the tv heroines of fifty years ago. No surprises, then; but the examination is still worthwhile and also makes very entertaining reading.

One great attraction of tv and movies is that here, at last, we have the authorless text that was promised to us many years ago and signally failed to arrive in print fiction. Try as you may, when you're reviewing a novel in terms of the society that made the book, the intentionality of the writer is always a barrier. In *Fantasy Girls* the essayists are dealing with texts that genuinely were produced by committee and shaped by the impersonal, Darwinian forces of the marketplace (although not forgetting vested interests that aren't so democratic). These critics are free to theorize, to unpick the conflicts behind the scenes, and often to recognize women's complicity in their own fate, without accusing or traducing any individual. They are also free—a convenience rarely enjoyed by the critic of a novel—to *gossip* about these household names in a loose and easy style, with the reasonable assumption that readers won't lose track... and there is a lesson here, a piece of news that could even contradict the gloomy re-iteration of the glass ceiling story. Fantasy girls may be compromised, but they are BIG; and despite our society's insensate striving to reduce the actresses involved (Gillian Anderson, Sarah Michelle Geller) to mere sex-goddesses, the *fictional characters* survive: iconic, heroic, genuinely aspirational.

But whose aspirations are these? That's the interesting question.

Some of our tv fantasy heroines are still trapped in the traditional feminine sphere, where nothing much has shifted (apparently) since the dawn of television. Being restricted to the domestic stage and traditional feminine pursuits doesn't mean you have to be second rate. Jane Austen and the Brontes had no trouble tackling the human condition, and Emily Dickinson isn't a bad poet for an American (that's a reference to a Giles quote, by the way). The Alicia Silverstone vehicle *Clueless* (directed by Amy Heckerling) demonstrated, some way after *Emma,* that the most reactionary feminine scenario can be fun and even wise. *Sabrina the Teenage Witch* does not come near this category, and I would agree with Sarah Projansky and Leah R. Vande Berg in placing it as weak, sliced-white, and exasperatingly muddled in both sexual and social politics. *Third Rock from the Sun,* on the other hand, is a favorite of mine. The conceit that the four primary characters are aliens in human bodies has, of course, long been subsumed into a classic situation comedy of random quirkiness; but (as Nicole Matthews and Farah Mendlesohn discuss) the role of Sally (Kirsten Johnson), warrior-turned-woman, is a definitive text of female embodiment in post-feminist society. Sally is big and strong and (running joke) devastatingly attractive to men when she's in her war paint. But she is the slave of her female instincts (which are assumed to be biologically, not socially or politically, determined) and therefore doomed, however cynically she may wax on the topic, to be secondary, submissive, etc. In their treatment of the gendered body, however, I feel that the Third Rock team are more even-handed than the essayists allow. By happenstance I had the chance to re-watch the first episode of Third Rock, which is treated at length here, while I was reading *Fantasy Girls.*

It's true that a great deal of fuss is made about Sally's boobs; but Dick and Harry spend an inordinate amount of time in that episode fondling phallic objects and remarking (bemusedly) that it feels really good, reassuring, and fun, to hold on to your phallic object... I think the writers took that as far as the small screen and general certificate sitcom expectations would let them go.

Dana Scully and Lois Lane (examined in essays by Linda Barry and Rhonda Wilcox) are two more heroines whose tv and movie antecedents go back a long way: the equal-but-different female partner in a thriller format, and the sparky girl reporter. I should confess that I never became an *X-Files* fan. I always seemed to catch the episodes about mystery psychic nosebleeds, never the main plot, and the teleplay was so unbearably STUPID. I refuse to be grateful for an "empowered" female character who has to come out with lines like "You can't question science, Muldur." For heaven's sake. What else are you supposed to do with it? But I remember watching the evolution of the Gillian Anderson effect, in the early nineties, and how it seemed to me that she was being read as a babe, (re-)constructed as a babe, because she *must* be overpoweringly sexual. Otherwise, the audience would be watching a woman just because they found the fictional character interesting and exciting, and we can't have that, can we? In the *X-Files*, and in *Superman*, what we see are the defense mechanisms of the woman who has invaded a man's world. Gillian Anderson can fight her battles over pay and status, but on the screen Dana must become more and more sexual (and this particular fantasy girl story goes beyond the centerfold into extremely disquieting territory). Lois Lane began her long career in an era where the occasional successful female professional was considered harmless—effortlessly outgunned by the male superpowers of physical size, strength, and competence. These powers may be "secret" in the setting of a newspaper office, but everyone knows they're there. In the nineties (played by Teri Hatcher) she has to be a lot more careful. Male superpowers are not as secure as once they were: it's necessary for Lois's skirts to get shorter, her cleavage more pronounced, her mistakes and frailties to be emphasized. As both the essayists make clear, women who work on shows like these are as complicit as the fictional characters have to be in the sexualization process, because they too have no choice. Women use sex to avoid the backlash, men treat women as sex-objects to reduce the threat. It's a time-honored peace strategy in the battle of the sexes, but it's never yet brought peace any nearer.

Mystery Science Theater 3000, here treated by Jessica A. Royer, sounds like a strange relation of *Third Rock*, where a throwaway science fiction conceit provides the vehicle for whimsical comment on contemporary mores. Apparently the show depicts a young man and a team of robots, trapped on a satellite (as if in a deserted office block) watching ancient B movies to pass the dead-end job time. The fun is in their zany comments on lunatic productions like *The Amazing Colossal Man*, and the show has a lively chat room and website following. I have no knowledge of the program, but the concept of the post-feminist *male audience* is highly significant. Shows like *The Simpsons* and, in the UK, a whole raft of post-Python post-pub surreal quiz and sketch shows have been tailored for this altered male gaze, designed for the self-image of post-feminist man: the dumb, loveable slacker whose only surviving superpower is an *astonishing* ability to get out of doing the chores. The phenomenally successful *Buffy the Vampire Slayer* targets this audience, although Buffy also attracts a huge female following. One of the discoveries of the fantasy tv explosion has been, indeed, that the young tv audience today is unisexual. Really, who wouldn't want to be Buffy? To be feckless, cool-looking, wisecracking, full of energy for play, stubborn at avoiding drudgery and yet, (not least) always on the side of the right and the good…? But there's a price to be paid. The *Buffy* essay in *Fantasy Girls* takes issue with the racism of the series. Buffy good guys are middle class and cozy; bad guys are basically immigrants and homeless. The reading of demons and vampires in the Buffy stable (*Buffy, Angel*) as poor people and members of ethnic minorities is hard to avoid; and the effect is subtextually doubled, as Kent Ono points out, when the cute vampire with tenure (No, I don't mean Angel. I mean Spike!) is as white as could be, while black vampires and non-white secondary characters are invariably dismissed in short order.

The post-feminist male eagerly embraces moral inferiority as a masculine privilege, moral superiority as a feminine given (Lisa Simpson is *The Simpsons'* conscience). But as Elyce Rae Helford's chapter on *Xena Warrior Princess* explores, the fantasy series that seems nearest to getting right inside the women's locker room does not support this view.

Admittedly, the whole series is completely bonkers and a law unto itself, but whatever you make of the relationship between Xena and Gabrielle, you can't call it exactly *healthy*. Master and servant games, sexualized violence, the self-abasement of the "submissive" partner…this is not a model fairytale. I'm sure it's right to point out the shortcomings of these much-loved programs; I'm not so sure it would be right to try and "improve" them. The multi-racial Disney "Cinderella" described by Marleen S. Barr might be a case in point. Paradoxically, the authorless text disappears when the committee deliberately decides to make a statement, and we can't read the truth about ourselves in that kind of production. All we get is the artificial conversation of people who know they are being overheard.

The final section of *Fantasy Girls* deals with the Manifest-Destiny American future depicted in the *Star Trek* family and *Babylon 5*. The examination of *Star Trek* itself (Robin A. Roberts) takes a moderate and affectionate feminist line: ST1 is just silly, but has an inexplicable charm; *Next Generation* is detestable; and *Voyager* is the pick of the bunch. The relationships between Captain Kathryn Janeway and her female officers is surely the most soothing depiction of women working together on sci-fi tv, and maybe in all of American television. Janeway, B'Elanna, and Seven of Nine are heroic and noble-hearted but not without human weaknesses; they do their jobs as if they love the work. What more could you ask from your escapism? A cat suit supported by some very alarming-looking undergarments is a small enough price to pay. We have learned. You always have to do some horse-trading; and unlike the unfortunate Lois Lane, at least Seven of Nine gets what she pays for: freedom to be a scientist and even (as a special treat!) freedom to have no social skills.

Science fiction, unlike the horror genre that gave birth to Buffy, has a tradition of concern for social issues. The treatment of race in the *Star Trek* family of shows is typically very careful, even *too* careful not to give offense. This makes me curious about the wheelchair episode of DS9 discussed in Hanley Kanar's chapter, "No Ramps in Space." I'm not a DS9 fan, but I wonder if there may have been something else going on, other than what sounds like extremely crass treatment of a story about a visiting wheelchair user. But the raging against exclusion in this final essay is a reminder of the battles for civil rights, the battle of feminism: those battles which are over now, without having been won—or exactly lost. In Sharon Ney and Elaine Sciog-Lazarov's "The Construction of Feminine Identity in *Babylon 5,*" we get a reminder of the way things used to be: female characters struggling to survive as powerful individuals in a patriarchal world, their need to "retain feminine characteristics" seen as a problem that they must solve for themselves, because the world isn't going to change.

I don't know what the chronological distance is between *Babylon 5* and *Third Rock* or *Buffy*. (One thing I regret about *Fantasy Girls* is a shortage of that kind of information: we're told that the events of *Babylon 5* take place, allegedly, between 2257 and 2262, but not when the series was first aired or when it was written.) In terms of the perception of gender roles, there is an abyss. But again I want to ask—whose head is on the coin? Who is selling us this story of the fabulously empowered, heroic, hyper-sexualized young woman—and why? Some of the answer can be found, it seems, in *Men, Women, and Chainsaws: Gender in the Modern Horror Film* (Princeton University Press, 1992), a work cited by Kent Ono, where Carol Clover discusses "gender displacement" and "cross-gendered identification" in the typical slasher movie. "On reflection," she remarks, the girl who usually saves the day may provide "a congenial double for the adolescent male." I have myself observed and commented on a related phenomenon in post-feminist science fiction. So many male sf writers (many of them with absolutely zero credibility as "feminists") feel compelled to create cute, feisty young female heroes!

The fantasy girls of today's tv shows are still, as these essayists reveal, created and constrained by a male-dominated industry and the gaze of the male audience, just the way things used to be. But there has been a strange sea change. It's not that girl power, for better or for worse, has replaced feminism. It's what's happened to the boys. It would not have been unthinkable for a red-blooded heterosexual girl (excuse my appalling language, it's required by the plot) to dream of being a feisty heroic tomboy twenty years ago—or fifteen hundred years ago, for that matter. But for so many young heterosexual males to be dreaming of Buffy Summers, not as a sexual conquest (that's the cover story) but as an aspirational hero-figure: now that's really got to be called different.

Or maybe it's just another cunning way to stay in charge of the remote control.

String of Pearls

First presented as a Guest of Honor speech at the World Fantasy Convention 2004, Tempe Arizona; later published in the *New York Review of Science Fiction*, Vol. 17 No. 4, December 2004.

Sex and Horror: Better Together?

I was talking to a friend about genre. We got onto the area of horror and sex, as you do, and he asked me, why is there no sex in any of your teenage fiction? (the books I write as Ann Halam). Well, there's several answers to that, such as, on the whole the market says no, or I'd never get any kind of sexual content past my UK editor, nohow; or—maybe closest to the truth—I feel I'm writing for teenagers of the same geeky, immature kind I was myself, who see the kid-sexual arena as a trap, to be avoided like the plague (and who keep up the honorable tradition of finding the hot pages in adult novels, if looking for useful and rewarding information). But the question was about mixing sex and horror. (I'm writing science fiction for teenagers now; at the time of that conversation, it was all ghosts and demons.) I said I didn't think sex and horror were compatible. Bring sex into the picture, you dilute the fear. A horror story with love, sex, or even frankly porno interest can't be truly terrifying. If I'm writing a scary story, I want to FRIGHTEN my readers, not titillate them: take everything away, show them a cold abyss of nothingness—

Charles was amazed (yes, I was talking to Charles Brown, the emperor of *Locus*). What are you talking about, he said—or words to that effect. Sex and horror are inextricable, the whole horror genre is ABOUT sex, about unmasking and facing the fear and revulsion secretly, shockingly implicit in all sexual relations… I was amazed myself, when I gave my answer a second look. Of course horror and sex are intertwined. Look at Bram Stoker's *Dracula*, the quivering white woman-flesh of it all; look at Buffy and those indispensable vampire boyfriends of hers… Charles reminded me that the one actual *horror* story I've ever written as Ann Halam (usually it's ghosts, no viscera), *Don't Open Your Eyes*, is also the only Ann Halam with any kind of romantic content. Okay, the story in *Don't* is that a good girl, a go-to-church-on-Sunday, never-skips-her-homework, high-self-esteem girl, falls for a bad boy, car-thief, truant joy-rider who hates himself. She knows their romance is going nowhere, *because he hates himself*, not because he's "bad," even before he gets killed in a police chase as a passenger in a stolen car. He becomes a ghoul, he visits her in her bedroom at night: this is when he begs her not to open her eyes… This Ann Halam gets fairly ugly, in parts. But Diesel still loves Martin. She still wants to touch him, feels no revulsion, only pity and longing, when she's more or less convinced a rotting, flesh-eating living corpse is sitting on the end of her bed—and it's the survival of her physical tenderness in this dreadful impasse that gives the situation hope, that holds the possibility of redemption.

So there you are. Sex and horror go together, traditionally, intuitively, deep in the back brain. That *Augh*, the open-mouthed O of horror, that red yell of terror we spread to greet the gaping maw of the fiend about to devour us, is obviously, instantly sexual…[1] We're agreed on that. But while sex and horror have positive interference for Charles, the interference is negative for me: sex damps the horror down. After that conversation, my first, spontaneous, contradictory answer stayed with me. I found I'd given myself something to think about. Maybe I'd struck a genuine, innate male/female divide, not imposed by social construction: which is something I always find interesting, because it's so unusual. As many of you must have noticed, there are a lot more female horror and "dark fantasy" writers around these days. How do they treat sex? And how do they treat the nexus of sex and horror?

Conventionally, traditionally, women have been the preferred victims of the fiend (possibly acting as permissive alter-egos, so the notionally predominantly male audience for horror can safely "imagine" being vulnerable, as well as imagine the fun of being the fiend[2]). Females are deadly: women can be evil in more sophisticated variants, but male sexuality is the horror writer's weapon of first resort, the immediate threat: and to a degree, you have to admit it works. The flimsy nightie and the bare feet and the gothic darkness, that's just decoration: I'm *always* in danger, because men can so easily be monsters. There's a notorious James Tiptree story from the seventies (written as Racoona Sheldon), called "The Screwfly Solution," where an alien race intending to colonize Earth decides to get rid of the pesky human population. They use the same expedient humans have used in controlling insect pests: tweak the reproductive process, make it destructive. This—in Tiptree's vision—is easily done, because in the human male psychotic, murderous violence is just a protein expression away from sexual arousal. (A percentage of the men would end up killing men, of course, but that's not a problem.) Is this true? If it's even partly true, then women ought to be terrified of sex. Men are big and strong and naturally violent and often, as much psychological research attests, deeply resentful of the drives that urge them into the dangerous reproductive arena. Women ought to live in constant fear of sexual assault. But do they? Forget the received wisdom: look around you. Think of what you see on the street, on your tv, every day. Need I say more? Women ought to be totally cowed, but clearly they are not. Far from it. They should be afraid; there are mighty books of law telling them to be afraid; but something older than reason, beyond their conscious control, the *agrapta nomina*, the unwritten law of female mammal psychology, keeps telling them a different story.

"The Screwfly Solution" is an important marker for me. It's the stark, powerful psychosexual message of "James Tiptree's" agenda put into in street clothes, given a human, everyday reality. But there's another sex/horror story, Angela Carter's "Company of Wolves"—translated, by Neil Jordan with Angela Carter beside him, into one of the first and among the greatest of the animatronic horror movies (remember that transformation scene?)—that I find more viscerally convincing. Men are wolves. When they become sexual they open up their human skins and reveal the naked, swollen, glistening animal: before your very eyes. Sex is a wolf, with big teeth and gaping red jaws; if you're a girl you know this when it tears at your young belly and makes you hurt and bleed. But fear is an old wives' tale. No, scratch that, of course there's fear. The fear is huge. But it's not the kind of horror you would want to escape (though you might run away screaming, just a little bit). It's a wild ride; it's part of the delight.

How far can Darwinian evolutionary psychology be trusted? Not very far. We humans don't have an oestrus period, for one thing, which means that female choice is not protected, although women behave as though it is. We're rather out on a limb as hominids, anyway; there can be no comparative studies, as all the other hominid species are extinct (fer some strange reason…). Yet the way women persist in their display, as if sex cannot harm them, no matter how often they are proved sorely mistaken, suggests there has to be some enduring truth in it. As surely as the top men rule, finally, by violence or the threat of violence, women rule by sex, or the promise of sex. This is written, inverted but perfectly legible, in all those books of law—in every dress code, every sexual mutilation, every economic and cultural repression imposed through the ages on the weaker party. In every high-culture dramatic medium for the last many thousand years, even the drama of cultures where women had no place at all in public life, the assumption that sex gives women mighty power is deeply implicit. In so-called fairytales, ancient hearthside, genre works, it's the same. The very thing that's supposed to make women vulnerable, makes them impervious. Sex is the maw of the beast, but it will save your life: it's a paradox.

The theme of this convention is Women in Fantasy and Horror. What I plan to do, for the rest of this presentation, is to talk about what happens when the Chosen One of a fantasy epic is a woman. Not a chaste woman-warrior, but an emphatically sexual, feminine woman… I want to look at how such a characterization twists the thread of manifest destiny, and what it does to serial fantasy's rich resources of sex and horror. And because I always work best when I'm telling a story, I'm going to use a particular epic as my example. (I'm also paying a debt, because this is a topic I promised to tackle a long time ago; hello Kathryn.) Some of you may know I'm writing a sex- and horror-injected fantasy sequence my-self at the moment, but I'm not going to talk about *Bold As Love*. It isn't finished, and it doesn't have that kind of heroine anyway. I'm going to talk about a very striking, three-volume historical fantasy novel by a US author: the Kushiel trilogy, by Jacqueline Carey.

This is the story, briefly, for those who don't know it. Phèdre nó Delauney, a whore's unwanted get, sold into the sex-worker industry at an early age, is talent-spotted by a nobleman for her intelligence and her supernatural appetite for pain as pleasure. She's trained as a courtesan, a diplomat, and a spy, and becomes a special agent for her country… Actually, the "whore's unwanted get" part is harsh. Phèdre's parents are just a pair of rather sweet but feckless bohemian airheads with no desire for parenthood, who thought they were doing all right for the kid, giving her a decent trade. In Terre d'Ange, Phèdre's beloved country, the Night Courts are a highly respected guild. Kushiel mainly happens, I should explain, in a fantasy version of mediaeval Europe, based on the Courts of Love and a tradition that says Mary Magdalene fled Judea and settled in Provence, after the crucifixion. Terre d'Ange, roughly geographically and culturally equivalent to France, was founded by a band of sensual angels, Blessed Elua and his companions, created when Mary Magdalene's tears mingled with the blood-soaked earth at the foot of the Cross. Its people are known the world over for their beauty. Its graceful, pleasure-loving culture is backed by the immanent presence of those earthly angels and by a highly baroque, not to say camp, New Age Theology. Love as Thou Wilt is the whole of the law, but Kushiel (of the rod and weal) is worshiped as fervently as the rulers of gentler passions. Phèdre was born with the rare mark of his dread favor. She has a scarlet mote in the night-dark iris of her left eye, which is how her patron, Anafiel Delauney, recognized her. This is Kushiel's Dart; it makes her an *anguissette*, born to experience pain as sexual pleasure, the first of her kind in a hundred years.

Now, you may be thinking, in a nation dedicated to sex and sensuality, can she be the only babe who likes pain? Or who will pretend to like it…? Well, suspend your disbelief. There's a Night Court called "Valerian," where the trained, professional staff will take a whipping or a session with the flechettes or whatever and act delighted, or fight, or beg for mercy, as per the client's fancy. But, as you can tell from that "whore's unwanted get" slur, society in Terre D'Ange isn't *really* that much different from ours. Most of the courtesans in this land of courtesans are on the game because they were born poor and pretty, and either they like the idea of commercial sex or they'll put up with the indignity because the money's good. They're making a living. Phèdre is something else. She is a true artist, possessed by the divine. You strap her up on the wheel and whip her, you get to bathe in the glow of her supernatural ecstasy. She'll make you feel like a merciless god.

A Literature of Arousal

I like the mind of the woman writer who sees her feminine epic pro-tagonist as a whore. It's so rational, so *French*, indeed. I'm fondly reminded of the hot feminine epics of my childhood, Anya Seton's *Katherine* and the Angelique series by Anna and Serge Golon (not that Katherine is ex-actly a prostitute, and as I've been reminded by one distressed reader, An-gelique remains the chaste wife, however often her bodice gets ripped...). A whore, a woman who sells her body, is the *logical* female equivalent of a warrior hero; because a warrior is above all a soldier, *soldari, solidus*, a man who has sold himself, his will and his body's strength, to be used by an-other—hopefully in a cause he can believe in. And I have problems with women-warriors. I understand the allure, but there's something Uncle Tom about them. They're buying into the whole second-class citizen deal on condition they get a special rate for themselves. Every other female character in this book is a serving wench or a chattel of some kind, but not me, pretty please, I'm just like a MAN, aren't I? It's a bit grovel-ing... Phèdre is no special case, she has no ticket out of the ghetto, she's a woman in the same way as a soldier is a man: all function, not much left over for personal use, reproduction, or any form of bourgeois indi-vidualism. She's just very, very good at it. She has matchless prowess; she can take any amount of punishment in her chosen sport, ooh; she's *well* hard, as we say in my country. She'll come down in the morning, after a session, covered in welts and bruises, agonized in more intimate places, but glowing with pride. She's the champion of champions. At one point she's perfectly ready to tough-out getting flayed alive in her country's service. The whole thing gives her boyfriend problems—she has a very nice boyfriend, eventually, called Joscelin, kind of a motherly bodyguard type. Of course the sex isn't exactly to her taste, but there you go, they live around the issue.

I also like knowing that this Chosen One is not going to turn out to be the legitimate heir. In time Phèdre will have lands and money and a title, as any hugely successful *grande horizontale* might: but as I said, Terre d'Ange isn't all that different from Kansas. When she steps out of the bubble of the *demi-monde*, where nobles and whores are pals and the queen can call Phèdre friend, she's just a high-class hooker, and there are plenty of people who make sure she knows it. But I prefer that. (Frodo tops Aragorn, right?) Real heroes should remain outsiders. They ought to *give* their life and courage to achieve the quest, not trade them for reward. They should not stand to gain a material kingdom.

The feminist in me reads Phèdre's story, and it gives me chills, especially after I realize that the S&M set pieces are the exception. The kooky accessories are light relief, as are the perversely cruel and inventive clients (some of them female, by the way: Carey is even-handed). Most of the time, Phèdre caters for rich, powerful men who simply want a classy-looking babe they can thump and no reprisals. Getting smacked around, that's her bread and butter… I think of women living with domestic violence, living out the real world version of this extreme feminine sport. Victims who are *paid,* in some sense, to take beating after beating, and who are proud of their ability to take it, and keep up the façade, and look as if everything's okay. Who feel it's all worthwhile when they see the guilty respect in his eyes, after one of those sessions… The clients, these high and noble gentlemen, are chilling too. Cut away the glittering fantasy splendor of the balls and masques, the excitement of the intrigue and adventure, and what we learn from *Kushiel's Dart* is that a high proportion of the men who rule Terre D'Ange, this ideal, chivalrous and morally superior land, where Love is the whole of the law, get their preferred sexual satisfaction from beating the living daylights out of a beautiful young woman who never did them any harm. That's a disturbing thought to bring back from Neverland to the twenty-first century; and to Jacqueline Carey's own beloved country in this world of ours. Isn't it?

(Where I come from the top blokes prefer to dress up in nappies—diapers—and have a woman dressed as nursie smack their botties. Or so I've heard. Different strokes.)

But to return to the fantasy. The Kushiel trilogy gets called many things, mostly very complimentary, but the terms "adult" and "sophisticated" crop up a lot; so, if you have any experience at all, you will know, dear reader, that these are books that will tend to fall open at certain instantly rewarding passages (I can provide a list of page numbers, on request). Paul Bleton, a French-Canadian critic of genre literature, has said that pornography is one of the ur-forms, one of the strongest roots of paraliterature, by which he means all the genres: sci-fi, horror, fantasy, thrillers, romance. In a pornographic "novel" the sex passages are the business. The narrative that links them is a pretext, almost non-existent, absurd. Oh, there I was unpacking at my new flat. A knock on the door, who can that be? It's the plumber with his wrench! So there we were, getting my pipes sorted. The door bell rings. It's the electric-man with his toolbox! So there we three were, testing my circuits, when along came the carpenter-lady! So there we four were, busy putting up my shelves, when… Well. I'm sure you all know the sort of thing.

Paul Bleton calls this style the string of pearls. The narrative is a thread, holding together a succession of arousal-freighted incidents, and the reader doesn't care how poor the story is, because he or she is reading purely for the arousal bits. Hence the expression, *sensational* novels. Pulp-fiction pornography is perhaps the most ruthless form, but you can discern the same structure in horror, in thrillers, in sentimental romance, war stories, adventure stories, and of course in imagined-world fantasy. Maybe even science fiction—which combines elements of all the other genres—has its own special string of pearls. There's an intense thrill in writing a passage of fantasy science, when you feel you've understood something difficult and you are mapping your personal understanding of molecular biology or high energy physics to the added value of your story's drama. It's when you can translate an idea into another form that you know you've got it, of course… I suppose there may be sci-fi readers— *Analog* fans?—whose well-thumbed paperbacks fall open at the science passages.…

Okay, so genre fiction is a literature of arousal. Genre readers are utilitarian. They press the lever; they get the jolt of pleasure—whether it's sexual, sadistic, or sentimental—the fairground ride of printed-terror, or something more esoteric. Literary fiction may have sprung from entirely different roots and acquired sensationalism (because it certainly uses sensationalism) late in its development, by one of those accidents of similar function in a similar context that we call "convergent evolution." We know such things happen all the time in nature. Still, you can plot a Bell curve, from the pulp fiction where the pearls are patently obvious lumps of sticky, glowing arousal, to the kind of literary novel where we are asked to give our attention (and often we do, and find it worthwhile) to a bare, unsullied, very interesting piece of string. But there's a middle way, which is the wide space in this pattern occupied by genre fiction in its developed forms. The pearls are there, defining the structure, clearly discernible—it's possible to pick out the tell-tale luster of those vital incidents, the stirring, treasured scenes the writer was *impelled* to include. But the arousal has diffused through the whole narrative, so that we say, with approval, that every sentence of the thriller is implicit with menace, every domestic detail of the six-hundred-page horror story makes us jumpy. It's as if the thread between the beads has become encrusted with nacre, the whole story a single pearl: layers of gleaming, colorful words wrapped around that inveterate itch of disturbance, the shock that tugs the mind into hyper-awareness.

There are few passages in the Kushiel trilogy where you'll cease to be aware that you are reading for thrills: where you will surrender yourself to a work of art instead of expecting the book to deliver bang for your bucks. But the narrative is not negligible. It has grown. It tells a life, a life full of adventures and journeys, shared struggles, moments of wonder (as all our lives are). Kushiel is not a very magical fantasy: the supernatural element is theological. But there is always magic in the way the glamour spills out, from genre fiction's passages of fetishistic arousal, and spreads its glow over the sticks and stones; the snowy wastes, forests, caves; the firesides; the boat piers and mule trains; the trees, rivers, and mountains. We often say, of the most beloved fantasy epics, that the writer has contrived to *fall in love* with a whole borrowed culture, a whole imagined world. I remember getting that particular praise myself, long ago, for a book called *Divine Endurance*. Maybe what we mean is that the world of the book is infused with a lover's superbly jacked-up brain chemistry—if you'll excuse my sci-fi—a constant state of excitement. In the Kushiel trilogy it's mediaeval Europe getting *sexed up* (as the revealing phrase has it); in my current Bold As Love series, it's a version of England. The impulse is the same. Is this state of passion that fantasy nurtures a good thing, or a bad thing? I don't know. There are other excitements beside S&M that flirt with uncontrolled destruction. But I do know that something inside us, all of us, not just genre readers, calls any access to heightened arousal good. We love to be thrilled, so we walk that line, just as Tiptree said.

Mother of Pearl

The first time I attended a Fantasy convention (it was in Birmingham, England in 1986), I was shocked—no, disgusted—at the complete ascendancy of the Horror genre. It wasn't that I thought the serial fantasy of the time was so great. The kind of fantasy I liked reading was either classified as science fiction or unclassifiable, the oddball, old stuff: C.S. Lewis, David Lindsay, Charles Williams, William Morris, Nicolas Stuart Grey... It was because I found the genre Horror of those days so irredeemably *fake*, infantile, about as scary as having a bucketful of chicken entrails tipped over your head. I remember one panel where a member of the audience asked celebrated Horror writers to say what had been their most frightening experience in real life. One man (I think it was Shaun Hutson) said, recently he'd been to the first funeral he'd ever attended, and the most scary thing he'd ever seen was when his aunt's coffin was lowered into the grave... Well, my God, I thought, if you know *that*, why don't you write about it, instead of this ludicrous guff about microwaved babies???

Ah well, at least nowadays I can relax with one of Laurel Hamilton's Anita Blake stories, Kelley Armstrong's engaging *Bitten*, or something gothic and high-concept by Poppy Z. Brite, and console myself that gender determinism is a crock. Not all horror sets out to excite pity and terror, as Aristotle says it ought. Most of it is *supposed* to be shallow. I note, however, that this wave of new women writers has, notoriously, brought a rush of pornography to the chaste shelves of the black covers and embossed foil titles—and with the clear agenda, which some find extremely shocking, that their most gruesome sex scenes are part of the solution, not part of the problem. But the increased presence and increased influence of women in the twin genres—as both producers and consumers—hasn't merely made the books raunchier. There's been something more vital going on; something that throws a different light on the whole nexus of sex and horror over the past twenty years. I'm talking about the rediscovery of the traditional material.

Looking back now at the Horror and Fantasy of the seventies and eighties, I see the modern, commercial genres of that day like cargo-cultists in schism: one party carrying off Bram Stoker's *Dracula* to be the centerpiece of their blood-daubed orgies, maybe with a stolen page or two of Orc material; the other founding their Numenorean temple of high and manifest destiny on the teachings of Tolkien, neither congregation having the least idea that they'd grabbed two fragments of a single scripture. (There was a breakaway cult, went off down the beach to do something unmentionable with a tattered copy of Mary Shelley's *Frankenstein*, but we won't talk about them…) Writers, editors, and publishers, like Ellen Datlow, Terri Windling, Jane Yolen, Sheri Tepper, Anne Cameron (and many others) have changed all that. Just as in the UK, where the rediscovery of fairytales started in the seventies with Angela Carter, Marina Warner, and other artists and scholars, the reformers have been predominantly women, and that's fitting, because the old scary, sexy, hearthside tales were always regarded as women's business. But this isn't a case of seventies alternative Cinderellas who reject wimpy gender-role stereotypes. This is a roots issue. For both male and female writers, reclaiming the night of "dark fantasy" we find in fairytales has been a reconnection, a restoration of continuity; and I know I said I don't trust legitimate heirs, but you don't have to trust a mighty force to feel its power. The schism is over. Horror is not just Fantasy's evil twin (or vice versa, depending on your taste). The relationship is closer than that. In fairytales, wish-fulfillment has never been separated from horror. Even Disney never tried to separate them—remember Snow White's stepmother? The hideous family crimes, grotesque punishments, vengeful demons, callous step-mothers, incestuous fathers, savage ordeals share a bed with the beautiful princess and the handsome prince. It's always been that way. And it's always been that way because that's how our minds work: arousal is arousal. It's quite true, what Tiptree said; though let's hope the psychosexual divide is not so black and white as she imagined. The palace of delight is very close to the pit.

The Kushiel trilogy doesn't have a very strong story arc. The Chosen One's standard career path—boy meets destiny, boy and destiny have a big fight, boy and destiny get back together—can't be feminized for Phèdre. Not least because she's never going to fight her destiny: her strength is to yield. There's a quest, and it spans the three books, but it's a sideline. Instead of the arc, the action quickly falls into an episodic pattern: a dire threat to the realm will emerge, which somehow only an *anguissette* can handle. Inevitably this works best in the first volume, when it comes as a surprise. By the time she undertakes her third commission, in *Kushiel's Avatar*, Phèdre is a superb, mature, internationally famous celebrity, and at times it's weirdly like reading Elizabeth Taylor's account of how she single-handedly defused the Cuban Missile Crisis... There's something inimitably Hollywood, inimitably suburban and cushiony about the adventurous travelogue. Anyway, this time the threat involves a mad Middle Eastern tyrant (surprise). Phèdre has to smuggle herself into his harem of doom, and there's a huge, filth-encrusted, knobbly iron penis, but we won't go into that... (oh, all right, you want chapter forty six, pages 319-325). *Kushiel's Avatar* is the most theological of the books: for a while I was afraid Phèdre was going to use her art to save the villain's soul. I'll leave you to discover what really happens and the momentous events that follow, but you'd better be prepared for the iconography... Personally, I have to say I wasn't worried, and I've been a Catholic all my life. I don't think a religion that makes the beautiful, near-naked body of a man dying by slow torture the center of its worship can complain too vociferously about the Goth fan club... Actually I found the Kushiel trilogy's daring use of Christian theology refreshing. So many fantasy epics and serial fantasies are set in approximations of Mediaeval Europe, but the culture is given a vaguely Pagan Bronze Age religious base, or, blindly following the fashion set by Tolkien, a spirituality you might call Wagnerian Stern and Solemnism. Very few writers have given the fantasy glamour of chivalry and courtly love the psychic background it ought to have. But women, especially courtesans, ought to notice details and décor, and Phèdre gets it right. In the Kushiel books, Jacqueline Carey has invoked the monstrous, fairytale world of the fourteenth century with its proper complement of demons and angels, love to the utmost, splendor and sacrifice. I don't aspire to write historical fantasy myself. The research sounds too much like hard work. But I loved reading this series because I felt I was getting a true revision of the original of all our romances; I was glimpsing the place invented by Malory and Chretien de Troyes: a mirror of longing, where our double nature is understood and forgiven, wreathed in pearl and held up to a world as beautiful and terrible as the one we know ourselves. The same land that Petrarch wrote about in the radiant sonnet he composed after the death of his Laura. If we're right about the real identity of the person he called Laura, and it seems likely, she was thirty-seven when she died, by the way, and she'd had sixteen pregnancies. But Petrarch remembered…

I vidi in terra angelici costumi—

(but I won't try to recite in mediaeval Italian)

I once beheld on earth celestial graces
And heavenly beauties scarce to mortals known
Whose memory lends nor joy nor grief alone
But all things else bewilders and effaces
I saw how tears had left their weary traces
Within those eyes that once like sunbeams shone
I heard those lips breathe low and plaintive moan
Whose spell might once have taught the hills their places
Love, wisdom, courage, tenderness and truth
Made ill their mourning strains more high and dear
Than ever wove sweet sounds for mortal ear
And heaven seemed listening in such saddest ruth
The very leaves upon the boughs to soothe
Such passionate sweetness filled the atmosphere

(Petrarch, sonnet 123)

That beauty co-exists with horror, and that they spring from the same roots, is the message of the fairytale, and the gift that women have brought to the twin genres.

Notes

1. Compare with Jean Marigny, *Le Vampire Dans la Litterature du XX siecle*, 71.

   "Cette être ou cette chose qui se jette sur vous pour vous avaler, votre bouche s'ouvre tout grand pour le contr'engloutir. C'est la béance meme de l'origin menacant que vouse singez Rien ne dit mieux le fantastique que cette image: l'attaque du requin, l'effroi du nagcur, duez geules affrontées. Une face-à-face qui voudrait virer bouche à bouche, pour un baiser mortel en forme de dévoration…"

   (This creature or thing that leaps on you to swallow you, always opens your mouth wide, as if for a counter-swallowing. No image speaks the fantastic better than this gape-mouth made at menace: the attack of the shark, the terror of the swimmer, two open throats affronting each other. A face-off of open mouths, leaping into a deadly kiss that becomes a devouring…)

2. See *Men Women, and Chainsaws*, Carol Clover, Princeton, Princeton University Press, 1992.

Principal Works Cited

Bleton, Paul. *Ça Se Lit Comme Un Roman Policier*. Quebec: Éditions Nota bene, 1999.

Carey, Jacqueline. *Kushiel's Dart*. New York: Tor (Tom Doherty Associates), 2001.

———. *Kushiel's Chosen*. New York: Tor (Tom Doherty Associates), 2002.

———. *Kushiel's Avatar*. New York: Tor (Tom Doherty Associates), 2003.

Halam, Ann. *Don't Open Your Eyes*. London, Orion Children's Books, 2000.

Petrarch's Sonnet 123 is taken from the translation of Thomas Wentworth Higginson (1823-1911), most famous for his long correspondence with the "dark and tameless" (his words) Emily Dickinson.

A Short History of Vampires

Review of The Vampire in 20ᵗʰ Century Literature

(Le vampire dans la littérature du XXᵉ siècle). Jean Marigny, Honore Champion, Paris, 2003).

First published in *Paradoxa*, ed. David Willingham, No. 20, 2006, 301-306.

There are two stories to be told about vampires. One is the psychological, social, and even political history of a pervasive nightmare figure: a human predator, dead and yet still possessed of a physical body, that preys on the living by sucking blood. This folklore creature—as is well-established in Jean Marigny's compendium of the nightmare—has appeared independently of printed or oral transmission (but presumably always without foundation in fact) from Japan to Aztec Mexico. The idea of the active, blood-sucking corpse, typically a woman, often dead in childbirth, encapsulates fear of the dead; fear of the incalculable powers of gestation and lactation—and our pre-scientific conviction, near-universal, that blood is life and has a supernatural meaning and utility. In this narrative the vampires of Slavic and Central Europe might appear as an interesting variant, along with a few vampire figures in the eighteenth- and nineteenth-century printed literature of Western Europe, just part of the same folklore-collecting craze that gave us the fairytales of the Brothers Grimm and Perrault's *Contes des Fées*.

But the vampire has another history, a phenomenal new life, founded by a single novel—Bram Stoker's *Dracula*, and this literary narrative is the primary concern of Jean Marigny's study. From 1897 (when Stoker's founding-father novel was published) to the present day, the vampire has been one of the markers whose trace we can follow through the explosion of mass-market, and then mass-media, popular fiction, from the sensational *feutillons* that entertained the newly-literate, newly leisured urban masses, through the "pulps" and the flood of genre magazines—*Weird Tales, Strange Tales, Amazing Stories*—in the US between the wars, to the teeming tv and movie "novelizations" of globalization. By studying the vampire we can discover how a specific fictional character may come to prominence, almost accidentally, and take hold, like a genetic trait spreading in the population of a paraliterature: expanding in scope, exploding in numbers; changing in response to changes in the environment; finding new uses for old features and ways around the constraints of the original conditions. As Marigny's acute dissection of the nature of sensational fiction demonstrates, at the opening of the discussion, there is a real, logical difficulty at the heart of this fictional afterlife. Where fantasy literature (and especially "the fantastic," as distinct from the more prosaic make-believe of fantasy) relies for its effects on disquiet and surprise and must be continually pulling the rug from under the reader's feet, the vampire anti-hero is by definition predictable. Must be dead, must suck blood, must have fangs, must be able to infect his (or her) prey with the supernatural disease, may not go out by day... The complete list is formidable, and would soon leave *strangeness* no place to hide, if the Bram Stoker character of Dracula were taken as a literal model. But as the ensuing detailed and inclusive exploration demonstrates, there is something in the vampire concept that overcomes familiarity and continually finds new pathways, while always at the risk of a slide into banality.

Inevitably, the first and more substantial part of *Le Vampire dans la littérature*, "Le Vampire Dans Le Texte," is primarily a scholarly catalogue: an annotated list of titles and story-synopses, from the first incidence of the term in print (probably in a Latin document called "Visum et Repertum," dated 1732, in which a surgeon tried to analyze an alleged case of vampirism, for Emperor Charles VI). We learn of vampire children, vampire fetuses, vampire plants (even, in one instance, a vampire rock); vampires descending from Dracula's lonely castle to adopt a bewildering variety of professions and vocations: vampire artists, vampire musicians, vampire bike-boys, vampire nazis, vampire doctors, teachers, priests. Fictional vampires, it almost goes without saying, have often been found active in Ceausescu's regime in Romania... Lesbian vampires, following Sheridan LeFanu's entrancing Carmilla rather than Dracula, have become a minor industry in themselves. We follow the ingenious developments in vampire physiology, as different writers have struggled with the hemoglobin. Does the active corpse of a vampire *digest* the blood? Does that make any sense? Or is the blood-sucking symbolic of a psychic parasitism? We know about those marks on the throat, so thoroughly popularized by the movies, but how exactly is the fluid taken? Is it sucked up through hollow, retractable fangs? Lapped? Licked? Some vampires crudely rend the victim's throat, with maximum Grand Guignol splatter; some have cat-rough tongues and penetrate the skin that way. Suzy McGee Charnas, creator of one of the great modern variants, supplied her "ordinary" vampire, the urbane Dr Wayland, with a kind of fleshy dart on the underside of his tongue. The issue of infection, meanwhile, has been the ground for the whole development (unknown in pre-Stoker sources) of vampire culture and society. When Dracula was a solitary predator he could develop a rapport with his still-living prey; in time it has become very generally accepted that vampires kill to eat but choose an elite of victims to join them in their immortal torment and regard those "sired" in this way as their compatriots or their offspring. The pulps, including those of a coterie of modern German writers adopting American-sounding pseudonyms for their prolific output of blood-sucker shockers, are not forgotten. Nor are the thriving, if heterodox, subgenres of sentimental and erotic vampires. The rationalization of vampires, sometimes used rather speciously to recover the element of surprise (as in Conan Doyle's Sherlock Holmes story "The Adventure of the Sussex Vampire"), has in other cases recovered the disquiet of the fantastic or—notably among science fictional vampires—opened a huge new philosophical area. If a vampire is not a dead human, but a human with a helpless need to ingest blood, as in Theodore Sturgeon's very strange tale of perversity, *Some of Your Blood*, one can have sympathy for the monster, without the farce of the "nice" vampires of sentimental romance. If a vampire is not human at all then the exchange of blood or energy may be neutral, or benign, or may be the key to a universal system of psychic commerce—that questions the nature of good and evil and takes us far beyond the crude morality tale of Stoker.

Despite those prolific Germans and a scatter of representatives from other nations, an overwhelming number of titles are in English, which is easily explained by the relative size of the US market. The stand-out, landmark texts, discussed at length and often referred to, are also, almost without exception, Anglo-Saxon. Stephen King's *Salem's Lot* (1975), technically the first of the modern vampire blockbusters, broke no new ground. Anne Rice's *Interview with a Vampire* (1976), although it cannot supersede *Dracula* as founding text, is the definitive novel of the third wave (the second wave, a renewed popularity of the original themes, having been launched in the Sixties), stunningly original, endlessly copied. Meanwhile Richard Matheson's *I Am Legend* (1954), with its transformation of vampirism into a plague of otherness that will supplant humanity, remains the great vampire science fiction novel; and the psychic vampire, supernatural predator with none of the gory trappings, is chillingly captured in "The House of the Vampire," George Viereck's very early riposte to *Dracula*. As Jean Marigny notes, perhaps with regret, the French are too rational to have supported a vampire folklore (though I would point out they've always had a thriving *loup-garou* population, including flowers of the nobility like Gilles de Retz; maybe it's just diff'rent strokes). Fittingly, the single non-Anglo-Saxon novel awarded truly classic status, *La Mante au fil des jours* (1977) by Christine Rénard, is, according to Marigny, "one of the few vampire novels of the twentieth century truly faithful to the spirit of the fantastic…" and treats of a "femme fatale" (which I think is English for "La Mante") whose real nature, vampire or innocent victim, eludes definition, even to the end of the story.

Vampires for children are forgivably gentle and funny (and under this heading I'd have been proud to have found my own science fiction vampire story *The Fear Man*, which won the Children of the Night award in 1995; though it has slightly more bite than the beloved tv cartoon, *Count Duckula*). Vampire police detectives have such a time of it, explaining why they can't move around in daylight, one wonders whether this combination was really worth trying. Christian religious items like crosses and crucifixes persist, but have an unconvincing effect on the undead as we approach the almost entirely Godless popular culture of the twenty-first century—although may I recommend Pat Cadigan's terrific "The Power and the Passion" (1989, collected in *Patterns*, Ursus Books, New York) as a successful re-vamping of this theme.

But with few exceptions the trend of the literature has been, inexorably, from mystery to explanation, and this has its pitfalls. *Tout comprendre c'est tout pardonner;* which is not the effect one seeks in a shocking scary story. The "realization" of a fantastical threat, tempting though the project must be, ends in creating a monster who no longer has the least power to disturb. Can they eat and drink ordinary food? What's it feel like to wake up in a coffin and realize you've become a dead, bloodsucking immortal…? Can they enjoy sex…? Do they have emotions? What do they really think of us…? These are dangerous questions, the downfall of monstrosity. Chelsea Quinn Yarbro's Comte de Saint-Germain, the typical late-period vampire, is entirely benign: barely a bloodsucker at all, but merely the conveniently long-lived and widely traveled hero for a series of charming historical novels. Anne Rice's Lestat and Louis (at least in the early books of the series) were beautiful but also genuinely damnable, even while they became very human, mixed-up predators. Her imitators have reached a distressing nadir of sugared dullness and display an ever-stronger tendency to anodyne, poisonous neo-conservatism, the brutality of the vampire-elite "domesticated" by admiration.

The literary history must predominate, but it would not be complete without some account of the psychological, social, and even political development of the vampire as a cultural icon. In the second half of Jean Marigny's study, and also woven through his examination of the texts, we find a discussion of what the monster has meant to different non-literary interests over the years and of what the monster reveals about us. Bram Stoker's Dracula was a wealthy nobleman, eccentric, ugly, immune to restraint and above the law: a brutal overlord at home, a merciless marauder abroad. The adventure of his defeat can be seen as mildly democratizing (not so much "power to the people" as "power to the jolly decent Anglo-Saxon upper middle classes"). It is also, along with John William Polidori's satirical portrait of Byron as *The Vampyr* and his employer's own treatment of the theme, in *The Giaour*, the first locus of the sexual heat that seems inseparable from the vampire concept now—though it was, ironically, unknown in the bloodsuckers of folklore. In the years *entre deux guerres*, the vampire—invariably supplied with a difficult, foreign, aristocratic name, not necessarily Romanian, even French would do—was to become a hate-figure easily read as the personification of any alien undesirable. Jean Marigny reports—unfortunately without a precise reference—that US troops, on their way overseas in the Second World War, were issued with copies of *Dracula* and leaflets caricaturizing German soldiers as typical vampires. Post-War, in the witch-hunt years of McCarthyism and the Cold War, US propagandists found the Stoker novel again a powerful portent, a fable of the triumph of the West.

So where is the vampire now? The last decades of the twentieth century saw the end of the Cold War, the collapse of the Soviet Bloc, and a paradoxical escape (for Anglo-Saxon dominated consumers) from the "peace" of the long impasse into a future of war abroad and terror at home, where plenty and horror seem inextricably entangled. In those same years the vampire was finally democratized, socialized, and humanized; and does this mean our everyday lives have become monstrous? This unassuming yet masterly study takes us from Victorian England, where Gothic thrills may have represented an escape from censorship—permission, under license, to admit that death, disease, and other dirty secrets had not been banished from the world—to the brink of a new age, in which vampires are our neighbors, their wicked ways not so shocking, in fact not much different from our own. In the early twenty-first century we seem inclined to go further and identify *ourselves* with the evil aristocrats, the luxurious and despairing Byronic heroes of these wonder tales. As Jean Marigny puts it, in his closing remarks, not only are the vampires among us, they hold up a mirror in which (instead of the empty glass that greets a classic vampire, the monster who doesn't exist) we are shown our own reflection.

Note: Jean Marigny was awarded the Grand prix de l'Imaginaire Essai, 2004, for *Le vampire dans la littérature du XXᵉ siècle*. Le Grand prix de l'Imaginaire, created in 1974, at first restricted to Science Fiction, has covered the genres of Science Fiction, Horror, and the Fantastic since 1992. The award was presented to Jean Marigny at the Festival Utopiales at Nantes on November 10, 2003.

[Re] Reading for a Chapter on Feminist SF: An Annotated Book List

I was asked to write a chapter on Feminist SF, for "The Routledge Companion to Science Fiction." The chapter is a fair, informative round-up and overview for the general reader; at least I hope so. But the assignment drew me on, through the back pages of the seventies and eighties, one title suggesting another, and this is the reading list that resulted. It's not so much the Big Names or titles that have remained visible, continually discussed, established in the canon. It's more of a miscellany, some well-known texts, some hidden gems, and some... Well, a mixed bag, anyway.

Native Tongue: Suzette Haden Elgin

No use, not for me. I feel the same now as I did then. The concept sounds fascinating. There've been secret feminine languages and writings for millennia, notably in China for example—but a language devised by women *linguists*, that cuts up the world in subtle new ways unknown to man: that's something else. Sadly, the execution is narrow and prosaic. Every science fiction is about the making of the present, and classic feminist sf is (typically) a satire and a rebellion against a very particular place and time, namely the fifties, post-WWII USA. But this is just too transparent.

Venus Rising: Carol Emshwiller

Space man. Sea woman.... A fable about our foremothers, the Aquatic Apes, written after reading Elaine Morgan's *The Descent of Woman*. I like the Aquatic Ape hypothesis. We're naked, we're fat, we have voluntary breath control, we weep. Sure, I'll buy it. We were driven from the savannah in a period of global overheating and became human on the ocean shore, frolicking like sea-otters in the waves.

I liked the fable when I first read it. Second-time around, I wasn't so sure at first. Emshwiller's sweet style can charm you, or irritate you. Venus, the proto-human narrator, is so careless in her oceanic, happy innocence, she could seem vapid. Zeus (the non-aquatic hominid, whose people have already invented patriarchal society, violence, paranoia, and banishment) is very much the regulation bad guy. But there's a subversive, rug-pulling twist. Gentle Venus gets nasty to deal with Zeus and save her people. In the process she has to become tough, progressive, and ambitious (Adam tempted her to eat his apple?); and we leave her setting off in search of new worlds to conquer.

The Wanderground: Sally Miller Gearhart

Generally held to be the most embarrassing "Seventies feminist" sf text in the world, ever. *Who can read* The Wanderground *now?*, a highly sympathetic male respondent demanded, rhetorically, on a mailing list I belong to, a few months ago. So naturally I had to check it out. Actually, it's not that bad. Along with *Despatches from the Frontiers of the Female Mind*, this is the book that really brought back the flavor of those strange days of The Women's Press SF imprint. Like listening to Leonard Cohen again, first time since *circa* 1973. What you have to realize, first of all, is the tiny scale of the operation. This isn't Wimmin for World Domination. This is the yoga class that meets above the whole-food store, Bay Area, West Coast USA, daydreaming about getting back to nature, rejecting the cruel city and all its works, and developing their psychic potential. *Let's everybody curl up in a ball, arms around your knees. Now imagine that you're lifting off the floor, imaging that you're floating, floating...*

Can you buy it? In certain moods, I can wish it might be so. David Saxton, reviewing for the *Guardian* around 1987, called the Wanderground women "something between robins and hobbits"; sounds about right. Take over? Kick ass? No, no, we're pacifists! Gaia Herself is going to do the dirty work. Can the boys play, too? Yes, if they promise not to spoil everything. But they have to build their own treehouse.

The Female Man: Joanna Russ

Most of the canonical texts got displaced: I felt I could wing it on prior knowledge and received wisdom introducing, e.g., Ursula K. Le Guin or Suzy Charnas titles to the readers. But I had to read *The Female Man* again. What did I notice? (Apart from the fact that I still found the four-ply story gripping, the elliptical style sharp and compelling.) The Probability Mechanics, the "braided possibilities" that also turn up in this year's *In War Times* by Kathleen Ann Goonan, for a different satirical purpose. And the theatre of operations. Once more, it's not about the human world, as I assumed in my salad days: it's about the good old USA. The planet Whileaway has two continents, North and South. Little girls cast out to do their spirit journey in the far north (aka Canada, I surmise) kill wolves, and bring back the paws as proof.

A feminist Utopia where children are treated rough, leave their mothers at five, and grow up shooting straight and taking no shit... The longings of someone deprived of not just *any* set of "male-coded" freedoms, but of a specific, culturally defined set of "male coded freedoms"; almost a Hollywood Woodsman version of what it means to be human (as in, the defining human being, to whom *woman* is the yielding, supporting complement). I'm reading these texts historically. Should I apologize? I'm seeing them in context, and I don't think any the less of them for being more personal, less universal, than I imagined.

Machine Sex and Other Stories: Candas Jane Dorsey

"Machine Sex" is the definitive feminist cyberpunk story. Everything about it says so, from the babe programmer's inside-out street costume, the white silk shirt over the black leather jacket, to the way she's introduced: sexy, naked young woman at the computer keyboard. I could wax intellectual about the take on the zeitgeist, but hell, why ignore the obvious? Cyberpunk's central myth is about the "fusion" between man and machine, and Dorsey's story says: oh, you mean masturbation? You mean: guys *actively prefer* to jerk off, alone with the little tool? Well, why didn't you just say so? Funny, vicious, and broken-hearted... Deft anti-gender fantasy in "The Prairie Warriors" and "War and Rumors of War"; chilling existential grief in "Sleeping In A Box"; "Black Dog" and "Willows" provide different takes on the people who stay behind on earth, when everybody has gone somewhere else, and the people who return—both beautiful, so evocative of beloved landscape. In case you haven't noticed, I loved rediscovering this collection.

A Spaceship Built of Stone and Other Stories: Lisa Tuttle

Ghosts. Probability ghosts. A subtle account of how we discover that the aliens are among us, and then we forget. A touch of gothic family horror in the saga of the Thing Lurking in the Back Room, once a sentient creature from another star; but that was long ago. Probability ghosting turns up again and again in feminist-sf, and everybody has their own reasons, but isn't it always, deep down, a way of saying, the way things are is not immutable? *It ain't necessarily so...* Most notable story, the powerful, often anthologized "Wives." The defeated non-m/f inhabitants of an invaded planet have literally been forced to become women, squaw-brides, to submit to the male humans' alien version of sexual reality. One rebel soul thinks (s)he can fight back, defy this miserable regime, become a person again. But (s)he's wrong. "The old way is not waiting for our return, it is dead."

A Door into Ocean: Joan Slonczewski

One of the first books I (re) read. As I've said elsewhere, at the time I didn't want to like this. Don't do it! was my cry. *Don't* claim the moral high ground; the sf guys' club will love you for it; doesn't that tell you anything...? A woman doing just what she's supposed to do, being gentle and nurturing, looking after our spiritual growth, being moral so we don't have to be... That's not the revolution! I feel differently now, because these are very different times. Best feature: *A Door into Ocean* works like mainstream sf. Okay, it's about the sixties US *under the skin*, but the skin is proper, sciffy, rich, and strange sfnal skin.

The Warrior Who Carried Life /Air: Geoff Ryman

Cara needs to be something other than a weak female so she can avenge her family. She takes on the fake magic that the old wives peddle, makes it real, and becomes a man, her slight body hung with slabs of muscle, massive thews, and flesh-like living armor to wrap it all... Why can't she wish to become a woman warrior and kick ass that way? Because that's a different book. Because she's got to experience the weirdness of inhabiting a male body, that's the whole point. *The Warrior Who Carried Life* is fantasy Gilgamesh, a past distant beyond my imagining. (I can't get Gilgamesh to stick in my head, although I've tried.) Gruesome in the extreme, a pungent, meaty adventure that turns out to be a re-writing of Genesis, with Man as the serpent and Woman as the good guy. I think now as I thought then: a fine example of a story that's all about gender and not at all about politics. Give this guy a Tiptree!

Air: Twenty years later, he did get a Tiptree. *Air* is a pleasure to read. A skilful, affectionate celebration of feminine culture, both in the imaginary near-future Asia (where the telephone and the tv are morphing into spookily pervasive forms) and in long ago Ontario where (as the author makes plain in his dedication) these impressions were first formed. Only thing that worried me: Mae's grotesque pregnancy and abortive birth—a motif that also features in *The Warrior Who Carried Life* and in Ryman's wonderful novella *The Unconquered Country*. It's creepy. What's it supposed to mean?

Nothing changes. The haves are still the haves, the have-nots are still the have-nots. Women find ways to live with this eternal verity; they make the best terms they can with their *lords and masters. (*I suppose I should say "including their own coded-masculine alphas," but I don't feel like it. You'll just have to paste Condoleezza in there for yourselves.) The trouble with celebrating feminine culture is that it's impossible to do so without also celebrating male supremacy. Male supremacy is the condition of feminine culture's existence. Discuss.

The Godmothers: Sandi Hall

I count this one a missed opportunity. Written by a New Zealander living in Canada. The central narrative is a low-key urban thriller: women's liberation and community activism, the people going head to head with a wicked developer, plus a strand about a lesbian in danger of losing her teaching job through machinations of a nasty piece work, also lesbian but in the closet. Then there's the rich media folk in the far future, then there's a mediaeval girl about to be burned as a witch, then there's the quasi-religious Godmothers, who are on another plane, but I couldn't figure out what they were for. I liked the urban thriller strand—a gritty, normalized version of the *Wanderground* scenario, with real people, tragedy, and a touch of psychic powers. Couldn't get on with the overtly sfnal elements. Like Margaret Atwood or Jeanette Winterson's sciffy bits, amateurish and disorganized. Shame.

Despatches from the Frontiers of the Female Mind: Jen Green and Sarah Lefanu, Eds.

My, this takes me back. I did readings from this book at gigs for the Women's Press. I don't believe I ever read from my own bizarre story—I'd have cleared the room. Whose idea was that title, eh? Lesbian separatists whose only interest in sf is the opportunity to do away with men. Feminine, not to say *girly* sf; polemic sf; surreal sf; sf written by feminists (the excellent Mary Gentle makes this distinction about her own writing in the intro). A stellar collection of names, including a grim morality tale from a certain Racoona Sheldon; a brave outpouring of madness and painful longing; a respectful and very decent review in the *New York Times* by Jewelle Gomez, which is worth reading for itself. [Review can be found at: http://query.nytimes.com/gst/fullpage.html?res=9B0DE7D 9173BF93BA15755C0A961948260]

Memoirs of a Spacewoman: Naomi Mitchison

In many ways my top favorite. Hard to believe this novel is over forty years old. Mitchison, upper-caste maverick, has no fear, no howls of Tiptree anguish, no pleas for equal rights—she just takes them. Writes about women doing science, a feminized science that has become the mainstream, NOT a soft option or an inferior version. A xenozoologist (think I've got that right) recounts her career, her students, her expeditions to various planets, her adventures, her pregnancies (two of them very bizarre indeed), her lovers, her children, her friends the lab animals. One of the best vintage science fictions, still fresh and compelling. Seek it out.

Woman on the Edge of Time: Marge Piercy

Along with *The Left Hand of Darkness* and *The Handmaid's Tale*, a "feminist sf" novel the general public has heard of. Stands up well. The Utopians of Mattapoisett remind me of Early Christians in the Acts of the Apostles, with their touching conviction that they're going to get it right this time, that they have the magic code for a truly humane civilization. A likely story. And yes, they are flimsy, but now I can see that they're identified in the text as Connie's daydreams, made of the stuff of her life, her stifled anger, her longings. Utopias have a right to be flimsy, in fact the flimsier the better. They are hope for the present, not street maps of the future. The more solidly they're constructed the more these New Jerusalems, ideal societies, start to sound like totalitarian states.

Dreamsnake: Vonda McIntyre

Post-global-thermonuclear-war with added aliens and normative polyamory. A wander-story, gentle in pace, in which Snake, altered-venom physician with a painful work-related arthritis condition, leads us through a melted and healed over scar-tissue US landscape. Criticized as *too* gentle at the time, mainly due to the characterization of the male lead. Compare and contrast with McIntyre's visceral recent short story, "Little Faces," where the "male leads" are treated very differently!

The Power of Time: Josephine Saxton

I wanted to read *Queen of the States*, but could I find it? I could not. My loft ate it, along with Nicola Griffith's *Ammonite* and Elisabeth Vonarburg's *Silent City*. This collection comes under New Wave sf, but there's more New Woman, sixties-style, than women's lib. Notable stories: "Love From Beyond The Dawn Of Time," subversive Lovecraft sex-demon in a totalitarian far future; "The Power Of Time," the wish-fulfillment-sf title story with a great last line (*really I have never had any power. If I had, I'd have made everything go very differently…*). And the one I liked best, "Living Wild": where the heroine thinks the world has ended and goes to live naked in a cave on the winter moors with a friend-ly lion that she rides.

Not Before Sundown: Johanna Sinisalo

A sex-and-horror lifestyle story, very readable and stylish; blink and it's gone. Cryptic, rather worrying subtext equates male homosexual de-sire with the Beast of the Apocalypse. Trolls (sexy beasts) called up by Gaia from the Finnish forests, in response to the human threat to the planet, draw patriarchy to its nemesis, one worthless lover at a time.

Parable of the Talents: *Bloodchild*: Octavia Butler

I'd never read the Talents series; I stopped at *Xenogenesis*. Couldn't get hold of *Parable of the Sower*. I'd already spent a mad number of rainy summer hours buried in this heap of books, my family had declared me missing, so I made do with Episode 2. A different, nineties take on the savage death-throes of patriarchy. Butler sees no need to imagine a nightmarish satirical future, well-removed from middle-class experience (as in *The Handmaid's Tale*, or *Walk to the End of the World*). Everything is ready right now. Outside the shrinking bubble of affluence, many millions of women are being treated as chattel slaves, stripped of all human rights, kept as prisoners; and the figures are going up, not down… Nasty, grim, streetwise reality, awash with guns; pacifists going to the wall; kill or be killed is the only law. Women, girls, pretty boys are specially vulnerable, but no one's safe. Me not too happy about the New Religion with Female Messiah strand. Manifest Destiny as the palliative for unrest and the hope for the future, hmm, is that a new and better idea? I prefer Mattapoisett: party hard, garden hard.

Bloodchild: Butler's rare short fictions, powerful sketches for the novels, spanning a lot of years. The title story, an *Xenogenesis* out-take about "male" pregnancy (or possibly about bot flies), left me feeling maybe ANY human relationship involves a grisly invasion of the self.

Octavia Butler is an extraordinary case. A very private person, compromise not in her vocabulary, a great loss. A Black US woman with a powerful literary and educational presence, a certified "genius," and a writer who may be read as an sf-feminist: what a combination! Yet her material is unremittingly harsh towards women's chances of finding a solution. Moments of spiritual illumination, sure, but scarcely a glimmer of hope. Rather like Doris Lessing (the Nobel laureate) in this respect. Major works, minor key, little comfort. Difficult to sort out the personal message of a powerful writer from the "message" she delivers about her times.

That's all, folks. Please note, these are not considered reviews, they're tactless off the cuff remarks, scribbled at the reader's elbow; and only marginally cleaned up for a blog post.

PS: Some critical studies

Daughters of Earth: Justine Larbalestier, Ed.

What a great idea for a format! (collection of sf stories by women, each with accompanying critical essay, stories chosen by the essayists). I especially enjoyed revisiting Pat Murphy's "Rachel In Love" and reading Karen Joy Fowler's "What I Didn't See" for the first time, which lead me to the annals of an interesting controversy. Is it sf? I don't know. I can't really envisage reading this story without realizing it's a commentary on "The Women Men Don't See."

Utopian and Science Fiction by Women: Worlds of Difference: Jane Donawerth and Carol Kolmerton, Eds.

Very useful historical background and academic overview.

Women of Other Worlds: Excursions Through Science Fiction and Feminism: Helen Merrick and Tess Williams, Eds.

Ditto, but definitely not a dry academic text (which the Donawerth and Kolmerton tends toward). Especially rich in vintage writer interviews (a long one with Suzy McKee Charnas) and fandom history.

True Life Science Fiction:
Sexual Politics and the Lab Procedural

First published in *Tactical BioPolitics: Art, Activism and Techno-science*, eds Beatrix da Costa and Kavita Philips, MIT Press, Cambridge, MA, July 2008.

Science/Sci-fi/Feminism

Science fiction writers and "science" have a dysfunctional relationship. The core audience for science fiction, especially print fiction, tends to be drawn from those in science and technology related employment, self-identifying geeks, "anoraks," coders, nerds. Readers have a high tolerance for details of lab procedures, engineering problems, high energy physics phenomena, gadget specifications (astonishingly high, relative to the rest of the fiction audience)—yet many express indifference to the *content* of these demanding passages. "You wade through that stuff to get to the story and the characters," is a typical comment. Meanwhile the writers, a group that includes many passionate amateurs, attempt to keep up with the future. Their preoccupation with "science" is an accident of the twentieth century, their *desire* is to be at the cutting edge of everything, dress codes, black holes, radical politics, melting ice caps. Science fiction writing lives poised on the edge of now, always about to be out of date. The vital element that research lab life shares with the genre could be that mood: the addictive stress of novelty, the pride of stepping out onto empty space—

The genesis of my novel *Life* was in the nineteen seventies, when science fiction took on the novelty of the Women's Movement.[1] It was a paradoxical meeting. Defining feminist sf texts, notably Monique Wittig's *Les Guérillères* and Joanna Russ's *The Female Man*, were (and remain!) lyrical, intellectual, experimental, with passages of theory, a painful naming of parts, at once too alien and too accusing to be ignored. The average recreational sf fan, male or female, was appalled. Yet the popularizers of this epiphany, the developers who made the novelty saleable and took the goods to market, were Ursula K. Le Guin and the late Octavia Butler—two US writers whose sheer quality and gravitas has had an immense and lasting impact on the genre. A third figure, using the pseudonym James Tiptree Jr (later outed as a woman called Alice Sheldon, which brought about her downfall), wrote novels and stories that combined startling sexual themes with devout sci-fi convention and swiftly collected every honor the community could bestow. It was a Camelot moment, a brilliant anomaly, soon buried.[2]

Iconic female futures speak bitterness. The most famous, the mainstream novel Margaret Atwood's *The Handmaid's Tale*, features affluent North American women reduced to the chattel status of Pakistani peasants by an ultra-conservative administration. Genre versions anticipated the same theme, i.e., of women crushed under the iron boot of patriarchy, sometimes dragged-up in role-reversal fantasy, sometimes unrelieved (Suzy McKee Charnas, *Walk to the End of the World*),[3] sometimes in diptych with a sweet Red alternative (Marge Piercy's *Woman on the Edge of Time*). In the last pages of any of these novels a light glimmers ahead. But don't go there, for if you do, our Utopia will sound as fascist and covertly vengeful as any other; end here, it sounds hopeful… Issues of science and technology permeate these narratives, but the encounter is tragic. *Positive* feminist sf (Joan Slonczewski, *A Door into Ocean;* Vonda N. McIntyre, "Of Mist, Grass and Sand"; Kathleen Ann Goonan, *Light Music*)—imagining a ravaged planet restored by the new, experiments in reproduction and post-humanism, gender-neutral societies; high-tech symbiosis with the living world—is far less likely to be known outside the genre, or to be recorded in the academic canon. Feminism cast as daring scientific endeavor is not easily read as radical politics: the dissonance is too great; women are not supposed to occupy this space. And yet, as those writers of the seventies discerned and as we see all too clearly in this hell-bent, regressive young century, embracing futurism and assimilating *les accidents de féerie scientifique*[4] (if only in art/drama/fiction) is our only hope.

I saw Joanna Russ's *The Female Man* (1975) in a bookstore in Singapore, where I was living at the time, and walked past it several times before

I picked it up. I found the expression "Female Man" disturbing, and I did not expect to be *disturbed* by the Women's Movement. I expected feminist theory to tell me only things I knew already. Curiosity got the better of me, and I bought the book and discovered that Joanna Russ was none other than the writer of *When It Changed*[5] — a new wave sf story, radically feminist yet impeccably science-fictional, that I greatly admired.

The Female Man is a hatchet job. It strips feminism of all sentimental illusion, exposes the (sf) writer as a daydreaming schizophrenic, and presents its women-only world as a dazzling high-tech playground, where duelists strut and genius "IQ" is advisable if not mandatory. I was an instant convert to Russ's view of women as *human*, dangerous, powerful, and fallible. Overnight, the veiled women in the novel I was writing (set in a far-future South East Asia), stopped being piteous victims and became rulers of the health, who had abandoned the public sphere to their menfolk or "studs" of their own free will—with disastrous consequences.

Russ appeared to be a disillusioned fellow-traveler of US (regular flavor, not feminist) underground politics: of urban terrorism, secret maildrops, layers of deception—a world I deeply distrusted. She probably ruined my chances of a career in commercial sf, for which I thank her, sincerely; and she set me the task of stripping down my own, very different illusions.[6] My writing was a means of naming the parts and, by building functional models, finding out by trial and error what happened when I discarded one unit or another. I produced a series of novels, reiterating in variant forms the only story feminist sf can tell.

But *The Female Man* had shifted my focus. I was no longer describing the battle of the sexes, speaking bitterness and imagining a more hopeful outcome. I was investigating the causes. What is femaleness, what is maleness? What exactly *happens* in the wiring of human sexual behavior? Is the dominance of a male-ordered culture (supported by the women, apparently of their own free will) one of the great problems of our world? Or am I just deluded? Like Ramone, the perennially angry-young-woman who shadows the protagonist's career in *Life*, I did a huge amount of reading: at first seduced by the blank canvas of the question, then increasingly fascinated by the material itself, the naked equations of sexual difference.

By the mid-nineties the idea of *the female man*—the proposition that our treasured *difference*, the moral identity of women, cannot survive the success of feminism—had brought my fiction to a gender-neutral space that many sf feminists considered positively hostile. I was writing of a future in which the world had divided into two camps of a global low-intensity war: between the Traditionalists, fanatically intent on preserving hallowed male/female characteristics, and the Reformers, who were prepared to let the difference go into freefall. A lot of the Traditionalists were women, a lot of the Reformers were men. The don't-knows had a particularly hard time. There were some aliens too, who had no conception of the sexual other, the either/or, dark/light, active/passive divide: it was the challenge of their arrival that had triggered the gender wars.

As I came to the end of this project I knew it was time to move on from sf feminism. I had nothing more to say. But before I left town I wanted to do something with my research. I'd discovered a collection of articles from the first conference devoted entirely to sexual difference, in which I'd read Jennifer Marshall-Graves's original "SRY" paper, among other despatches from the front line.[7] Drawn by her reputation among feminists, I had encountered Lynn Margulis's endosymbiotic theory and her stubborn fight to break down the establishment's resistance—on a point of doctrine completely innocent to lay-persons, yet *immediately* recognized by the priesthood as a challenge that shook the pillars of the universe. One meets the same bewildering acuity in all holy wars. I felt there was a story to be told, which would trace the checkered career of a visionary woman scientist and the equally checkered career of a controversial discovery. It would be a fantasy about something going on in the human sex chromosomes, the impossible made plausible by a wealth of technical detail. But crucially, vitally, this change in sexual molecular biology would turn out be profoundly important for all life on earth… And it would be nobody's fault, it would be something inevitable, neither good nor evil, working its way to emergence. (It was nobody's fault that Galileo saw the moons of Jupiter.)

There would be no alien invasion, no divine or demonic intervention, no mysterious Rapture. No single-sex colony on a distant planet, no Born-again Bronze Age matriarchs, no gender-selective genocide, no sex-linked plague. I would return *ad fontes,* to the source of all modern folklore, whether or not labeled "sci-fi": science itself—the marvelous in its street clothes.

Shadowing a Scientist

Ideally, science fiction writers should be scientists, tossing-off best-sellers in their spare time. Ideally, they should be working in theoretical physics or engineering; astrophysics, astronomy, and branches of computer science may also apply. This is our long-established, male-typic elite, the standard by which we judge ourselves. (The genre is conservative. Life sciences, until recently considered more suitable for women writers, are coming up fast.) Even now I feel slightly shocked when I hear that one of their number has quit to "become a full time writer." What a fall! The rest of us are camp-followers, groupies, cargo-cultists, collectors of antique packaging.

I had been writing science fiction for more than a decade without ever going near a lab. For the Anna Senoz novel I needed to enlist a scientist, and this was alarming. I had been working with Richard Crane (now the Convenor of Creative and Dramatic Writing, at the Centre of Continuing Education, University of Sussex, UK) on community writing projects. I asked him to be my matchmaker. Could he find a molecular biologist, preferably female, who would be willing to talk to a sci-fi writer? Who might even let me come into a lab and be a fly on the wall?

My first approaches were not successful. I find an entry in my notebook, after one phone call in which I'd been given a short, sharp answer. Here's the catch. Women in science are likely to be hard pressed. *Oh dear, I've hit the busy people. This isn't going to work; why should anyone make time for me?*

Eventually, Dr Jane Davies agreed to see me.

I prefer to do my own research. I read everything I can get my hands on. I do my best to understand, or at least to capture the ambience; and then I make it up. Conformity to today's knowledge base is beside the point in sci-fi. The Higgs boson discourse will no doubt have moved on, two hundred years from now—if anybody cares at all. When I have to call in a specialist, I try to use (and not to abuse) a personal contact. I don't tend to ask questions, because I fear I'm too ignorant to think of the right way to frame them. I tell my story, explain how the device or special effect is supposed to fit into my plot, and the specialist makes objections. This seems to work. I had no list of questions with me, no tape-recorder either, when one morning in November I set out for Sussex University, my old *alma mater* (where I had wasted three years of my parents' and my government's money, once upon a time).

At Sussex, four miles from Brighton, on the edge of the south downs, the Great Divide between arts and science is physical and dramatic. Arts is in the green valley; Science occupies a concrete hillside. I announced myself at the porter's desk in BIOLS, a building in a part of the campus I had never entered when I was an undergraduate. I approached the corridor lined with office doors expecting very little. I thought I'd state my case, go away and wait for Dr Davies's decision. I was concerned because I was going to have to talk about feminism right away, or I'd be under false pretences, and I didn't know how she would react. In my experience successful professional women are often very wary of that word. It's demeaning.

Feminism? Special pleading, whiney nonsense. Get out of here!

I saw a woman in a white coat, maybe a few years older than myself (but I'll feel childish 'til I die), with a warm smile. I stumbled through my intro, and Dr Davies showed no sign of impatience. Unprepared, and babbling I'm afraid, I began to tell her my story—

"The important thing to remember is that Anna isn't interested in sexual politics or politics of any kind. She's not *anti*-feminist, she'd say she just wants to be treated like a human being. She's ambitious, secretly and wildly ambitious. When she's an undergraduate she dreams of finding a missing link—some mechanism to bridge the gaps in evolutionary theory, giving a better model of life itself. But that's a daydream. In real life she's an idealist; she wants to do good. She decides on a career in plant biology, improving food crops (sustainably of course). Feed the world. But she gets derailed by bad luck involving a male student who probably resents her talent. She ends up in human fertility studies, and then she spots something going on, a tiny change in a sample of male sex chromosomes, which she sees at once might have a very weird explanation…if it's not an experimental artifact. She checks it out and is convinced she's on the track of something, and I'm not sure how, but in the end this will happen *fast*, become visible and unstoppable *fast*, within a generation.

"Is it possible? I know they don't usually but do the X and the Y ever exchange bases, would it be obvious or could it appear and disappear, the way I need—? At some point she's forced to sacrifice her career to her domestic responsibilities—

I trembled every time I had to use a technical term. *Mitochondria*, how do you pronounce that? I rambled around, explaining about taking things apart, identifying er, the basic components, as if that's what's important... I remember Dr Davies gently prompting me. "Reductionism—?"

"Uh, yes."

Reducing dramatic situations to their component parts, isolating them from the real world, is science fiction's most treasured technique, borrowed from science itself. But Anna's story had to be natural, complex, full of inextricable connections, like a novel about real life. And here I was asking a scientist to help me—

I was extremely exposed. All I could do was cling to Anna.

She keeps coming back to the thing she saw, and finding it again, and getting more and more excited. She knows it's the key to a BIG discovery, but she knows, and it turns out she's right, that the sex angle will be her downfall. It's what happens to women in science in real life. Because they have children, or a husband who doesn't like their long hours, or a superior, or a grants board, tacitly, unthinkingly, marking them down, or because they make male colleagues feel insecure (though you can never say that). It's meant to be read doubly: a young woman who wants to be a *pure* scientist and has a very idealistic notion of what that means, but she keeps being brought up against the sex angle—

I have pages of scribbled notes from this interview; it was astonishingly successful for me. There are no notes about my state of mind, but I know how I felt. I'd been trying to teach myself molecular biology, from a half-page of misunderstood notes washed up on a desert island: and was plunged into a masterclass—

Interview Notes

A transfer of material from the Y to the X, with some selective advantage?

The X and the Y don't usually exchange recombination, they're too different in shape, but there is a small area where this male donation could happen —

A benign mutation, fixed in the population for thousands of years?

A tiny change in the amount of Y (more)

Conveying resistance to our increasingly toxic environment?

What's needed is a horizontal transfer

Transposons. What about transpons?

(Transposons were my big idea—)

What do you see? When that happens? A band changes in size?

Spontaneous change causes transposable elements to mobilise.

At least 10/15% of our DNA is made up of transposable elements.

They can act like viruses...

She would note this change, publish a paper in "Trends in Genetics"

a scientific journalist would pick it up from a database

Very bad news if your supervisor doesn't know what's in your graduate paper. If it's published without her supervisor's name, that's a crushing blow —

I had not decided *when* my story would start when I walked into Dr Davies' office. Possibly the near future? As we mapped out Anna's career for her, as if she were setting out now (a game of snakes and ladders: that's not going to change), I made an instant decision. She starts from here—

She knows nothing about seventies feminism (although she's going to meet a ferocious, defiant young feminist). She's eighteen, proud and brave, and the Spice Girls have just released "Wannabe." She's *disgusted* by girl power—

She gets a good first degree

A science department gets a quota of grants

Your supervisor puts you on a project

For three years. It's not enough time.

The nature of lab-based science makes it impossible to survive for the fourth year. Industry sponsored studentships, for top-up grant support. Student works w. industrial partner, but no guaranteed employment.

Many supervisors use their students as technicians, you could end up without much choice of work.

In academic science you can keep going on short-term contracts. But you have to have a permanent job by 35-40. Teaching, administration, grant organization.

Publish! Publish! Publish!

Her own research is always going to have to give —

Serendipity: I was very lucky to have encountered someone who was prepared to countenance my proposal: to recognize and nurture what faint resonance it had with her professional knowledge. Perhaps even luckier to meet someone—outside science fiction or academic literary criticism—who grasped the idea of a *doubled* narrative, where the information, the sequence of events, is meant to convey at least two meanings at the same time. Or perhaps that wasn't luck. The genome is the original complex, layered, looping, interactive narrative. A gene may "mean" several different things. Depending on the location, depending on the bases upstream and down; depending on the weather in the cells...

Simplicity as a result of complexity: this is a historical document. I met Dr Davies in 1996. The human genome project had begun in 1990. The Y chromosome would not be sequenced until 2003. In 1996, horizontal transfer of DNA, in a population, between species, was verging on science fiction, to coin a phrase. I was to spend the next few years, as I wrote and rewrote this book, rearranging my fantasy science so that it could live in the chinks between real world discoveries (conditions, current affairs): my understanding of the science growing more sophisticated, and the surface of my fiction growing sleek as flesh and blood.

Some things certainly haven't changed. In 1996 there were initiatives, conferences, workshops, on the Women in Science question. The hemorrhage of female graduates, from both public and private sectors, was being debated. "Everyone" knew about the hoops women had to jump through to get grants, the scandal revealed by blind testing of the funding application process; the dearth of women reaching high-level, role-model, influential posts. And yet, just as now, girls like Anna, talented and liberated, were supposed to be having it all. If Equal Opportunities didn't work for them, there must be something wrong with the girls.

(My memories: *Once, when I was twenty or so, a fellow undergraduate jumped on me. We were alone in a student rented house, a grimy front room with a mattress on the floor, posters of Ché and Dylan. He was one of the circle of friends, by no means a close friend of mine. What did I do? I fought him off. He came back for more, I kept on fighting. I did not scream; of course I didn't. I went on fighting, silently, until he finally quit. But if he had persisted, I would have had to give in. I would not have called it "rape," not unless he'd beaten me unconscious or tied me up or something; and I wouldn't have dreamed of reporting the incident. Girls usually don't. What would you say, in the face of his convinced denial? It's true, I let him do it. He didn't rape my body, he raped my mind, he forced me to accept his version… Nah, better keep quiet. Expect to be insulted; understand that you always have to be careful.*)

After about an hour, I took away the ideas I'd been given, the insights into the feudal relationship between a student and (her) supervisor, and the promise that I could have a lab visit. My sense of astonished daring, my feeling that I'd entered a sanctuary, a holy place where I had never expected to tread, was no part of the interview. But it was to become part of Anna.

She spent the lunch break lurking in the crowd, unmolested. In the middle of the afternoon she presented herself in good time. Professor Reeves of Computer Science, who was running the symposium, greeted her distractedly.

"Who are you?" His grey curly hair fizzed with anxiety.

"I'm Anna Senoz, from Parentis."

"Good, good. Now look, er, Anna, we're running late, it's going to be very unfair on the last group, so could you make it short. Get through your stuff in fifteen minutes, instead of twenty. Can you do that for me, love?"

"Of course."

"Good girl! Now where the hell's Eswin? Anyone here seen Terry Vick?"

She scanned her pages and made instant cuts. It was better this way: hustled, badgered, no time to think. It would be no worse than talking to a nearly empty hall, the way she'd imagined. There was no one here remotely interested in "Transferred Y." This was a rehearsal, harmless as practicing in front of the mirror. Her heart beat wildly, she felt like a half-fledged bird crouched on the rim of the nest: "*Ca, mon ame, il faut partir...*" Who said that? Rene Descartes, as he lay dying. My soul, we must go. But she was not dying, she was being born. She was about to join the edifice, the organism, thousands of years, to which she had given her life and heart. To speak and be heard. She checked the OHP, made sure her acetates were in order— and saw K.M. Nirmal, sitting erect in the middle of the front row. She hardly recognized him. Her supervisor was wearing a very smart suit. She'd never seen him except in a lab coat or a shabby sports jacket. He hadn't said a word about attending the symposium. Her head started to spin. To speak in front of Nirmal was *completely different*.

She began.

That evolution is still a mysterious process, with many unsuspected byways, and perhaps she had found an example of one of these. That her predecessors in sequencing the Y chromosome had worked like this.

That she was analyzing samples of DNA from healthy, normally fertile contemporary human males and from recovered medieval tissue.

That her technique was like this (including the tweaked modeling program). That she had repeatedly observed an exchange of the same sequence of bases, between the Y and the X chromosomes in the modern samples. That she had found no sign of this polymorphism in human male DNA from a similar geographic location at an earlier date. (The Huit Bories samples.) Further investigation was indicated. Was there a female version of "Transferred Y," passed on by affected males to their daughters?

Meanwhile here was a distinctive genetic variation, apparently fitness-neutral, that had established itself in a human population in a relatively short time. How this happened—if it was not disproven by further evidence—and whether there were other instances of the same mechanism, continued studies might reveal.

The previous speaker, Eswin Holmes (Bacteriostatic Effects of Food Preservation) had overrun his fifteen minutes a little. Therefore, after about thirteen minutes and a quarter, Professor Reeves started making urgent *wind it up!*, signals. Anna wound it up. She was pleased with herself for being in control enough to do that and still more or less make sense. No one was listening, anyway—except presumably Nirmal. She dared, as she delivered her final sentence, to risk a timid glance in his direction. He was staring right at Anna, his eyes blazing with naked fury. As she watched, horrorstruck, he got to his feet, pushed his way along the row, and marched out of the hall.

There were no questions.

The symposium had been on a Saturday. Nirmal kept her waiting for a week before he called her to his office. No one else had mentioned the symposium except Ron Butler (m), who made an attempt to congratulate her on breaking her duck. Anna thought the delay was a refinement of cruelty; she realized later that Nirmal had been giving himself a chance to calm down. The worst part was that Anna hadn't an idea what she had done wrong. He'd accepted her Transferred Y outline without comment, merely telling her to carry on, and she'd been too unsure to ask to talk it over. She'd handed him a copy of her final draft and waited hopefully for his input. She'd been disappointed when he failed to make any response, but it was typical of Nirmal.

The best and worst thing about the interview itself was that everything became very clear very quickly.

"So, Miss Senoz. I gather that the work we have been doing together has been far from worthy of your undivided attention. When I suggested that you give a paper at the Young Scientists' symposium, I think I had a right to assume that your presentation would focus on the doctoral project you are undertaking with my supervision."

"I'm sorry," she whispered.

"But no. Your mind is elsewhere." He lifted a copy of Anna's "Transferred Y" paper and slapped it down on his desk as if he hoped to break all its bones. "If it cannot be distorted into the service of your much more interesting private preoccupations, your work in this lab does not engage you at all. I trusted you implicitly! It was extremely, extremely unpleasant for me to discover, in public, that you had chosen to present a peculiar hobbyhorse of your own—"

Anna was dumbfounded. It dawned on her that Nirmal had not read her outline or her paper. Of course, he'd assumed he *had* read it. He knew everything she'd been doing on the pseudo-genes. He'd assumed she would be going over that ground. He had not made time to check up on her, or it had slipped his mind, or he'd let it go because he hated one-on-one meetings. She stared at her hands, clasped in her lap to stop them shaking, and wondered, how on earth did someone as allergic to personal contact as Nirmal get to be a postgraduate adviser? It wasn't because she was a girl, he was as distant with the male members of the team. Everybody complained about it.

That's science for you. The better you are at what you do, the more time you're doomed to spend doing things you're no good at. Her terror was strangely dissipated. *No way* was she going to remind him that he'd told her she could do what she liked. *No way* was she going to point out that he'd had every opportunity to find out and had omitted to make sure he knew what his student was going to say in her first public appearance.

"Until you are free to return to your beloved potatoes," Nirmal was saying, with withering politeness. "I expect you to concentrate *mainly* on the tasks in hand here."

Anna nodded: accepting her lessons. Anything you say in the lab, your supervisor is going to hear. Anything you do, it is your responsibility to make sure your supervisor knows about it. Don't take chances with the natural human vanity of your boss.

"Professor Reeves intends to publish a transcript of the colloquium. Needless to say, *this* will not feature. It will never be published. I cannot consider putting my name to it."

She nodded again. She was no longer devastated. She knew he would not be unfair in his personal record. Neither of them would say it, but he knew he'd been neglectful.

"I'm sorry," she said, standing up. "I got carried away. It won't happen again."

"Good. I hope I can trust you from now on."

She reached for the paper. Nirmal's thin hand came down upon it, the nails almond shaped and calcined, thick as seashells. He didn't speak, so she headed for the door.

"Oh, Anna—"

She quailed. What now?

"This is very good work," said her supervisor dryly, tapping the Transferred Y paper. "Wrong-headed, even absurd, in the implications, which you wisely didn't spell out. But bold, original, well-reasoned, and well-presented. Your technical work is also very good. You have a formidable talent, young lady. But you must focus. Focus!"

"Thank you," she muttered. "Thank you, I'm sorry, I will."

"A formidable talent," repeated Nirmal. "Don't waste it!"

[Extract from Life, *Chapter Two: Anna Anaconda]*

(My present: *I watch the extreme sports programs on late night tv, with my son. I see those young men leaping into the empty air, their preternatural confidence: as if they have an immediate, physical sense of their place in the whole of this state of all states, this state of affairs, a path they follow that will never let them fall. The truth is that they DO fall, crash and burn, smash their elbows, snap their collarbones. But they don't care. I wonder, is that leap into space testosterone, or nurture? Is it something I could never learn, or is it something I could find in myself, an atrophied skill? What kind of human being am I?)*

Shaking B. Polymerase Chain Reaction
28.1.97 Martin shows me round:
A Biology lab, too warm. Long islands of benches, clutter of
equipment, screwtop jars with masking tape labels. Post docs in
jeans and teeshirts. Names of the machines: a microwave oven
bought from a chain store, various devices for long-term shaking of
things. A squat pyramid with a rubber cone let into the top vibrates
a microfuge (eppendorf) tube. The fridge freezer, the PCR machines,
the gel trays linked to a row of transformers. Designed so you can put
your hand in the electroporesis liquid with the current running. For
sequencing the voltage may be very high, today it's not critical. The
prep room where tech support staff make up mixes from enzymes
and proteins bought in bulk. The fume cupboard, the camera in a
closet, Eagle Eye, where people take pictures of their gels. Moments
of tension, sometimes no bands appear.

βlots and Ꮐels

Anna wanted to tell them that when she studied a protein sep-
aration gel, it was like a negative image of the starry sky. She
was an astronomer, a cosmologist, a particle physicist: knowing
events by their traces, through a chain of mathematical infer-
ence, never able to perceive her quarry directly. She wished she
could make her friends understand the vast *distances*: which
was far more important than worrying about vanity parenting
or whether men or women owned the jargon. It is so far away,
you can't imagine how far. We don't exist there. They don't direct us, no more than the stars direct human affairs. We are part
of the same system, obeying the same laws, but we hardly begin
to understand what the laws are. Maybe we're still waiting for
Galileo's telescope…

[Extract from Life, *Chapter* One: *The Spirit of the Beech Tree]*

Dr Davies had advised me to listen-in on some lectures. I turned
up and snuck in at the back of the theatre for Janet Collett's Eukaryotic
Genetics (1996/7), "Heritability; Genetic Constraints of Selection; Rec-
ognising, Saving, and Using Genetic Resources." The lecturer was a tall
woman with a graying braid, dressed in work shirt and jeans; unpreten-

tious and kindly. The students liked her, evidently; so did I. My way had been prepared for me. When I first appeared, someone came up at the end and asked, "Are you the science fiction writer?" I nervously agreed, and that was all. I copied diagrams; I made adjustments to the ideas formed by my amateur reading. I discovered how fluid, how interactive the genome was becoming, how much unsuspected complexity had been uncovered by the failure of early attempts at "genetic engineering." It's not that the processes aren't predictable, they're just far more intricate, and there are far, far more variables, combinations, feedback loops, than had been dreamed possible. I pondered on transposons, viruses, cohorts, methylation, environmental factors.

Polymerase Chain Reaction #2

The project involves a gene in Drosophila called Shaking B that affects nerve/muscle junctions. The object of this exercise is to try and pinpoint the working part of the code. Martin is using a different technique in this reaction-a section of DNA with an added long tail of nucleotide bases that will help him to spot his target. PCR record sheet, check boxes. Use the micropipette to make up the mixture of cutting enzyme, buffers, template, de-ionized water etc. Add a thin film of oil to prevent evaporation. The enzyme is a special one that is thermostable to 95 degrees centigrade. Shake the tubes, using the machines that shake them, and insert in the PCR machine.

Micropipettes are robust, practical looking dispensers, disposable tips, use and eject into beaker (bin) Care must be taken to let no part of the pipette beyond disposable tip touch microfuge, DNA is everywhere. Names on masking tape, like on food in a student fridge. Post-docs are in their late twenties. Pressures on labspace, supervision hours = many undergrads do no practical work, except by-rote prepared experiments. A few will be lucky enough to do a 3rd year project.

In the late nineteen-thirties (this was before Crick and Watson, before the dramatic revelation of the structure of DNA) something highly critical happened to genetics, which until then had been a patient science of organisms and cells, where the result of a cytology experiment had to be read in the variegated color of a flower; in the shape of an insect's wing. The technology improved and the physicists moved in, notably Max Delbrück, bringing their mechanistic, reductionist (that word again!)

world-view. For more than thirty years thereafter, DNA was the miraculous blueprint (this was what they taught me in school, in the nineteen sixties): changeless as the fixed stars—except when a random mutation, conveying an advantage at some level, propagated through a population via fitness selection. It was a beautiful model, pure and simple, and essentially tragic. Every organism, every gene, was an isolated warrior, forging alone through the ages, ruled by arbitrary fate. And it was wrong.

It was wrong, but inescapable (it remains, with grudging concessions, "received wisdom"). You believed in the physicists' version or you didn't work; or if you worked you were a crank, unpublishable: you were nobody. The heroes of the resistance (Lynn Margulis, Barbara McClintock) suffered quite horribly, especially McClintock. It was like being nailed as Un-American, except nobody talked about a blacklist. I was proud of them. Yet if I had been a female biology student in the fifties, the sixties, wouldn't I have been *very* careful not to associate with anything cranky? Can't be too careful. Wouldn't I still be wary today? I felt my native caution welling up: if someone is called a crank, there's usually something in it. No smoke without fire. Just because I write sci-fi, doesn't mean I'm gullible.

But I took comfort—I take comfort—in the big mistakes of science. Sun still going round the earth, anyone? There's no mystery as to how a revolution happens. As long as the accepted theory works and produces good results, a few mavericks can easily be ignored. When cracks begin to show, they are shored-up and painted over. All human structures protect themselves. The life of the mistake is prolonged by peer-pressure, by witch-hunts, by more or less wilful blindness: whatever the market will bear. But sooner or later, the mistake is defeated by its own success. The bigger and more pervasive the system gets, the more the contrary evidence begins to mount up, too, until a tipping point is reached. Anyone can suppress the truth. You can suppress the truth as often as you like. But there comes a point when you can't suppress the facts, because there they are! All over the place.

The idea that gender is all important could be simply wrong. Down among the chromosomes, among the bases, the science is neutral. Every human body (right now, no fantasy intervention required) is a mosaic of male and female cells. If we were to look for sexual identity on that level, we'd be very puzzled to exercise our apartheid, our decree of either/or. The whole idea that humanity is divided into two halves could be a chimera.[8] One day it might vanish, like the Cold War, like the crystal spheres, like canals on Mars and jungles on Venus. People born with currently recognized X/Y pair problems would be treated only for the medical ill-effects. Parents and doctors would be less concerned to have babies with "indeterminate" genitals corrected by surgery. There'd be people who felt themselves to be men getting pregnant; people who felt themselves to be women at ease with their penises. People who just couldn't see the problem, letting their "sexual identity" go into free fall. And then everyone would—

Be happy?

Better than that. Everyone would be the same as before, or that's what they'd tell you. Successful revolutions vanish, nobody realizes they happened.

Dark they were, and golden-eyed.[9]

Random Lecture Notes

The rule is not "if you have a Y you're male"

It's 1X+2 sets of autochromes and you're male

2X+ 2 sets of autochromes and you're female.

A molecular mechanism that can distinguish one from two is sophisticated

Triggered by meiosis sorting X from Y or X from not-X

Y in flies, not necessary for male identity, is necessary for spermatogenesis

Environmental cues can also be used to determine sex, e.g., reptilians (temperature); sea worms — an embryo develops as male if near another embryo that's developing as female.

Genetic determinism = the genotype drives all subsequent behaviors = wants to ascribe all behaviors to one part of a process

Vast fruit fly chromosomes looking like the Alphabet necklace in "Just So Stories"

1966 refined specific enzyme assays in plants = wild type alleles were hugely variant! = we are extraordinarily variable, not only between genes but inside genes, in the coding systems of proteins

1944 Oswald Avery, Colin Macleod, Maclyn McCarty, identified DNA as the "transforming principle"; but cautiously hedged their conclusions. It was in the middle of the war but Avery isn't a legend, nobody's heard of him, because he wasn't the alpha male type. Discuss.

You have to be ruthless and driven to get to top, in science as elsewhere, but a woman with full domestic support immediately becomes a man — a man who makes time for his personal life, his family, in the chinks allowed by lab science.

A Feeling for the Organism[10]

In our first interview, Dr Davies advised me to read Evelyn Fox Keller's biography of Barbara McClintock, *A Feeling for the Organism*. All I knew about Barbara McClintock at that time was that she'd discovered "transposons" in maize—the jumping genes I'd read about and pounced on as a possible mechanism for my "Transferred Y" idea—; and won a Nobel Prize. It took me a while to get hold of the book. When I finally read it, chills went down my spine. The parallels between the story of this dead woman scientist of genius and my Anna were startling.

Barbara McClintock was born in 1902 and got her PhD from Cornell when she was twenty-five. There were no careers for women in scientific research in those days. She spent her life on the margins, amassing awards and honors, collecting fellowships that financed her research: never appointed to a post to match her reputation or her achievements. Her gender was "always there, always intruding" (Fox Keller 76). Male colleagues acknowledged that she was brilliant; they were in awe of her "surpassingly beautiful investigations" (Fox Keller *xviii*), but considered her "difficult," if not slightly deranged, when she protested at being passed over for jobs.

She became increasingly isolated after the advent of Molecular Biology, and her discovery of "transposition," announced in 1950, was dismissed as invention. Her results did not fit into the model of the gene as a fixed, unchanging unit of heredity. It would be more than twenty-five years before "transposons" were recognized in bacteria and the connection with her work was made. She was awarded the Nobel Prize in 1983. The implications of her work are still expanding, still causing controversy: perhaps, who knows, she'll be remembered in the end as the woman who discovered a better model of life itself.

Most biographical summaries, articles you'll read on the web, gloss over the "delay" in recognizing her discovery. Actually, you see, McClintock *was* difficult, and more than a little strange. She saw things nobody else could see; she had ideas nobody else could conceive. It was no wonder people found her hard to understand—it was her own fault, really. So was Richard Feynman a little strange, by all accounts. So was Albert Einstein hard to understand. Don't get me started on Isaac Newton. Being difficult and hard to understand didn't do *their* careers any harm. They had permission to be extraordinary. And here lies an issue for women in science that I had not suspected and that had no part of my original plan.

"Keep a cobbler's job," Einstein once said. But isolation from the mainstream has a high price, especially in lab science. By the time Barbara McClintock announced her "transposition" discovery, her vision was so differently trained, she was so preternaturally expert in the field of one that she had created, that other scientists literally *could not* see what she was seeing through the microscope. Even modern Molecular Biology is a "black art" (the organism fights back!). Samples behave differently in different culture mixes, visual acuity and deft hands make the difference between success and failure. Talented experimenters can produce perfectly genuine results that nobody can replicate… I'd walked into Dr Davies's office with an idea for a story about a woman scientist. I hadn't intended for Anna to be a "genius." But maybe it's the discovery that makes the genius, and not the other way round: a compelling insight that gets hold of a trained mind, and will not let go, and forces that mind to grow, to become the equal of the thing it glimpsed… Because of Barbara McClintock and Lynn Margulis, too (and others, the roll call stretches back), the issue of fame had to become a part of my novel.

But at least Anna was no longer alone. She was part of the ongoing drama in her field: life science riven by passionate loyalties, cold-blooded feuds, vicious disputes. She was a samurai serving her lord, then she became the handmaid of a visionary recluse; eventually she was the team-leader of a furious, sleepless race to be first past the post, with the proof that everyone in the game was madly chasing—

Coda

At the end of January, 1997, I had my last session in the BIOLS building. I sat in on a team meeting, in Dr Davies's office, keeping quiet, taking notes.

Business

JD: hopes the building work won't be too disruptive. The radiation area will go, needs a new home at the back of the lab, must have a separate room, nice surfaces—

Martin: says he needs to upgrade Word on the PowerMac. Can't defrag the hard drive any more. Is anybody in charge of the computers?

Work

Trying to make antibodies to Shaking B. There's a commercial firm in Belgium that will make them for us. Martin and Lucy have been designing peptides for the anti-serum. When David Beckham (not the footballer) came here he was talking about a wonderful new way to couple antibodies. Keyhole Limpet hemocyanin.

Unfortunately he still hasn't sent us the references—

Tanya is still doing hybridization, been doing Southern Blots, got v. high background and can't wash it off—

Do you have enough leech DNA to make another blot?

If you're doing some, give the carcass to Tanya

It's impossible to grind up that elastic skin—

This is how it sounds, looks, this is how things are done that have never been done before. The Shak-B gene, neurogenesis, gap junctions, CNS, wonder if I'll ever find out what happened... Wonder if *any* of these notes will turn up in my book, in any form? I was thinking about an expert system who was almost, arguably a person (call the Turing police!), and a storming guardian angel who would keep pestering Anna to get radical. I was preparing to take away with me, folded down small, the slightly rank smell of the big warm lab, the calm atmosphere in here, and a feeling for the vast complexity, the intricacy and individuality of the very small. Creatures of another world, speaking to us in their own language. How far away, how far—

I was supposed to go back for an internship, maybe in April '97, but I didn't. Perhaps I was too busy. I was on the Committee for Amnesty International UK's Women's Action Network, I was helping to set up a "feminist" website (short-lived!) for my local internet provider. There was always something. I have a last note: not referenced or attached, "you're going to have great difficulty getting this published." True enough. In 2003, when the latest rewrite was wandering the Western Seaboard of the USA, passed from hand to hand, my friend Timmi Duchamp contacted me and asked if she could publish it, for her new venture, The Aqueduct Press. *Life* won the Philip K Dick award for 2004. In 2006, I was invited to speak on a panel on Women in Science, at a literary convention, where I had to field some entertaining questions. I don't *know* much about the secondary school science curriculum. I did my best.

I watch my son's friends. How unaffectedly physical the boys are with each other, how easily they relate to the girls; now the segregated years are over. But still the young girls dress up in spike heels, fragile blouses, and tight little skirts. Maybe it's meant for dominance display (Spice Girl style), but I think of the Chinese proverb, *binding one's feet to prevent one's own progress.* More than likely there'll be another Women's Movement along soon. Right now there's a war on, that's the main story, and permanent warfare isn't good for women's rights. Or men's rights, really.

The story I told in *Life* is true. I wonder when it will be out of date.

Eppur si muove.

With grateful thanks to Dr Jane Davies, Dr Janet Collett, and the Shak B team, 1996/7.

Notes

1. The sf feminism of the seventies and eighties could trace its lineage in the USA through crusading women writers and editors of previous decades, to the Utopian New Woman fictions of the early twentieth century (Charlotte Perkins Gilman, *Herland*). But knowledge of this genealogy came after the fact for most of us.

2. Jeanne Gomoll, in her "open letter to Joanna Russ" describes the situation, and the swift reversion to the status quo that followed. It can be found online (http://www.geocities.com/athens/8720/letter.htm).

3. "Only one science fiction book in hundreds manages to convince the reader that it ever could have happened anywhere, and at least that few are worth reading at all. In *Walk to the End of the World*, Charnas has created a future that is at once believable and fascinating."
    —William S. Burroughs

4. "Que les accidents de féerie scientifique et les mouvements de fraternité sociale soient chéris comme restitution progressive de la franchise premiere…" Arthur Rimbaud, *Illuminations*

5. "When It Changed," Joanna Russ, 1972. First published in *Again, Dangerous Visions,* edited by Harlan Ellison; subsequently much anthologized; text online at: http://www.scifi.com/scifiction/classics/classics_archive/russ/russ1.html.

6. I've written about this experience, find it here: http://homepage.ntlworld.com/gwynethann/OSLO.htm.

7. *The Differences Between the Sexes*, eds. R.V. Short and E. Balaban, Cambridge University Press, 1994;reviewed here: http://tracearchive.ntu.ac.uk/frame/freebase/free2/gjones.html.

8. This is not my story; it's a story told as a science paper, with great verisimilitude, by a writer called Raphael Carter: "Congenital Agenesis of Gender Ideation," *Starlight 2*, edited by Patrick Nielsen Hayden, Tor Books, 1998.

9. "Dark They Were, and Golden-Eyed," Ray Bradbury, *Thrilling Wonder Stories*, August 1949. Bradbury's poetic vision of cultural change, mysterious and absolute, resonants beyond his times.

10. Evelyn Fox Keller. *A Feeling for the Organism*. New York: Henry Holt & Company, 1983, 1.

W.I.S.E.R... Shouldn't We Be?

A Blog post from: The Women in Education, Science and Research Conference, Maastricht, 4-5 October 2007.

Stand we at last...

I got turned away from the opening foray, on the grounds that I don't speak Dutch and the Jankerk was stuffed: which was a bust. It was the one with a slide show, academic tradition on females in science held up to sarcasm, and the choir singing Ethel Smith's "March of the Women," audience participation encouraged. That's a rave from the grave, thinks I. I went to look around the Basilica of the Redeemer instead (much restored; I liked the Paradise). Got into the next item, which was pretty entertaining. Such a crowd! Several hundreds of academics, all ages, usual sex ratio reversed, a lunch counter with coffee. The Minister made his opening address. In which he derided Larry Summers's immortal line, "a different availability of aptitude at the high end," and then went off to have lunch with the celebs, while the rest of us—and a platform of female profs and politicos, including the Spanish ministry delegate, the Norwegian Minister (who lives in a different world), and Miet Smet, Belgian Minister of State and long-time women's rights defender, who knew a lot about how to get things done, and how it's never easy or simple—debated four propositions on how best to make Netherlands academia (and/or the world) treat women and men as equals.

Legislation: making obligatory 40% women or men on any decision-making body; 60% maximum, either sex.

Visibility: What we need is a massive media campaign, changing public perceptions, especially children's and the short-span masses, of women in science, education, and research (especially science).

Psych-it: The numbers speak a clear language (the present sex ratio of top end academic jobs in The Netherlands is very poor indeed). The women are missing. Raise women's expectations, student expectations, daughters' expectations. Change from within!

Gender Mainstreaming: Stop trying to fix women so they'll fit into academia, or whatever other setting. Change the culture of academia, identify and change the gender thinking and discriminatory practices embedded in the organization. Have an Equal Opportunities police with the right to walk in anywhere, and nail sinners.

Blair's Babes, I'm thinking. Blair's Babes (referring to the massive increase in female MPs, in Tony Blair's 1997 government, achieved by Labour Party initiatives not unlike the proposals above). Did they really love Tony? Nah. They loved being in power though, and Tony soon made it clear that they served the One Man, or they were career-dead. Doesn't matter what you do. The thing about women is that they really *are* no different from other human beings, as corruptible and malleable as any brother... But I love this sort of thing, and waved my colored cards (like in *Ready Steady Cook*, you know) like a good 'un. At first I went for yellow (Image), but then I wavered and thought I should go for red (Quotas), but then some bright spark says, I think they're all essential, and I don't want to choose, and everyone thought this sounded fine, and practically all of us held up all four colors.

The Minister's Minions (young and female, did you guess?) who'd been left to our mercy were teased, but gently, with some suggestions from the floor. What would the Minister's response be? They couldn't possibly comment.

Later, I got worried about that *let's include everything* decision (so typical!). The object of the exercise was supposed to be to identify one of those four propositions to present to the Minister, as is traditional in these affairs. Four ideas is at least three too many. Ah, well.

Miet Smet made a point of saying one other thing: Women should distance themselves from "Diversity." Don't get bundled up with Lesbian, Gay, Transgendered, etc. May seem righteous, but it does not further political equality. Women are not a minority group. Moves addressing women's needs in academia, in the workplace, or in politics are not special measures, special treatment. Discuss.

So then we were asked to leave quietly, and we would get a surprise as we went out the doors. The surprise was that we were issued with orange whistles (with a transfer of a soccer ball on them, one more indication that the frugal organizers had not wasted any funds on decorative trim for this con) by a corps of stewards in lab coats, bootees, and hairnets, armed with klaxons, and we were to march. Shouting a Dutch slogan that I didn't quite catch, but I gather it said something like More Women On Top Now! People smiled. Especially the young teens, who had been issued with the extra whistles. Everybody gives you a whistle these days. It's from all those whacking big clubs, people getting lost. Is it the same everywhere? I wonder.

Couldn't get into the critique on male leadership in academia in the Derlon Theatre, so I milled around a bit on the 1992 Plein, the actual birthplace of the EU in its current form. Not so strangely, there is a lack of municipal sculpture on this momentous site. Nor are there any tourist kiosks selling fridge magnets featuring the Flag of the Union or anything of that kind. There is only the river Maas, also known as the Meuse, and the Moselle, with the barges gliding along it, beautiful and calm under the brilliant blue sky. The same river that runs through Rimbaud's home town and causes the Netherlanders no end of vigilance and expense at the delta.

Birth of the Superstate sightseeing soon completed, I went along to Science à la Carte at the Bonnefantenmuseum and caught Averil Mac-Donald, Professor of Physics at Reading University, UK, giving a presentation called "Living The Fairytale." "I celebrated my fortieth birthday as plain Mrs MacDonald, soon to be divorced mother of two. I will soon celebrate my fiftieth with a whole new life opening up before me..." An irresistible success story, with an award to prove it, Woman of Outstanding Achievement in Science. Awards are great, she says; they open doors; they make the Vice Chancellor listen. Any questions? "Did you meet any enemies?" I asked. I am such a clown, so juvenile.

When I'd failed to get into the Leadership epilogue and was sitting on the Plein 1992 eating my second lunch roll, Averil came and sat down next to me and sparked up a conversation… She says she didn't recognize enemies, only obstacles, and found a way around them. That's the spirit!

Good Utopian/Bad Utopian

Finally got into the Derlon Theatre, for the "NL2020" item, another debate, a show organized by the Dutch Network of Female Professors, using the results of a consultation exercise. First, we got two views on the situation in 2020: the reforms have been instituted, what changes do we see? Good Utopian/Bad Utopian.

Good Utopian (Saskia Keuzenkamp: Women's Emancipation Studies) is having a wonderful time. Her meetings are virtual, her hours are flexible, she gets to nurse her PhD students without leaving her desk, like everyone else on faculty she has her own PA, so she doesn't spend her whole time on paperwork; she's just been assessed (transparently) and given a great new job on a global master class program. Oh, and the Dean is always around (this got a laugh), popping in for a chat, etc.

Bad Utopian (Jenny Dankelman, Medical Engineering) says, grumpily, well, at least I don't feel so out of place, and since I'm NOT the only woman, I can get some work done. I'm not continually being dragged off into meetings because they're obliged to have a token female...

We were asked to vote, electronically, on fifteen statements from the consultation exercise, and the Good Utopians got some surprises:

It's 2020. The percentage of women in higher positions in universities has grown tremendously. What conclusions can be drawn? Here's a short sample of the more controversial issues:

Culture, Statement 2: The academic culture has become nastily competitive.

We were supposed to disagree strongly; we agreed weakly. Our feedback was displayed, and we were quizzed on it. The younger members of the audience said: women can be nasty, as nasty as men. It's competition that makes people nasty, and the international competition is bad enough now. In 2020, everything will be more globalized, *more* frantic; and that doesn't make you a nice person—

Working Practices, Statement 1: Working part time is the norm for both men and women.

We were supposed to feel strongly that this was a positive development. We were quizzed on our rather strong feeling that it was not. "This is about child care," said one respondent, tartly. "I don't see thirteen years making that much difference to male attitudes to parenting." (And I recalled the Minister, speaking wistfully of his gut feeling that mother ought to be there, when the children come home from school...) Other respondents said, yeah, we know that one: part-time pay, full-time work. Neither futuristic nor an improvement. And yet others said, you can't do lab science on twenty hours a week. The people who resist this change will still be the ones doing the great work and getting the good jobs. We *want* to be driven, we *want* to forget all else, we are creative scientists.

It's always about child care, apparently. (And it takes two, thinks I. If men won't change, it's because their wives and partners have let them know, one way and another, that they don't have to.)

The old guard are out in force, but many of the younger women at this conference are not at all sentimental about Women. They aren't here to sing "Stand We At Last;" they've been born and raised in a world where women in science have been colleagues and bosses, not a noble few inspiring heroines. They're here because their lives, their careers, their dreams, depend on reforms of a mightily unfair system. They don't expect Utopia. Just a better chance.

And then it was my item, "A Writer's View on Academia," with Joke Hermsen, a PhD in Philosophy who quit her philosophy department in some disgust a few years ago and is now principally a novelist; Gwyneth Jones (University of Life); and moderated by Maaike Meijer, "one of the voices of Dutch feminism in the Seventies" (it says here, a modest tag that no doubt covers a wild career). I can't really tell you what happened as I was not taking notes, but Joke Hermsen, Virginia Woolf scholar among other things, read an essay on *Granite and Rainbow*, about biography; and I read a bit of *Life*. Good house, and seemed like a positive response.

Anna Senoz's career, and naïve mistakes, really seem to strike a chord with the young, gifted, and female science and research contingent.

Ah, say the delegates, with one voice. Science fiction! *Woman on the Edge of Time*! Wonderful book, Marge Piercy, have you met her? Ursula Le Guin, have you met her? For some reason, nobody seems to have heard of *The Handmaid's Tale*. Couldn't possibly comment.

Municipal drinks and nibbles in a municipal hall, where an Alderman spoke rather movingly (in English, of course) about his long ago experiences on a literacy aid program in Nicaragua. If funds are short and you want to make a lasting impact, what do you do? You *concentrate on the girls*, he told us, with the force of long-ago revelation. Educate the girls, you're educating their children and their children's children. Ah, Mr Man, what are you saying? Are you saying that your own people, your own kind, are shiftless selfish layabouts, and spending money on *them*, in the hope of giving the people a better life, is pouring water into the sand?

Here I met up with Bernie Williams, Liz Faye, Averil again, and the rest of the SET UKRC crowd, some of whom I'd met in Hay on Wye last year, and we went off and had a meal together in the Holy Virgin Plein, and then, I'm afraid, we persuaded each other it would be a good idea to come back and go to the WISER disco. Ah, well. You're only young once.

Friday, 5 October

I spent the morning sightseeing; bought some tulip bulbs (orange); paid my respects to the *Star of the Sea* along with a constant stream of Maastrichters popping in to light an e.60 candle. The Basilica of the Holy Virgin is tenth century, on the site allegedly of the first Christian church here, founded by Bishop/St Servaas, 384. He killed a dragon, I think. The statue, a pliant curve in her red and blue robes, her gilt crown, is sixteenth century. Couldn't leave her out, could I? Not here, where the blue flag with the gold stars was anointed. I do not worship the Goddess, but I thoroughly respect her capacity for survival. After all, somebody has to hold up half the sky.

In the afternoon I went to JIVE, the UKRC event, which was mostly PowerPoints about data collection, employment research practice, and the problems faced by returnees. The star of this show was undoubtedly Maggie Aderin, a remarkable young woman. She's "the UK's only black woman rocket scientist, she's conquered dyslexia, and she has chosen to get into science education." Could she tick more boxes? Actually, she's an astronomer not a rocket scientist, that's just press-release talk. What she does is build custom instruments, novel instruments for big, big, telescopes. She showed us a video she's made for UK Teachers' TV, in the Cape, where she was visiting SALT (South African Largest Telescope)—an astonishing installation, with a 10 meter mirror, brand new (2005), standing alone in the empty Karoo. She joined a Scifest over there and talked to ordinary kids. Fantastical, dazzling, romantic, end note.

But in JIVE, probably because we were all speaking the same language (second language conversations tend to be effusive, polite, and sunny), I heard the hard things said. Small hard thing: returnees feel they've not got a leg to stand on when partner is earning more. His career has to come first; her (relaunched) career has to come second; it's a quality of life issue. So, women in science, yes. High-flyers, no. Or not until the children are reared and gone. Other hard thing: women are interesting now, because of the ageing and declining population problem (not in England, but in other UK nations and throughout NW Europe). The loss of female graduates is a drain industry can't afford. But what about when the economic crash bites? It doesn't have to be the end of the world, just a normal recession. All Utopian agendas will be dropped, instantly.

And the hardest thing, the one we still hope will just go away. Isn't it a beautiful day, teeshirt weather in October, where are we right now? Balmy California, I suppose. So, where will we be in 2020? Could be somewhere rather less idyllic. And the 10 meter telescope in the Karoo will still be there, but where will those kids be? Who'll be living in Sunderland and Grahamstown?

In the Bonnefanten Museum there was a show by Mai Thu Perret, Swiss artist, a multimedia presentation called "Land of Crystal." Here's a quote from the artist's program notes: "Mai-Thu Perret has been writing a fictitious story entitled 'The Crystal Frontier' since 1999. Employing part-imagined and part-annotated diary fragments, letters, and texts from handbills, she sketches a kaleidoscopic image of a group of women who have retreated, disillusioned, from the city and from Western, i.e., capitalist, society. They pick up their lives again in the desert of New Mexico but on a different footing with work, nature, and themselves."

Ha! This is where I came in! *Girls like a pack of wolves, sorry we disappointed you, nobody gets mothered here.* I didn't linger. I've read *Les Guérillères*: not when it was written but a long enough time ago, in the second wave. So there's an end to another fly on the wall, or chameleon on the wall, visit to an academic/science/feminism conference. Events like this are really useful to me. Utopians: talking, arguing, trying out ideas, getting things wrong, getting things right, speaking the language a writer of Utopian fiction must know. Oh, you thought I was a fem-sf writer (or ex-fem-sf). You didn't know I wrote Utopian fiction? Is that a job that only a male writer can do? Hm.

Back home on the Eurostar, massive queues at Brussels Midi, for the Thank God It's Friday train to Waterloo. I wouldn't mind, but the placards on the UK passport control raised my hackles a bit. "You'll find it rather more difficult to get into the UK, from September 2007." As if that was something to be proud of. Not a word of apology.

Art, Forward Slash, Science

First published in *PMLA*, the Journal of the Modern Language Association of America, Vol. 119, No. 3, May 2004, pp. 526–529.

Synasthesia… One day in 1997 (soon after the National Gallery acquired the picture), I walked up the familiar marble stairs, crossed the rotunda, and was confronted, for the first time, by George Stubbs' *Whistle-jacket*,[1] the stunning, naked portrait—no groom or rider, no landscape—of a chestnut Arabian stallion. I smelt the stable, horse manure and leather, and I had the thrill of knowing what was happening inside my skull. How the *attention* response had sent a cloud of fire leaping through my brain, tugging on associated traces, map on map of firing and partial-firing neurons springing back into existence (never the same twice, yet continuous with my earliest childhood and the millions of years before that). Surprise and the power of the artist were making me read internal stimulus as external: recall had become once again perception. This is an iconic memory for me. It holds, packed down and ready to unfold, both the direction my work has taken through my career and the context of that work: my own life and times, the history that made me, the Next Big Thing in science, and my privileged, difficult position as a science fiction writer, an arts graduate, and a woman.

In 1984 there was a revolution in science fiction. It involved a book called *Neuromancer*, by William Gibson, and a manifesto[2] compiled by Bruce Sterling: declaring (among other matters) that the rocketship fantasies of the fifties were finally dead, the galactic empires played out. From here on the only true science fiction was to be about *the future of now*; its hallmarks would be close extrapolation from the present, contemporary referents, political and emotional realism. Labels and brand names would be vital, style would be understood as content; *appropriation*, scratching, riffing, sampling, would be the palette. It was to be an Impressionist literature, where there'd be no attempt (or as little attempt as possible) to smooth out and hide the real world behind the futuristic mask.

This was a dramatic change. Classic science fiction writers always lied. They set post-WWII visions of world-dominating empire and benign totalitarian control in galaxies far, far away. Writing about the *realpolitik* of their times, radicals like Ursula K. Le Guin set their Vietnam War or Equal Rights scenarios on imaginary alien planets. In the US cyberpunk caused a furor. It especially upset people to see *progress* dethroned as a power for good: to have the future shown as uniform with the present, where globalization and advanced technology were not noticeably reducing the dark side of the human condition. For me, here on the island George Orwell had named, bitterly but accurately, *Airstrip One,* the cyberpunk message was a different liberation. I leapt to the task of creating the science/fiction of a European woman and an arts graduate, writing about the future of *my* now: my science-bothered, art-impregnated society, my world, the place where I live. I spent the next ten or fifteen years (along with my UK sf contemporaries, call us the cadre of 1984) trafficking across the divide between art and science as I searched for the truth about gender/racial superiority, trying to uncover the deep structures of inequality in a science fiction series that became known as the Aleutian Trilogy. I was influenced by the radical science of Lynn Margulis,[3] by Claude Shannon and Warren Weaver[4] on information theory, and by the dawning of evolutionary genetics—but equally fascinated by Jacques Derrida (especially a collection called *Writing and Difference*) and Roland Barthes (especially the iconic S/Z). Science fiction writers develop their own strange mental musculature. Those people who think Derrida is a difficult writer should try attempting to get a grip on General Relativity with nothing but a BA degree in History of Ideas and a dim memory of convent school physics classes. I watched, thrilled as if I were observing a rare planetary transit, the tide of relativism that had risen from linguistics and from physics, from Einstein and Sassure, as it swept through the disciplines, the poststructuralists unaware that they sounded just like the paleontologists, the historians measuring the irreducible plurality of truth as if straining the past through a lattice of quantum indeterminacy. Potent ideas (like the frame of Alberti; like fitness selection), like good books, escape from genre. As the Aleutian

Trilogy proceeded, mapping measures of humanity and alien-ness in a future Europe, I found myself increasingly drawn to *narrative images*: the common ancestor, the ur-craft, where ideas about the nature of the world, technical skills, and poetics are fused. The movies were important, but the older visual narratives, framed pictures, postcards from the past, seemed closer to me, at least *seeming* to be the lonely creations of a single artist, without the mediation of a crew and cast. I looked into frames in the National Gallery to find meanings for what I was doing myself: Géricault's *Raft of the Medusa* (a cyberpunk revolution there); Renoir's *Les Parapluies*; Caravaggio's *Supper at Emmaus*; Monet's water lilies. Monet's project of representing simultaneity, *the same light everywhere,* gave me the epigram of the last book. And it all went straight into my writing (true to the code of '84). Here's a sample of the art/science impulse at work. One of the empire-building humanoid aliens (they call themselves "Aleutians" from the accident of their landing spot) is browsing the Tate "Pre-Saatchi" gallery, trying to explain to her native guide the superiority of Aleutian art-forms: which are alive, which have a living, chemical communion with whoever approaches—

> "An Aleutian poem is…it's alive. When an Aleutian takes a wanderer cell from his skin and feeds it to a friend, he's saying *this is me, now. This is my state of being.* When I compose a poem I'm trying to do that with the world. When another Aleutian comes along, maybe generations later, and 'looks at my picture' the biochemical meaning of that moment of composition is shed from the picture and enters the viewer, becomes part of him. The picture is a communication-loop. What's captured and released again is not the same, but evolved by everything that's happened since, the whole information system that's involved in the new gaze… It's not at all the same."

> She stared at *Les Parapluies,* the flower faces standing out like love-stories in the sober text of Renoir's narrative. Virtual particles of the dead artist's intention filled her air, entered her being.

> "I'm wrong. It is the same."[5]

Synchronicity... At the end of the eighties Chaos mathematics was the Big Thing in science. It was time to talk of butterfly wings and hurricanes, fractals and strange attractors. The number-crunching machines had reached critical mass: scientists would now be able to interpret the patterns in disorder. They would tackle raw, non-linear natural phenomena, instead of being restricted to a limited (though useful) set of special cases. As the Berlin Wall tumbled and the Soviet Bloc disintegrated—miraculously, blessedly—without overt bloodshed, it seemed as if the barrier between art and science was going as well. Science had lost its limits and its certainties; artists were achieving equality with the men in the white coats; it was even possible for the women to stand alongside the men. We were all in the same boat, fishing for connections out of an ocean of boundless complexity, stringing them together by accidents of history, never knowing if we had the *right* answer, only knowing that something seemed to work... Darkness at dawn soon descended on the New Russia; the constructed state of Yugoslavia, released from Soviet bondage, fell apart in hideous, genocidal warfare. But the change from monolithic stasis to the Pandora's Box of possibility remained a potent image, and this was the historical mood in which I began my Aleutian Trilogy.

Today, the hopeful time is forgotten. The end of the Cold War did not free us to tackle the awesome threat presented by humanity's success (forget the oil, we're running out of *water*!). The utopian achievements of the idealists who made me what I am (Eleanor Roosevelt, Clement Atlee) are falling into dust, and coincidentally, science fiction has reverted to the galactic empires and rocket-ship fantasies. I've moved on to another project, a near-future story that reflects these times,[6] but I'm still studying the narrative representation of the world, trying to understand my own art form by *looking back*, out of the imaginary frame of the future.

In William Gibson's *Neuromancer*, self-conscious artificial intelligence is conceived as the emergent property of a network of networks, an idea that was way ahead, in 1984, of much real-world Artificial Intelligence research. In those days neuroscience was still a black box, and probing the processes inside the grey matter was a branch of psychology. At the start of the twenty-first century there's still nobody who knows what consciousness "is" (which might be the wrong question), but we know the brain as a network of networks; we can watch the neuronal connections ignite, layer upon layer, skein upon skein. When I reached the finale of the Aleutian Trilogy, I had drawn the conclusion that information theory, which binds the visible and the invisible, the material and the immaterial worlds, would someday unlock the prison of gravity and isolation. It would be through inner space, through our ability *to image* the whole world in our minds, that we would cross the vast spaces between the stars. Now I'm back to the near future and inventing the route to that discovery. I'm still looking at pictures and movies. I'm also fascinated by computer games, as they grow toward complexity, and by those unborn confections known as "virtual movies." Today I can know (in some limited sense, as a lay person) what happens when I pay attention. How long before someone will be able to solve the emotions that a hybrid movie-game is meant to arouse into neuronal code, and deliver it to Electronic Arts as an email attachment? And what strange vistas open up beyond—

I'm walking around the National Gallery (as I love to do), thinking about Proust's involuntary memory, thinking about neurology, about the digital revolution that has engulfed us all; and about Stubbs's *Whistlejacket*. I'm thinking that art and science do not run on parallel tracks. They come together wherever and whenever one finds the cutting edge, the growing point of human thought.

Notes

1. George Stubbs 1724-1806, artist and pioneering anatomist, published his *Anatomy of the Horse* in 1766, four years after he painted the portrait of the racehorse Whistlejacket. His anatomical drawing ranks with Leonardo's, and the dissection techniques he invented are respected today. He was aided in his often difficult and laborious dissections by a mysterious female assistant, whose name went unrecorded (information from John Lienhard, University of Houston).

2. The preface Bruce Sterling wrote for the highly influential *Mirrorshades, the Cyberpunk Anthology*, 1986, has been regarded as the Manifesto for the cyberpunk movement. The Movement was short-lived, held to have had its day by 1988, but the anthology is still known as the best selling sf anthology of all time, while "cyberpunk" and "cyberspace" have passed into the modern lexicon.

3. Lynn Margulis, Distinguished Professor at the University of Massachusetts, Amherst, proponent, with James Lovelock, of the Gaia theory. Her early *endosymbiotic hypothesis*, which proposed (through suggestions about ancient symbiosis captured in the human cell, later proven in the laboratory) that Darwin's theory of evolution by competition is incomplete, was a key concept for much of the alternative, bio-centered science fiction of the late twentieth century.

4. C.E Shannon, "A Mathematical Theory of Communication," *Bell System Technical Journal*, vol. 27, pp. 379-423, 623-656, July, October, 1948. Claude Shannon, research mathematician at Bell laboratories, conceived of information as a measurable physical quantity, like density or mass, expressed in on/off yes/no "bits," irrespective of the content of a "message": an immensely powerful insight, one of the foundations of our digital age. Available online at http://cm.bell-labs.com/cm/ms/what/shannonday/shannon1948.pdf

5. Quote from *Phoenix Café* Tor Books; New York, 1998, 134/135.

6. My Bold As Love "near future fantasy" books can best be approached through their website, which is here: http://www.boldaslove.co.uk.

Works Cited

Gibson, William. *Neuromancer*. New York: Ace, 1984.

Jones, Gwyneth. The Aleutian Trilogy, *White Queen*, New York: Tor Books, 1993.

———. The Aleutian Trilogy, *North Wind*. New York: Tor Books, 1996.

———. The Aleutian Trilogy, *Phoenix Café*. New York: Tor Books, 1998.

———. *Deconstructing the Starships*. Liverpool, UK: Liverpool University Press, 1999.

Livingstone, Margaret. *Vision and Art (The Biology of Seeing)*. New York: Harry N. Abrams, 2002.

Margulis, Lynn, and Sagan, Dorian. *Acquiring Genomes: A Theory of the Origins of Species*. New York: Perseus Publishing, 2003.

McCrone, John. *Going Inside (A Tour Round a Single Moment of Consciousness)*. New York: Fromm Intl, 2001.

Shannon, Claude & Weaver, Warren. *The Mathematical Theory of Communication*. Urbana, IL: University of Illinois Press, 1963.

The End of Oil [In Three Acts]

A playlet commissioned by BBC Radio, first broadcast in May 2004.

1. Paper Tiger

Sunita had the choice of watching tv or having the central heating on. It was a cold and dark November evening, but she chose the tv and pedaled away furiously on the Powergen bike. She wanted to know what was happening in north London. All she could find was the President of the United States facing another grueling interview. "Mr President, the writing's been on the wall for Oil for decades, in letters a mile high. You went on squeezing the barrel, and now we're in that worst case, rapid decline scenario. What's your answer to the *social* collapse, that some are calling inevitable?"

"The end of oil is a paper tiger!" shouted Sunita's husband. "Meant to scare us! There's plenty of alternative fuels—" He was at their designer dining table, juggling clothing coupons. Polyesters and polymers are petroleum based: far too expensive. So you think you'll buy cotton: but the cotton needs expensive irrigation, which also uses insanely expensive power, hence these bloody coupons…

"Well, I AM scared," muttered Sunita, through a menacing burst of ordnance fire. The President had changed the subject and started talking about the oil wars, which seemed to be surviving an almost complete lack of oil. So now there was a half-screen of warzone footage on the tv, and a leap in volume.

"Stupid, stupid, how stupid do they think we are?" panted Sunita.

She tried again to get hold of her son. She'd heard about the awful fuel riots at Brent this morning; too close to home. She had thanked God none of her family were likely to be there. But Jati had phoned two hours ago, to say he and Sally were right in the middle of it. They'd heard, like everyone else, that there was a chance of getting petrol rations. "A million people," he'd shouted down the phone, then something about "guns," and "It's really frightening Mum!" And since then, his phone had gone dead.

Suddenly she couldn't pedal anymore.

"It's like the end of the world," she whispered.

Ravi left his figure-juggling and they stared at the blank face of their energy gobbling, flatscreen tv. Sunita's husband went to the kitchen and came back with a cold chisel and a claw hammer. Too little, too late, she thought—as they smashed it.

2. The Phylloxera Virus

"But you see, it wasn't the end of the world, Mum," said Jati.

Ten years on from the Brent Riots, which had left five hundred dead, Jati and Sally were moving into a new flat on Riverside Walk, with the latest flood-proofing. Both sets of parents had come along to help out. "It's like the phylloxera virus," continued Jati. "In the eighteen-seventies the phylloxera virus destroyed all the vines in France, but they found resistant strains and the crisis was over! Wine is wine, energy is energy. We have H-power and biomass; we have solar power, methanol, ethanol… These flats are so energy-efficient we'll be selling power to the grid most of the year! What are we missing? Long haul air travel?" He shuddered. "I don't think so!"

"You don't even have your own car," muttered Sunita.

"Who needs a car?" demanded Sally, "That's just old fashioned. We have modern luxuries, *and* a sustainable energy economy."

"We're having it all," remarked Ravi, pouring a glass of beer from the jug. You don't get beer in cans anymore, it's uneconomic. "Including the disaster stories. The canola oil fields of rape are almost as polluting as the black gold used to be. The huge plantations for cellulose plastics are ruining the environment, and even if mass air travel's over, soy-based aviation fuel is no better than the old stuff for global warming."

"They say the brown coal they use for power in the USA and China is so dirty it's causing a kind of "Nuclear Winter effect," added Sally's dad, Ronald, cheerfully.

Sunita looked out of the window, at the river that lapped the concrete skirts of Chelsea Wharf, higher every year. It's going to start again, she thought. The riots and the deaths, the cold and darkness. Changing one source of energy for another is no solution. We need something more, something we can't see—

3. The Future Is Another Country

Sunita moved into sheltered accommodation after her husband died. Her great-grand-daughter Sophia took her out for the day, and they went for a drive in the country. It was September: they passed the fields where Sophia's physical body was at work, harvesting the apples. The virtual Sophia who had come to visit Grandma directed the little disposable car by wireless nerve impulses, while the young woman sat there like a living ghost, the Kirlian field around her sparkling gently, her virtual skin glowing green with the chlorophyll the real Sophia had had implanted. "This is all too strange for me," complained the old woman. "It's altogether too much. And why can't you come and see me on your *real* day off, young lady?" "This is really me," said Sophia, patiently. "I'm here, *and* I'm picking apples. Grandma, every leap forward in human civilization seemed fantastical, before it happened. You know. Horseless carriages? Ships with wings? This is the same. No one thinks anything of 'the end of oil' nowadays: it truly wasn't important. Much more exciting things were beginning, in embryo, in the early twenty-first century. The petroleum age was just a phase we were going through."

The Games
□ Δ + O

First Presented as a Guest of Honor Speech at "Confuse," the Swedish National Science Fiction Convention, Linköping, 2002.

> One highly influential attempt at a logical interpretation of "fun" has been made by psychologist Mihaly Csikszentmihalyi, with his concept of "flow." Csikszentmihalyi was interested in the fact that musicians, rock-climbers, chess-players and other people engaged in very complex tasks reported an experience of ecstasy or bliss, losing track of time and losing the sense of self. He decided that although on the face of it each activity was markedly different, all his subjects must be having the same sort of experience, which he termed "flow"…

(Trigger Happy, Poole, 180)

> …You see, whatever you "see," whatever you "hear," whatever you "touch," et cetera, what your brain experiences is a pattern of fire. See that? How it washes over the whole brain, like, mm, a cloud of sparks? When I write my immersions I copy those patterns, and make your brains believe they've had the experience. I do it visually, and I'll explain why that works best in a moment. I write the code, and I deliver it on a carrier wave of visible light. I don't even have to fake the patterns very *well*, because brains love being fooled…yeah, what?

(Castles Made of Sand, Jones, 58)

On the screen, a cartoon-style landscape stretches into the faux distance. Center screen-right, foreground, stands a child-like figure with a big head, painfully cute features, and a peculiar hairstyle; he's hefting an *enormous* sword. A small group of diverse cartoon characters stands with him. They face another group, these figures not humanoid but garishly colored monsters: giant insects or maybe insectoid machines. Everyone is moving slightly, marking time as in some slow folkdance. The cartoon child springs forward from his phalanx of toys. Fireworks flash from the blade; a monster quivers, changes color; and then everyone's back where they were. Another champion springs forward, and back. A monster riposte... And so on. It's really nothing like a fight. The scene resembles (as much as it resembles anything natural on earth) the display behavior of certain tropical birds. This is a dancing ground, a *lek* where candidates show each other their DNA poker-hands, and the loser folds, bowled over by color and movement.

I wonder, who—and where—is the analog of the female bird?

I wonder, what is so fascinating here? Why am I doing this?

Make-Believe

Once upon a time, a long long time ago, there were no videogames. Little children played at make-believe. The girls (predominantly) played *house, mummies and daddies, shop*. The boys (predominately) played at chasing and killing each other. The children were practicing for life. They were building up repertoires of behavior, just as they had done when, as tiny babies, the flailing motion of a hand connected occasionally with a toy, and by the reinforcement of success the pattern of firing neurons involved in accidental capture became fixed: became the act of grasping, a complex of muscle and eye and nerve and cognitive reaction that could be called up at will (*baby thinks: grab rattle*)... The five-year-old selects scraps of unnatural, adult dialogue from her cache (a limited, somewhat arbitrary multiple choice menu) having deduced that these overheard words have something to do with the transaction she's imitating. She places make-believe money on the counter and receives the goods. The other five-year-old runs around the playground, copying actions and speaking dialogue lines more likely to have been picked up from the tv screen than from his real life—though of course it depends on the neighborhood. He is mastering the invisible controls of a game more "skill-oriented" but perhaps simpler: fewer variables, limited possible moves, more prescription.

From such beginnings social training is instilled, and the rewards are clear: play these games and you will gain added competence in the environment in which chance has placed you. You will amass useful tokens in your society's status-currency, and (crucially) your power to amass yet more tokens will be increased. You will not even be punished if you prefer the games assigned to the other gender or if you prefer both. Little boys can dress up and play shop. Many playground-chasing games are without any gender bias. The years pass. By the time the children of long-ago reach puberty nearly all of them have spontaneously rejected make-believe. Board games and card games are for Christmas, for the stylized socializing at birthday parties, for a rainy holiday afternoon. Passions may rise on those occasions, but emotionally involving role-play isn't a big issue. Physical games, meanwhile, are (predominantly) replaced by organized sports, a source of status for the talented, a universal social currency only among boys. But there is a child with a secret. Something is happening in her mind, as thrilling as the polymorphously perverse, unrecognized sexual fantasies of childhood—though it's not about sex (not exactly); and yet it's an even more vulnerable delight. No one must know. Adults would disapprove, peers would destroy the magic, shun the company of the self-confessed weirdo. She has no name for the activity, though what happens is vivid—swordfights, fast cars, feats of prowess, adventurous journeys, high romance, passionate friendships, tragic sacrifices, lovingly scripted betrayals and avowals. Above all the power to manipulate a world directly, by psychic fiat; like someone making magic.

The ability to fantasize existed in the pre-videogame world like a technology in search of an application. The clumsy young girl wandering alone at the top of the lacrosse field or shivering in a corner of the netball pitch had no Playstation. She had to invent virtual environments inside her head, and they were not solid places. She could control the libretto, so to speak (the plot and dialogue), but the scenery was elusive, glittering fragments like remembered scenes from a dream. But it was important that the scenery was there, because her fantasy was played out in three dimensions (at least). The action was *physical*, she could feel it in her heartbeat, in the quickened breath, in the tears that rose to her eyes, in the stomach-gripping tension. It wasn't like a book, or a tv program, or a movie, or music (though she could transfer her skill and use it to bring those other art-forms to life: set them alight). It was wonderfully addictive. A secret power that other people might share: maybe everybody did it, but if they did you'd never know. Later, she might have compared it to a sexual fantasy—even if your lover tells you, you can't know for sure he or she really shares your invisible experience. You can't ever *know* with this kind of magic, it is beyond intellect or cognition: you can only *feel*.

In the last twenty years the social status of the games has changed dramatically. The astonishing, and bizarrely under-examined, videogame phenomenon is not isolated. Organized sports have become very big business in these same years: transformed by the dead, Midas touch of major investment from passion into product. Children, young adults, and older adults who can presumably remember the time when they'd have considered such behavior bizarre, throng the shopping malls dressed in the uniform of sports training wear: Adidas, Nike, Reebok. Primetime tv viewing, the choice of the masses, is dominated by masochistic quiz shows and very strange trials of daring (eat the live worms to win a holiday in Jamaica). The work ethic dies. Leisure is the chief economic activity of the affluent, philistine mass-market. Even the workaholics clearly see that the work they do has little intrinsic value: it's just status-establishing display. Late capitalism returns to the pre-industrial patterns that are finally vanishing in what we still know as the Developing World. Indonesian village dance-dramas, Central Asian traveling puppet shows that date back to the time of Alexander, are tourist consumables now—or gone forever. But here, where we live, the games matter again. Entertainment becomes interactive: every movie has a website, tv soap-opera would be nothing if the punters (that's "the audience," US readers) didn't behave as if they were part of the show. Elaborate sex-games once hidden away in shame or embarrassment are served by high-street retail outlets for bondage gear and curious items of lingerie. Fantasy, in every sense, is big business.

Videogames have been part of this huge cultural shift: a secret, new youth-culture art form/entertainment-technology ignored by the establishment—marked down for its crudity, its anti-intellectual appeal to young males, and for its low-social-class associations. Even a couple of years ago, it was okay to play games on your PC, but there was a stigma (what are you? Some kind of back-bedroom lurking brainless spotty male teenager?) attached to owning a dedicated games console. Though the new industry has been boosted into wider public awareness (it already had its own mass market) by the success of icons like "Lara Croft," and the sinking of much money into spin-off movies, there's still a major breakdown in communication. To videogame aficionados, the making of a *movie* about Lara is totally beside the point. A videogame is not fiction…so they say. Conventional fiction can provide raw material (the legendary first person shooter "Goldeneye" is a James Bond movie spin-off), but the making of a satisfactory game entails field-stripping the fiction and discarding most of the working parts. Gameplay is the thing: racking up hits on the targets, amassing status-tokens through puzzle solving, filling-in your trick card on the digitally assisted snowboarding simulator. Aesthetic pleasure, in videogame terms, means superior graphics, high quality sound, an unusually gory blood-spatter effect. Dramatic exposition and insightful characterization are unnecessary distractions. So here's an ironic outcome. Fantasy worlds have become applied technology, and they can be accessed at will by anyone; but emotionally gripping make-believe, of the kind that I discovered for myself long ago, remains a solitary vice. You can still grow up thinking you're the only one in the world.

Few would deny the social importance of emotionally gripping make-believe in its older forms. Theatrical drama, epic and lyric poetry, classical symphonies, opera, print fiction, rock music, film. All of these (and more) are the means whereby artists hold up a mirror to their community, and for thousands of years, probably from the birth of modern humanity about fifty thousand years ago, the community has responded eagerly—with indignation, with outrage, with tears, with delight. Myths about ourselves bind us together. Violence, tragedy, and comedy enacted on stage let the audience share the artist's wider vocabulary of self-expression, bringing release and pleasure. Yet artists and audiences have been curiously reticent about the mechanism behind the dramatic artist's creations: the secret vice of virtual experience. "An artist," says Freud, "is a man who turns away from reality because he cannot come to terms with the renunciation of instinctual satisfaction which it at first demands, and who allows his erotic and ambitious wishes full play in the life of phantasy" (*Formulations on the Two Principles of Mental Functioning*, 224). Fantasy (however you spell it) has a bad name.

Catharsis is a medicine that we need—a purge and a corrective. Social cohesion mediated by inspired myth-making, the shared rhythms of the dance, stirring anthems is a morally neutral force (a lynch mob can feel uplifted by passionate togetherness) that has been vitally important in human history. It's strange, then, that so little attention has been paid to the dramatic artist's *technical* ability to re-present the world. Investigation seems to founder in psychology. Published material about fantasy tends to the anecdotal: collections, predominantly female-authored, of sexual fantasies, such as Nancy Friday's notorious, ground-breaking *My Secret Garden* (1973) or pathological studies showing that Freud was right. Serial killers are people who act out their fantasies. Weak-minded neurotics take refuge in daydreams. Artists themselves, when they meet, will talk about anything but the intensely pleasurable kick they get from world-building. Perhaps this is self protective. Yes, I freely confess, sex is a vital part of my fun when I'm making up the story of a novel. So is self-aggrandizement, wish-fulfillment, and violent aggression (though I keep that last one on a leash, even in my imagination). But whether fantasy sublimates these instinctual appetites or fosters them into hidden, twisted growth, the appetite is not the mechanism. Right back to the Neolithic shaman who dressed up in the deer's horns and hide and pranced around in the firelight, something physiological must be going on in the brain itself, in the neurons and the electrochemical signals, when the artist conjures up and voluntarily experiences a world that only exists within his or her skull. Sex, aggression, and wish-fulfillment are regarded as very basic, primitive drives and treated with solemn respect on that account by twenty-first century post-Freudian culture. But virtual experience is far nearer to being the *primum mobile* of our humanity. Some scientists would call the ability to re-present the world to ourselves the very nature of consciousness. The neurological machinery that makes it possible to create a virtual world (in which to run your routines of seduction and destruction) must be common to us all. If it's possible, through genetic predisposition or life experience or both, to develop and enhance this innate power to re-present, shouldn't we be interested?

Everyone has to construct a working version of the world for themselves, in order to walk around and function. Some people (Who knows how many? Who knows how the spectrum of ability shades?) are able to construct *other* worlds at will. The vast majority of people (apparently) are able to respond to these constructions as if they are in some sense real. But how much is lost between the charged mental construct and the stage, the screen, the printed page? How much of the most refined art of prose composition or the most elaborate artifice in lighting and staging a set of actors for the movie screen is no more than sleight of hand to cover the deficiencies of the medium? Videogames are at present regarded (if they are considered at all) as inferior, stunted, literally *deformed* (Poole, 151-154) substitutes for real drama, and videogamers themselves are (generally) far from eager to deny the accusation. Yet I begin to wonder if it might not be the other way round. The respectable dramatic arts as we have them now might be the bent-out-of-shape apologies. The games might be the medium our magical powers of creation have been waiting for.

When I was five, and eight, and ten years old, I made myself arrays of characters out of colored plasticine and directed these little bands of adventurers on prolonged adventurous quest-journeys around the house. I acted out, with my sisters and my brother and three trusted friends of ours, lengthy virtual dramas loosely derived (like "Goldeneye" from the James Bond movie) from tv children's programs and text fiction. We played "William Tell"; we played "Narnia"; we played "Swallows and Amazons." There were battles in these games, chases, and feats of heroics. There were corner-shop transactions whereby currency tokens were distributed and amassed. There were passages of exposition, when the action stopped and we discussed (in character) what was supposed to be going on. No one had told us what to do. No one had told me that the quest story was a universal myth or that the "spirit journey" has been an initiation rite into full humanity for millennia on millennia. No one had told me that the protagonist/hero with his (or her) band of talented supporters is a motif many thousands of years old, an ancient metaphor for the divided, multivalent self. We were recapitulating phylogeny, enacting routines that seem to be hardwired into modern humanity. But fascinating though it is to look back and trace the immemorial contours that come into being always and everywhere that *story* emerges, I know that the secret *raison d'être* of our play was not in the story... Shared make-believe can become a hobby, no different from Freemasonry or Sunday football. You get together with your pals, dress up, and perform the rituals. It may look odd to the uninitiated; it feels ordinary, cozy, reassuring. But the real kick doesn't come in the game play. It comes when, as a character, you revert to the secret world and find it enhanced, pumped up, by the added element of embodied movement. "And I die," says the little warrior—redoubled, both creator and created, both conscious and self-conscious: composing herself on the ground, a weapon falling from her lax hand, the other hand pressed to her breast, unable to staunch the scarlet rush of blood, on her lips a tragic and dreamy smile...

The first of the quotes at the head of this paper is taken from a contemporary study of videogames, the second from a science fiction novel of my own (the speaker is teaching a kindergarten master class on a new kind of multimedia art form). Psychologist Mihaly Csikszentmihalyi considers the emotional *qualia* reported by people performing a wide range of demanding tasks successfully and concludes that there is some common element, a high (or profound: up and down have equal meaning here) order of neurological pleasure-state that all these people can reach, which is independent of the content of the task. A gameplayer hammering at the controls can reach the same delight as the consummate rock-climber or chess-player, because absolute cognitive difficulty and physical danger are not the triggers of reinforcement. (Reinforcement is a term experimental psychologists use when investigating the neurology of pleasure. You can't know that the rat with an electrode stuck in its brain is having fun: you can only *know* that the animal will return to the "reinforcing" stimulus in question voluntarily, foregoing sleep and food and sex [Blakemore, 166]) So, there's a reinforcing response that's triggered by the bare bones of controlled, repetitive, highly focused attention, and that's what the joy of videogames is about... In the second passage, my fictional futuristic-artist describes the underlying mechanism of all virtual experience. As long as the right neurons can be made to fire, the brain *is having* an experience of the world. There is no logical difference between artificial stimulation and real experience, because just as the solid objects we perceive "are really" made up of spinning atoms, the whole world of our perception "is really" made up of clusters and laminations of neurons firing together in different ratios. Blue is not blue, red is not red, fire is not fire; up is not up, down is not down, anger is not anger… Not even our passions are unmediated, it's all electrochemical signals.

Slightly gruesome experiments on conscious patients have demonstrated that varied, vivid sensual experiences can be invoked from memory by the simple expedient of a doctor sticking a probe into a specific spot in the grey matter. It isn't far from there to the concept (though of course not the technology) of an artificially induced, entirely convincing, full, sensurround fantasy environment. I wonder if different experiments could establish exactly what's going on in the course of world-building fantasy? There are hormones, enzymes—corticosteroids, noradrenalin— that flood the bloodstream at moments of high arousal. It's no surprise if the fantasist in the grip of a thrilling plot development—and equally the audience sitting in the front row, reading the novel, or jumping around in the mosh pit at an exciting rock gig—should have the same chemical symptoms as if they were really facing stressful emotional events. The physical symptoms (flushed skin, racing pulse, dry mouth) of excitement are easily triggered and notoriously infectious. But I wonder if there's something more intriguing going on.

We live in a twilight world. Our treasured self-consciousness doesn't play as large a part in our lives as we suppose. Experiment easily proves that we report the onset of volition (I see the button light up, I'm going to press it) about 220 milliseconds *after* our motor-nerves and muscles have started gearing themselves for precisely the action we (will) decide to perform. Consciousness is the forward edge; anything that can be subsumed, will be subsumed. What we do well we do "without thinking," and arguably Csikszentmihaly's "flow" relies on some kind of reward system that encourages the passage of ever-more complex skills into the unconscious, intuitive mode. (Which explains why people love driving their cars and will continue driving their cars, no matter what the counter-inducement, until the planet is paved over.) But paradoxically it is also very good to notice the new. A third of a second after some surprise or novelty, there's a broad-sweep feedback over the whole brain, called the P300 response, damping neuron activity, clearing the screen to make the novel aspect of the moment stand out for conscious attention. It has often been said—

romantically or pejoratively—that artists feel things too intensely, and that their art consists in their ability to mediate the precious bane of too much reality. What if this were true? What if that response to novelty, and other, *detailed* responses of focused attention to sights, sounds, interlocution, emotional stimuli could be detected—with massively greater frequency than normal—in the mind of the fantasist, responding to a world that doesn't exist? Like a well-fed pet cat chasing a crumpled ball of paper, the videogame commando has managed to hijack brain-chemistry rewards that evolved around survival-fitness. The little warrior "dying tragically" must be doing something of the same kind, using world-building to hijack the thrill of intense arousal—without the costs that pain and grief exact in real life. Could this mean (reverse engineering) that everyone has the potential to interact with a fantasy environment? To experience a virtual world exactly the same as if it were reality?

The players of the games seem to be confused about verisimilitude. Complexity is good, because it makes the game more challenging. Photorealism is not essential, not even desirable. Final Fantasy VIII was a disappointment to RPG fans because the characters look like adult human beings rather than big-headed cartoon children. Fantasy sports with quirky customized characters are preferred to realistic simulation manuals. Role play, though consistently given low value by the players, is always an issue. Cut-scenes (passages of full animation with no game play) are criticized as a distraction, yet high resolution, explorable faux "worlds" and idiosyncratic soundtracks are crucial attractions. There is a mysterious, intuitive engagement between the player and the world on the other side of the screen—and I have noticed (speaking as a lay person) that many of the features in a videogame are discernibly closer to our raw perception, as recounted in current popular science. The pixilated landscape in the screen is strangely akin to the world as we initially perceive it: no homogenized mimesis, just light reflected from surfaces, *noted* by the brain not for their beauty but for their relevance to behavioral goals. The hierarchy of presentation, those big heads, the disproportionate size of weapons, may also be deeply familiar. *Significance* is not a code invented by the intellect, it is the primary, raw value system—a truth that has been recognized by the performing arts since masks and costumes, big heads and exaggerated height were first used to impress an audience. Perhaps gamers reject realism and embrace the cartoon style partly because the "deficient" representation places the game not *outside*, as a spectacle, but *inside* the mind of the player/protagonist. Videogames are not yet designed to produce heightened, emotionally complex experiences. Yet something is moving, there in the faux-3D depth of the screen, and in the protagonist/observer relationship between the player and the game, which shines with a very enticing allure.

But these games have another curious feature. Where other forms of art and entertainment technology arrived first and were discussed afterwards, videogames—spreading and growing in the real world at the same pace as the IT revolution—have themselves been thoroughly represented, imagined, developed by the practitioners of another art form. Before we go over there and pick up the potion, let's take a step back and find out what meaning—what significance—has been given to the games in futuristic fiction.

The Games in Fiction

> My heart pounded, my mouth hauled air. Across my shoulders a line of terrific tension knit my muscles, engaging in force with those other muscles, thrusting pistons of bone wrapped in blood and glistening hide. The pack surrounded me in thunder and bodily heat, little cold gouts of animal spittle hit my cheeks. I felt the thighs—my thighs—clench in a compulsion more violent than any amorous climax; and an enormous surge under me. I bowed my cheek against grey flesh running with a hot gloss of sweat, making myself light as air, standing on my toes, floating, no longer tense… Everything slowed.
>
> Ah. Good one…
>
> (Escape Plans, Jones, 1986, 13)

In 1984 (which is when I was writing *Escape Plans*) videogames in the real world were fairly primitive. I was playing Pacman like a bulimic, gobbling dots in idiotic late night sessions, reduced to a barely sentient food-gathering loop (Somebody stop me! I have to pick all these berries!). In my science fiction I imagined the *vicset* (vicarious experience) games by analogy from the catharsis of stage and screen drama. In the future, I said (no doubt recalling that lonely sports-reject, wandering the lacrosse field) people will be able to share the physical prowess, the risk, and the sheer mental and muscular work-out of an athlete, same way as they can now experience tragic or thrilling emotions through the mediation of actors playing the parts. It's suggested even in *Escape Plans* that there can be uglier forms of vicset. Other writers, notably William Gibson in his legendary 1984 novel *Neuromancer,* were giving fairly graphic descriptions of vicarious-experience torture, rape, snuff movies (12). Maybe the important point (because let's face it, evil deeds are not and never have been dependent on any particular form of applied tech) is the statement that *we can be wired for anything*: the announcement that our consciousness is malleable. The cloud of fire can be ignited by technology, and it will not know the difference. Virtual reality experience—for the moment quite detached from the "world beyond the screen"—had arrived.

The relationship between videogames and science fiction has been close and pragmatic. Videogame sensibilities and modern sci-fi special effects grew up together. Sci-fi game scenarios are ubiquitous. Games developers discerned long ago that violent, gorily destructive shoot-'em-ups are less alarming to society's watchdogs if the victims are aliens, robots, or bio-engineered dinosaurs. The players' preference for the unreal is equally well served, while the deficiencies of the graphics of eighties and nineties games could be glossed over by a pulp-fiction cover-art style. Print fiction, equally, has used the games as a source of special effects: and also as metaphor—usually minatory. In *Escape Plans* the games mean unearned privilege. ALIC's ability to hijack the experience of another human being (an indentured laborer from the gladiatorial pool), although mild enough, is dehumanizing. In other sf, the message seems to be that in future we'll be able enact our most sickening desires without the cost of actually getting our hands bloodied; and of course we won't be able to resist the temptation.

In Orson Scott Card's immensely popular and acclaimed novel of 1985, *Ender's Game*, there's a war going on between the humans and some kind of bug-eyed monsters. The war is happening far, far away in outer space, but children sent to Battle School (the hero, Ender is eight years old at the time of this extract) are trained for those traditional interstellar dogfights through video-gaming. Here is Ender on his first day—a boy of destiny, a militaristic Harry Potter.

> Within an hour or so it began to pall. Ender understood the regularities by then. Understood the rules that the computer was following, so that he knew he could always, once he'd mastered the controls, outmaneuver the enemy. Spirals when the enemy was like this; loops when the enemy was like that. Lie in wait at one trap. Lay seven traps and then lure them like this. There was no challenge to it then, just a matter of playing until the computer got so fast that no human reflexes could overcome it. That wasn't fun. It was the other boys he wanted to play. The boys who had been so trained by the computer that even when they played against each other they each tried to emulate the computer. Think like a machine instead of like a boy.
>
> I could beat them this way. I could beat them that way.
>
> "I'd like a turn against you," he said to the boy who had just won. (49)

Of course Ender wins. Before long he has learned to "think like a machine" and has been brought to the point where he will have no compunction in committing, still through the medium of a game, Xenogenocide. (We kill every last one of them, or they kill every last one of us, son. That's the way it works.) So, no fresh insights into the human condition here… Perhaps the only thing in *Ender's Game* that would startle a reader today is the assumption that only children play virtual reality games; but the underlying philosophy is still disturbing and all too familiar. Waste the buggers, using highly intelligent technology that has no moral sense, in Afghanistan, in Iraq, wherever. With this kind of warfare you don't have to be brutalized in boot camp before you are able to kill. All you have to do is press the buttons at a distance: you will feel nothing. Waste the buggers. Waste them *endlessly*, all around the deserted Martian base, all around the bleak future urbanscapes of *Metal Gear Solid*. Do it inventively, do it moronically, do it with rumble: but that's the whole story. That's all there is.

The games technology in *Escape Plans* is wireless, and non-invasive. It's only poor people who have to get plugged in. In *Ender's Game* there's a zero-g playroom for physical simulations, but playing "mindgames" is not much different from sitting in front of a screen and using hand controls. But since Samuel Delany's seminal novel *Nova* (1968) and James Tiptree Jr's acid satire "The Girl Who Was Plugged In" (1973), sf writers have been fascinated by the idea of physically invasive connection to the machines: a connection both inescapably sexual and laden with doom. Henry Case, the hacker-mercenary of William Gibson's *Neuromancer*, only feels alive when he is jacked-in, surfing the data ocean, leaving the "meat" behind—sex and death fused in the allure of "Black Ice," the ultimate computer security, that can zip down that cable connection, through the neural jack, and fry your brain. In Maureen McHugh's *China Mountain Zhang* (1992), in a Chinese dominated twenty-first century, neural jacks are a mark of privilege. If you can plug yourself into the machinery of the State it means you are part of the system. Sexual games with the digital machines (or played through the medium of the digital machines) then become a subversion—illegal, addictive, life-affirming.

> ...Someone else jacks into our table as the golden ball is gliding past me and I feel everybody shift. It startles me and without thinking I reach out like a jai lai player and sling the ball my way.
>
> When it hits there is an explosion of feeling. For a moment I am the golden ball and the golden ball is me and I am jolted with pleasure. It is orgasmic and threatens to unlock my knees, but before I can even react it washes through me and we drop out of contact. I blink and everybody grins at me. I look at them.
>
> Then I remember. "My point," I say.
>
> "Five points for a gold," says Liu Wen.
>
> Back into the light, where I find my sensitivity is heightened. Now when the red or black balls come near I feel a tickle of sensation, with the golden ball it is more definite. The silver balls seem colder. I become more aggressive in my play and catch the red ball twice. The explosion is less dramatic than the

golden ball, and I remember to say, "My point," each time…"
(151-152)

In Candas Jane Dorsey's feminist cyberpunk story "Machine Sex,"
the sexual connection is gender-defined and bleak. Angel, a woman in
the boys' world of software development, abused both physically and psy-
chologically by her colleagues, extracts a vicious revenge by inventing a
form of software sex that will give irresistible satisfaction to the male
users—and remove their power over women.

> It was very simple, really. If orgasm was binary it could be pro-
> grammed. Feed back the sensation through one or more touch
> pads to program the body. The other thing she knew about hu-
> man sex was that it was as much cortical as genital, or more so;
> touch is optional for the turn-on. Also easy, then, to produce
> cortical stimuli by programmed input. The rest was a cosmetic
> elaboration of the premise.

> At first it did turn him on, then off, then it made his blood run
> cold. She was pleased by that, her work had chilled her too.

> "You can't market that thing!" he said.

> "Why not? It's a fucking good program. Hey, get it? Fucking
> good."

> "It's not real."

> "Of course it isn't. So what?" (91-92)

Strangely enough, or maybe not so strangely, machine sex has never
taken off in the real world. "Virtual Sex" (that you pay for) nowadays
means a private interactive sex video, with a girl (predominantly, at least,
for the mass market) who may be on the other side of the world, who
can't see you, and who may not feel particularly sullied by the transaction
as long as she keeps her imagination in check. Touchie-feelie versions
will surely come, but since girls are so cheap and so readily available it
seems unlikely that they will be replaced by software. The sexual element
in commercial videogames themselves is controlled by censorship, but to
an extent, undoubtedly, also by the self-censorship of the (predominantly
young, male) market. Female characters proliferate and are ranked as

pinups in the magazines as if they were flesh and blood: but perhaps they are too close to being potent, desirable alter-ego figures (as suggested in Carol Clover's work on gender roles in modern horror films [1992]) for overt sexual behavior to be found appropriate in the gameplay.

In the highly influential 1999 science fiction thriller *The Matrix* (complete with phallic female icon Carrie-Anne Moss), the key to freedom, in a world that is in fact a videogame (though most people don't know it) is to *realize* (to make real) the fact that you have the same power to defy the apparently immutable laws of gravity, time, space as the oppressors who are running the show have. In my own nineties science fiction, the games became the means whereby my characters escaped from the impoverished, alien-occupied, war-torn environment of a future Europe…into other worlds, both natural and fantastic, where most players are punters and obey the rules, but some have magical powers.

> Towards midnight the monkeys entered the city with torches. The battle had been long and varied. Sugreeva was surprised that Angada was still with him. His arm had regrown, but now he'd lost a leg and it appeared not to be regenerating. He also had a grisly head wound. He hopped gamely along on a whole-tree crutch. This monkey was a spider of sorts, but he wasn't very good. The clumsier rule-benders usually avoided the experts. Angada wasn't going to be making any extra kills around Sugreeva. Sugreeva's count in this tranche was respectable, Angada was barely scoring.
>
> Indrajiit still lived. He and Sugreeva seemed well-matched.
>
> The city, oh the terrible sights of that city! Monkeys and demons stumbled through its fire and blood dabbled streets, limbs shattered, eyes blinded, choking in poisoned fumes, witnessing and perpetrating hideous atrocities…
>
> "Whatever turns you on," muttered Agreeva, as they passed a monkey holding up a demon child, to impale it screaming on another's armed mace. "I suppose it's therapy."
>
> (*North Wind*, Jones, 213)

While experiencing a full sensurround illusion, as monkeys and demons acting out the scenes of the Hindu mythic-drama the *Ramayana* or in some other engrossing scenario, the players—and the spiders, players who know how to trick the game's software—are not as divorced from the real world as they seem.

> ...Once you're in the game environment, or when it is in you, you'll run around and jump about in real space, with your physical body, in the arena beyond those doors. It'll seem like a whole world. The sensei will stop you from colliding with anybody, or doing anything to make you conscious of the real-world scruffy hall in there. Remember what a sensei is? The Master Control Program. It keeps everyone in the same envie in contact, by sensing the electrical activity in your brain and converting it into void-forces signals: it's light, but not visible light. Your world will be made of the libretto, the storybook that's been put into your brain. Plus the input from all the players who have entered the same envie, wherever they may be. You understand?
>
> She nodded.
>
> He took her by the shoulders, his touch circumspect and distant, and guided her into position, her back to one of the gates. He showed her a tiny vial, cupped in his palm.
>
> 'What's that?'
>
> 'This is your visor. This is how the games get into your head... Look up.'
>
> She heard the murmur of his voice, felt the liquid touch her eyes. She dropped, into infinite space. She was in the game...
>
> (*Phoenix Café*, Jones, 146-147)

Eventually, games technology would allow my characters to leapfrog the laws of physics and escape from time and space, and gaming technology would become the gateway to instantaneous transit, an interstellar future... But while I was leading them to this point I became more and more interested in the mechanics of the virtual environment.

In print fiction, as on the tv or movie screen, "cyberspace" all too easily becomes another Never-never land. You "jack-in," you swallow the pill, you program the holodeck, and you are in the land of dreams. I had signaled my resistance to this conflation by insisting on physical participation. My cyber-players are not lying in body bags hooked up to the machines, they are running around. The virtual world is brought to life through their muscles and nerves, through chemicals pumped into their blood; by what's happening in that cloud of sparks. But that's metaphor. I wanted to know what was actually going on in the minds of people playing present-day fantasy games, this new dimension of fiction: this storytelling that insists it is not about "stories."

The Game and the Players.

The game goes like this. You meet a girl, a flower-girl... Then you're on a train, urban metro, in a mysteriously empty carriage. You're with your companions, a strong man and a girl; there's another girl on the train in disguise. You are with members of a terrorist resistance group called Avalanche. You used to be a member of an elite Ideological State Militia called Soldier, but you have changed allegiance. Now you're on your way, with the group, to blow up one of the main reactors, and the bad guys will be trying to stop you. Industrial scenery, metal ladders, huge pipelines. Your friends tell you they can see the Mako glow in your eyes. Members of Soldier are exposed to Mako energy when they're recruited, and it never leaves them... Nothing looks futuristic, nothing looks romantically "mediaeval." Maybe the levels of the vast city are a little like the shabbier, lo-rise urban side of present-day Japan. Occasionally, as the game goes on, there'll be intrusions of "reality"—a boss in a suit, who leaves in a helicopter; but this is a world between worlds, just as the names of the characters (your name is Cloud, your companions are called things like Barrett and Jessie, the flower girl is Aeris) come from no particular lexicon. Action, movement. Up the ladders, down the ladders; bright colored arrows show you where you can go. Choreographed fights emerge out of nowhere. Fights are good, they earn you HP. You learn to approach the secondary figures (the extras, who are serving in shops and loitering around the scenery) to request their input, which will be delivered in text boxes, in lines of white type on blue. You remember to look around, and pick up any extraneous items lying in the street, or under the bushes... How is this different from the games you've played before?

Through flashbacks and illuminating dialogue you'll put together the plot. Mako is the energy of the earth (aka Gaia). Shinra's reactors are sucking out this energy to use as their power source, with the result that the earth is dying, polluted, ruined. As the game opens up you'll find yourself in mysterious communication with someone who turns out to be the ultimate bad guy, the boss baddie. His name is Sephiroth. Your connection with him is obviously intimate, but when you find out the truth it's worse than you could possibly have imagined. You are a construct. Sephiroth *made you*. All your memories, even your memory of your mother, even that sojourn in Soldier are false. You'll be devastated when you discover this...and if the theme of horror at the determinist constraints of human nature (or of God's inscrutable dealings with Man) comes to you with the shock of the new, the part of you that is not Cloud will be seriously impressed at the twist in the plot. But that's not all. The first ensemble of characters won't survive for long. Many of your friends will be casualties as the game progresses; one of the most beloved of the main characters (like Obi Wan Konobi, in the first Star Wars episode released) will have to die, in order to serve the Good... Yes, of course it's a battle between Good and Evil. Yes, the ending will satisfy you. It will be cathartic. You will feel, if you have surrendered yourself to the game, as if you've been put through an emotional wringer by the end: but you will feel triumph and peace.

In 2002, fascinated by the RPG phenomenon, I got my teenage son and his friends to answer a questionnaire for me. I'm afraid the names are lost, so I can't attribute all the specific quotes (the first is from my son); in the next passages I'll be discussing their responses. Final Fantasy VII (FFVII) says a fourteen-year-old player, "can only be described as an epic game. It was the first English Final Fantasy game [1-6 only came out in Japan] and was released near the launch of Playstation 2 [Sony's current game console]; it has provided inspiration for many future titles. It went multi-platinum and went down in history as a truly great game. I think this was because of its originality, plot, and gameplay/difficulty curve. It has a little bit of everything. It is basically about a boy and his nemesis, Cloud and Sephiroth, with many other interwinding stories as well."

What's the difference between playing an RPG and reading a book?

"I've read Philip Pullman [His Dark Materials trilogy] and Harry Potter. I think playing Final Fantasy took me about as long as reading Philip Pullman—it was a lot of hours of gameplay. The difference is that in FFVII you have a personal experience when playing and visuals to push the story along and add interest. When two people read the same book they read exactly the same words and meet the same characters. In a Final Fantasy game there are a lot more things to do. You can breed Chocobos [big cartoon birds that look something like dodos: magical steeds], play minigames, collect special items, and defeat special monsters. Often this enhances the plot but it is always optional—only the most dedicated player would completely complete an FF game."

Perhaps only the most dedicated reader could extract the whole meaning from a adult novel of comparable (remember, FFVII is written for young teens) length and sweep. I don't suppose I'll ever "completely complete" *War and Peace,* or *A La Recherche du Temps Perdu.* My young players were, however, aware of a contradiction. One of them told me that you couldn't *ever* put the whole of the Philip Pullman trilogy or *The Lord of the Rings* into a fantasy game, because "it would take far too long. No one could play it." For better or for worse there is something in the print fiction that is not compressible into gameplay. Can this change? Should it change? What exactly is the relationship between a role-playing videogame and any other kind of story?

Steven Poole, author of *Trigger Happy,* describes a games designer, Chris Crawford in Los Angeles, casting his vote for the liberation from linear storytelling. In a fantasy RPG: "the story is generated in real time, in direct response to the players actions…(and) is customized to the needs and interests of the audience…"(105) One of my young players said much the same thing—and no wonder. He's been exposed to Games criticism and theory, through Strategy Guides and Playstation Magazine editorials. He knows what he's supposed to think. Outside the marketing of the games, in real life, we can easily discern that this "liberation" is illusory. There are specific things Cloud can do, there are questions he can ask, that lead him through the events as inexorably as the reader is drawn through the pages of a novel by the incidents of the plot. A game may have many "authors" instead of one (just as in the making of a movie), but there is no slackening of authorial control. Though players sometimes complain about the restrictions imposed on them (Why can't Lara use her bazooka to blast down that door? Why does she have to find the key?), it's clear that they don't even want their freedom—they just like being told that they have it. They still want to be told a story. My young players made an interesting distinction, in this respect, between an exploration/puzzle game like Tomb Raider and the character-oriented Final Fantasy. You might get annoyed about what Lara Croft can't do with her armory: but if Cloud can't do something, *that's part of the story*. When I asked them how they felt about the secondary characters and would it be an improvement if they were able to choose to play from any viewpoint, I was told that you *do* get to understand the other characters, "you get a deeper look into everybody's background." The ensemble is felt to be an essential part of the game, but just as the fixed gameplay is perfectly acceptable, changing your character viewpoint in FFVII would be nonsense: "The protagonist is the protagonist—not the biggest or the best person, but the person the story's about."

It is not surprising that a role-playing fantasy comes several steps nearer to recognizable dramatic fiction than an action game. Tomb Raider, like those tv challenge shows with volunteer contestants, is the apotheosis of a board game—with an inexplicably, unisexually charming animated counter for you to move through the squares. FFVII is something different. But what struck me most, when I started to play, was how deeply familiar I found the set-up. What happens on the screen may have been choreographed by teams of writers and programmers, and discussed in committee like a Hollywood movie, but it *plays* like a child's game of make believe. I remember this! I remember the brief encounters, the vivid action-incidents: where are we? We're on an underground train. We're going to blow up the reactor... You do that, I do this, watch out for bad guys... I remember how these arousal points had to be strung together, and made plausible, by dialogue exposition and retroactive plot development. I know that my novels are still generated in the same way. Themes and plots are off the peg. The story that I write is a transcription of the imagined scenes that I have lived, vividly, in make-believe, as an observer magically able to experience the viewpoint and the emotions of the characters. The plausible, smoothly connected plot, the agreement with the conventions of mimesis in the novel form: these are illusions, laboriously created after the fact. My dialogue, like the dialogue in FFVII, is really a series of instructions, embedded in "conversations" that are mostly inactive matrix. I will craft a whole scene around one line that I know must be spoken, for the sake of my characterization or my plot, and in this supposedly realist scene my characters are no more free to express themselves than Cloud, or Barrett, or Aeris. My triumph is when you, dear reader, can't tell the difference and call the painstaking illusion "natural." And finally, when my story pauses, when one of those climactic action points is over (or about to start), I will relax and gather my forces in the stillness of a passage of pure description. Another quote from one of my teenage players: "You really look forward to cut-scenes, because they are things of beauty…"

In a big, prosperous Victorian-style novel, or in a twentieth-century modern literary fiction almost devoid of adventure, the lineaments of make-believe may be buried deep, but the evolution is always there to be traced. In Fanny Ratchford's critical study of the Bronte children (*The Brontes' Web of Childhood*, 1964), she lays bare the traces of the Brontes' highly colored childhood fantasies of Gondal and Angria in the improbable plots, the lightning vividness and the passion of *Wuthering Heights* and *Jane Eyre*—a famous and rare case of barely contaminated survival. But even Anthony Trollope must have imagined certain intense moments and dwelt on them lovingly, before rubbing them down into conventional form and fitting them into a polished, prolix false-reality. Final Fantasy VII is far from being a great novel, but it plays like the germplasm of a real novel, for the first time made available to the audience. It convinces like a clunky form of AI—that looks like a shoebox and talks like a duck, and yet, discernibly, the team is on the right track this time. Somewhere up ahead there's a game that is as different from a novel as print fiction is different from a stage play, a movie, an epic poem; but no less a valid, complex, and satisfying work of art. It will be a story, of course faked, of course full of deceptive "simplicities" that conceal multifarious tricks of the trade, but much closer to the original, virtual-experience of make-believe. The medium will be the message, but the message will be very old—it just took a long time to get through.

When I asked my teenage players how they saw the games developing in the future, they gave me standard answers. Brilliant graphics, more complicated gameplay, more freedom in the game to do what you want. One boy said "I can see the plot being built by personal decisions a lot more." I think that last idea is an illusion, something they tell the customers to think. Plot will remain plot, characters will remain characters, *story* will remain something that the game player experiences, rather than creates. But I can envisage a time analogous to the change in scientific research wrought by the availability of truly massive number-crunching computer power. So far, the "story" in videogames has been very limited. Gameplay has made a virtue of the necessity to concentrate on action moves, the same way hard sciences used to make a virtue of sticking to the narrow confines of those natural phenomena that would conform to rules of Newton and Euclid. One day soon, the games will offer gameplay that tackles the complex variables of human emotion and motivation, as fluently as SSX handles snowboarding tricks. That won't be to everybody's taste, but it will be an unstoppable revolution.

Society Is Going to Tear Your Technology Apart

Phylogeny recapitulates ontogeny. The games are valuable to society for the same reasons that make play valuable to the individual. From their earliest infanthood (from before birth), children play as rehearsal for life—developing the mechanical routines of movement, grasping objects, getting food into their mouths, moving on to the equally vital rehearsals of language development and social interaction. Throughout history games—for adults and children—have doubled as weapons training, narcotic for the underprivileged, ideological indoctrination, a means of wealth creation, and finally, paradoxically, as a safety valve for the resentments that the masses may feel.

The watchdogs of society should certainly be paying attention to videogames, not so much because a generation of young people (predominantly, not exclusively, the boys) is growing up, has already grown up, addicted to interactive ultra-violent cartoons, but because of the attitude to life that lies behind the spattering gore. Win. Collect tokens. Waste your enemies: that's all there is. The games did not invent the ideology, but they reinforce it, in the lab-rat sense of the term, like nobody's business. Steven Poole suggests as a corrective that players of violent games should be made to suffer the consequences of their actions—if you betray a friend, if you leave your wounded behind, if you kill without reason or do anything in contravention of the Geneva Convention, the game will swing around and give you a heavy shot of instant karma; and you'll know not to do *that* again. Doing wrong should hurt…(Poole, 233-236). It's nice idea, and intrinsically it should be acceptable to the players. (Good deeds are just a different form of currency, aren't they?) I've a feeling you'd have to change the assumptions of your society first, or nobody would buy your sissy game. But I don't know. Dramatic art, as I pointed out in the first passages of this paper, is a morally neutral force with a powerful kick.

At first glance it is quite startling to find the mighty Sony corporation peddling a passionate satire on the evils of nuclear power, validating the Gaia theory through Shinto religious faith, and actively promoting a fairytale in which the horror of the modern human condition is laid bare. You don't belong to yourself, son. You belong to the corporation. Everything you do, everything you think, *everything you think you want*—those aren't your own ideas. The corporation did it to you. You have no free will. Further consideration shows that this is no more than the usual role of fairytale, in modern dress. The tale of the goose girl who turns out to be a princess doesn't foment radical demands for social equality. It keeps the goose girl happy in her lot, because you never know. The lucky ticket doesn't have to come to everyone; it's enough that it is believed to exist. FFVII is one of those stories that acknowledges the evils of the world and redeems them (whether or not they deserve redemption) by weaving them into a rich tapestry of heightened experience: converting them into something that gives pleasure. If fantasy games carry on along this route they might have some effect on the brutal ideology of our century, without any deleterious implication for the profit motive, by the mere act of inoculating the players with complexity.

The first videogame I ever played was "Pong"—aptly described by Michael Dixon, news editor of the Internet magazine *Classicgaming.com* as "tennis that has been cooked down to a kernel. It's one grey bar against another grey bar hitting a grey square. These games were pretty good!" I was rather scandalized at the way the game usurped the tv screen, social hearth of the late twentieth century, but I was impressed, like Mr Dixon, with the instant success of this utterly simple idea, instantly addictive, to a completely non-sporting klutz like me. I've played the games, sporadically, ever since. But when I met "Pong" I was already adult, already set in my ways. The young people who helped me with this paper started playing videogames when they were five or six years old, but even they were already living in a world of books and tv. What will it be like for another generation, "born and bred" so to speak in the virtual world? I don't look forward to any great moral or social change wrought by the games, but I do look forward to a strange time: when people accustomed from childhood to virtual environments, to e-learning, to constructing alternate "selves" and setting them loose in chat rooms will bring to the videogame-art form the sensibilities, both ancient and very new, of make-believe turned into immediate, completely convincing experience. It's said that the work of science fiction is to make the strange familiar and the familiar strange. I often find that what we do is to take some persistent fiction of contemporary human life and turn it into (imaginary) science (Jones, 1999, 114).

One day videogames are going to complete the loop and make the persistent fiction of the fully immersive virtual world into reality.

Works Cited

Blakemore, Colin. *The Mechanics of the Mind.* Cambridge: Cambridge University Press, 1977.

Card, Orson Scott. *Ender's Game.* London: Century Hutchinson (Legend), 1988.

Clover, Carol J. *Men Women and Chainsaws: Gender in the Modern Horror Film.* Princeton, NJ: Princeton University Press, 1992.

Csikszentmihalyi, Mihaly. *Flow: The Psychology of Optimal Experience,* New York: Harper & Row, 1991.

Dorsey, Candas Jane. *Machine Sex and Other Stories*. London: The Women's Press, 1990.

Freud, Sigmund. *Formulations on the Two Principles of Mental Functioning*, translated and edited by James Strachey et al., Standard Edition Volume XII. London: Hogarth Press, 1958.

Friday, Nancy. *My Secret Garden*. New York: Pocket Books, (revised edition) 1998.

Gibson, William. *Neuromancer*. New York: Ace, 1984.

Jones, Gwyneth. *Escape Plans*. London: George Allen & Unwin, 1986.

———. The Aleutian Trilogy, *White Queen*. New York: Tor Books, 1993.

———. The Aleutian Trilogy, *North Wind*. New York: Tor Books, 1996.

———. The Aleutian Trilogy, *Phoenix Café*. New York: Tor Books, 1998.

———. *Deconstructing the Starships*. Liverpool, UK: Liverpool University Press, 1999.

———. *Castles Made of Sand*, 2002

McCrone, John. *Going Inside*. London: Faber & Faber, 1999.

McHugh, Maureen. *China Mountain Zhang*. New York: Tor, 1992.

Poole, Steven. *Trigger Happy, the Inner Life of the Videogame*. London: The Fourth Estate, 2000.

Ratchford, Fanny. *The Brontes' Web of Childhood*. New York: Russell & Russell, 1964.

Jane Yolen: America's Hans Christian Andersen and Briar Rose

An appreciation, for the program notes for Interaction, Worldcon 2005, held in Glasgow, UK, where Jane Yolen was a Guest of Honor.

It's 2005, the sixtieth anniversary of the Liberation, and everybody knows what Auschwitz means. But while Auschwitz killed by the millions, it was possible to live there. Belzec, Sobibor, Chelmno are unfamiliar names, because no survivors have told the tale... Jane Yolen had written one acclaimed and honored Holocaust story (*The Devil's Arithmetic*) for children, when she heard of the first death camp set up in Poland, in November 1941, at a place called Chelmno, on a small country house estate, beside an impenetrable forest of young pines. About three hundred thousand people died there, poisoned by carbon monoxide in the "gas vans." It's hard to be sure: the bodies were burned and all records destroyed... An eerie "castle," surrounded by barbed briars and impenetrable forest, where the unsuspecting inhabitants were put to sleep by monstrous enchantment... From this image Jane Yolen wove the novel *Briar Rose*: combining, unsparingly and daringly, the French fairytale we know as Sleeping Beauty ("La Belle Au Bois Dormant"), with the drama, reconstructed by her American grand-daughter, of a young girl who came living out of that hell. Which is in itself a fairytale. In the real world, no woman survived Chelmno.

A controversial tale of Holocaust survival—*Briar Rose* attracted criticism: it depicts a gay man as a partisan hero and pulls no punches about the fate of Jewish wartime refugees in the land of the free—may seem like a strange way to introduce Jane Yolen, beloved and revered children's writer, whom *Newsweek* has called "America's Hans Christian Andersen." But Jane Yolen is also the writer and educator who declared, in her trenchant study of that enfeebled Disney heroine "America's Cinderella," that "all the folktales have been gutted." She's one of the writers, editors, and scholars who have fought to restore the power of the "fairytales" of Europe that were carried to the New World by fugitives, adventurers, survivors. She knows there is horror, as well as beauty, buried at the root of these fireside traditions, that terrible episodes from history survive in story, and that a dreamlike tale may be the only way unspeakable things can be remembered. Where was the forest where Hansel and Gretel were thrown out to starve? We'll never know. But we can take the tales seriously and read them for what they teach us. It is for her work of radical analysis, of re-membering and re-connecting modern genre with the tough-minded old *marchen*, that I honor Jane Yolen, as much as for her array of awards (including a Nebula, a World Fantasy Award, and the Mythopoeic Fantasy Award for her adult science fiction novel, *Cards of Grief*) and her wonderful collection of children's books.

There's a host of good reasons for making the acquaintance of Jane Yolen, either in person or through her works, but if you love children's books—as I do—you should seek out *Owl Moon*, the thrilling, atmospheric picture book that won a Caldecott Medal in 1988, and of course, at this Worldcon, I have to mention her new Arthurian series, starting with *Sword of the Rightful King*, a tale which has already gained honors in the US as a notable young adult novel.

Out of the Deep: An Early Introduction to Supernatural Horror Fiction

An appreciation of *Great Tales of Terror and the Supernatural*, Eds. Herbert Wise and Phyllis Fraser. First published in *Horror: Another Hundred Best Books*, eds Stephen Jones and Kim Newman. New York: Carroll & Graf, 2006.

I was ten years old when I bought a massive volume of ghost stories at a Jumble sale. I think it cost me sixpence. My mother was horrified. She'd brought her children up to be rational beings: science fiction was entirely acceptable; ghosts, ghoulies, and things that go bump in the night, definitely not! But she didn't take it away. My mother and father never forbade me to read anything (though occasionally they'd implore me to wait until I was old enough to appreciate what I was reading). I didn't know I'd got hold of perhaps the greatest anthology of weird tales of all time, but the stories made a huge impact. I was impressed to the point of wake-up-screaming by "The Rats in the Walls" and "The Dunwich Horror" (H.P. Lovecraft), "The Haunters and the Haunted" (Edward Bulwer Lytton), "The Screaming Skull" (F. Marion Crawford). Oh, that pit, that squirming abyss deep under the old country house, where the dreadful shepherd tends his blobby, white-fleshed, naked livestock… The peevish, defensive tone of the madman who relates the tale of the skull in the cupboard. The unwise experiment of spending a night in that house "situated on the north side of Oxford Street, in a dull but respectable thoroughfare…" Not to mention that intensely horrible face made of crumpled linen. Nobody who has read M.R. James's "Oh Whistle and I'll Come to You My Lad" at a young age will ever sleep easy with an extra, empty bed in the room. It took me longer to realize that I was marked for life by the disquiet of J. Sheridan LeFanu's "Green Tea," by

Professor Guildea's nauseating admirer, by the hinting, shying-away, circling around, Chinese-boxes narrative of Arthur Machen's "Great God Pan," the invisible creatures of "What Was It?" (Fitz-James O'Brien), and "The Horla," (Guy de Maupassant); or the bowl of primroses delivered to a very sick boy, in Walter De La Mare's "Out of the Deep."

I don't much go for pretty ghost stories, so I was less interested in Rudyard Kipling's gentle "They," but I liked "The Ghost Ship" (Richard Middleton) for the sarcasm, and I loved the shapeshifting falcon in Karen Blixen's "The Sailor Boy's Tale." For years I ignored most of the "Terror" section. If there was nothing spooky going on, how was my skin going to crawl? I still agree with the editors: the literature of the tale of pure terror is limited, good supernatural stories are far more plentiful. But children delight in sheer bloody-mindedness, so I relished "Leningen Versus the Ants" (Carl Stephenson) and Richard Connell's "The Most Dangerous Game"; and when I realized what had happened at the punch line (I didn't get it at first), I considered "The Facts in the Case of M. Valdemar" (Edgar Allan Poe) very fine.

Most of the books I loved when I was a child had been handed to me with shining recommendations: from my sister, my parents, the librarian. Either that, or they'd been deemed necessary for my education. I loved *Great Tales* because I had found it and discovered for myself that it was vitally important to me. I don't know why I'm drawn to supernatural horror—just lucky, I guess—but four decades later I still love this book, because I'm experienced enough to know that the stories are not only seminal (*Great Tales* material is buried at the heart of modern horror and coils its mycorrhizoid tendrils everywhere), but also ingeniously, intuitively constructed. A writer's algorithm for creating terror in the reader lies here. You can read them for spine-tingling pleasure today, and you can read them and learn. You may examine the autobiography of Arthur Machen and suspect that his demonic visions of the unthinkable are child-sex-trade in fancy dress; you may spot a barely disguised account of the moral and social consequence of untreated syphilis in Edward Lucas White's grisly "Lukundoo." The causes of horror don't change much from age to age: we fear death, we fear the unforgivable crimes society denies. But the abyssal dimension, the stripping away of rational and material defenses, remains valid.

The horrific side of my writing owes everything to this anthology. You can read on my Ann Halam webpage how the newspaper "ghost" in *The Fear Man*, the book that won me the Children of the Night award for 1994, is a steal from "Oh Whistle and I'll Come To You My Lad," *especially the way it moves*; and how the occult mechanism in the house on Roman Road is sampled from "The Haunters And The Haunted" (the most haunted house in London also features in *Band of Gypsys)*. Arthur Machen's "The Great God Pan" and Lovecraft's "The Rats in the Walls" can both be traced in the circling, shuddering, Chinese boxes narrative of *Phoenix Café*, and M. Valdemar's fate recurs in *Castles Made of Sand*. Most of all I take my lesson from Sheridan LeFanu, whose "Green Tea" doctrine you can find quoted by a character in *Castles Made of Sand*...(the Gwyneth Jones novel with the most overt horror content, so far; though *Phoenix Café* runs it a close second). There are circumstances when the internal and the external world may change places. The horrors of the abyss inside may enter the world we fondly regard as material and a safe refuge from nightmare. Maybe that's a parable, a rich metaphor. Maybe it's the truth of a world to come.

Great Tales of Terror and the Supernatural is a very masterly collection: I could wish there were more stories by women. Charlotte Perkins Gilman's "The Yellow Wallpaper" should be here, and May Sinclair's "Where Their Fire Is Not Quenched"; women more expert in the hidden literature could name many more. But this is the canon: work with it, add to it, transform it to your taste. If you care about weird tales, you need to know this old book. Let the ancient sorceries touch you.

Women Writers in SF:
My Top Ten Books

First published in The Guardian, London UK, December 2003.

The Left Hand of Darkness: Ursula K. Le Guin

Ursula K. Le Guin's famous novel about sex and society is a po-litically sophisticated adventure story in which the non-gendered Geth-enians (who may take on either sex in their fertile period) are as morally complex and recalcitrantly various as the nations of earth. What sticks in my mind, aside from the sheer beauty of this book, is the winter journey at the heart of it, across the Gobrin Ice, and the elegy for an impossible friendship, between Genly Ai, the human male, and Estreven, the *person* whose sexual nature Ai cannot accept.

Where Late the Sweet Birds Sang: Kate Wilhelm

A bleak, fairytale account of human cloning, overtaken by the sci-ence and colored by the disappointment and alienation of the post-radical seventies. In terms of social mores it will seem *dated*, like no other book on this list. But nothing else has changed. This is still a chilling, gripping, and heartbreaking landmark science fiction novel, one of the greatest of its time, about the death of the living world: an sf writer's response to Rachel Carson's *Silent Spring.* You are living in this. Read it and weep.

Up the Walls of the World: James Tiptree Jr

James Tiptree Jr (Alice Sheldon) is famous, or notorious, for the very smart, harsh, and daring psychosexual stories ("Love Is the Plan, The Plan Is Death"; "And I Awoke and Found Me Here on the Cold Hillside") that were hailed as "ineluctably masculine" before she was unmasked. You can find some of them in the collection *Warm Worlds and*

Otherwise. Up the Walls of the World is in a far different mode, a joyous and positive starry-eyed sf, with great characters and *my* sf-outlaws team handling the ethics, instead of the smug might-is-righters, and featuring some of the most convincing non-humanoid aliens (the Tyree fliers) I've ever met.

The Female Man: Joanna Russ

I must have walked past this book about twenty times before I bought it. What's she talking about? I don't want to be a man! And I have a life, you know. I'm not just *female*. The futuristic dominatrix on the original cover, with her naked toyboy crouching on a leash, didn't impress me much, either. Eventually, I was sufficiently bothered to hand over my dollars (I was living in Singapore). It was a revelation. *The Female Man* is experimental, clever, funny, violent; and startlingly prophetic. Also a great source of ideas for techno-green utopia.

Cyteen: C.J. Cherryh

C.J. Cherryh is one of the major space opera authors, always impressive for the realism of her great ships, the fiendish complexity of the intrigue on board and planetside; and for her bizarre, *changed* human characters of the future. *Cyteen* is the magnum opus of a series about a clash of empires, both of them human in origin, differing in their methods, identical in their lust for totalitarian control. It's about domination and slavery, the monsters power makes, and the twisted lives of the children born to perpetuate the dynasties. A dark mirror for the State of the Union, Cold War era, and a horrific science fiction boardroom drama; it will suck you in.

Grass: Sheri Tepper

Sheri Tepper's novels are a big hit with the punters but can be alarmingly didactic: this one's different. *Grass* uses the sf device of a whole planet without habitat diversity to create a stunning pampas world (not a million miles from the oceanic vastness of the Great Plains of the US West) and brings to it a diplomat, horse-lover, passionate human being, whose engagement with the alien uncovers horror and takes over her life. The center of this book is the character of Marjorie Westriding and her encounter with the sublime, but the native sentients are fascinating, the power struggles highly recognizable from our present day: and the landscapes of Grass are truly wonderful. This is what science fiction is all about. Fabulously enjoyable.

Synners: Pat Cadigan

The Queen of Cyberpunk takes on the West Coast Entertainment Industry, in a prescient investigation of the unholy marriage between digital technology and the profit motive. What if we could grab the consumers *directly*, straight to a center in their brains? Just like crack, only it keeps them passive too! Oooh! A ragged band of music video makers, hackers, slackers, tattoo artists, all of them up to their eyes in the 0s and 1s world, must race against time to save humanity (well, the USA; the rest of us are relegated to a paragraph, but get real, this is the West Coast) from an awesome virus, which has "corrupted"—irony fully intentional—this brilliant scheme. Terrific. Some techno-sf dates quickly. *Synners* seems newer and hotter now than in 1991.

Sarah Canary: Karen Joy Fowler

A white woman, mute except for her strange "singing" and seemingly deformed, wanders into a Chinese railway workers' camp, in Washington Territory, 1873. A young man called Chin-Ah-Kin gets the job of returning her to her own community, and so begins a mystical journey, by turns brutal, weird, and lyric. True-life news snippets between the chapters reveal that the actual North West of 1873 was every bit as surreal as the events of the story. It's probably no coincidence that a Shoshone woman named Sacajawea, which means "Bird Woman," was the white men's guide, on Lewis and Clarke's epic attempt to open up this coast—and was treated with the same oblivious, uncomprehending "affection" as is meted out to Sarah Canary. But no historical explanation really covers it. Profound, disturbing, and mysterious, this is a novel about the first encounter with an alien intelligence that goes far beyond genre.

Light Music: Kathleen Ann Goonan

Radio Cowboy and Dana are willing, richly enhanced symbiotes of a living city that floats in the Caribbean. Cut adrift after a pirate attack, they wander through the deserted lands that were the southwestern states, *falling back* into their individual pre-histories and forgetting their vital mission… In ways, *Light Music* is a post-catastrophe novel, where an ensemble of characters discovers how shockingly the world has been changed by a bizarre cosmic plague. In ways it's a tour of the consequences of Lynn Margulis's radical thinking on evolution. This is how we might see ourselves, if we weren't Darwin's slaves: every self a community; every human being a symbiote city, a node in the richly permeable network of life on earth. But there's also a vision of a perfectly possible and *daunting* future. What happens when our organic, wireless, data/DNA information networks are so pervasive, so interpenetrative with the solid world, that we're just part of the software?

Natural History: Justina Robson

There was a time, not so long ago, when I was about the only native-British woman novelist active in science fiction. In spite of Mary Shelley we're extremely rare birds and always have been. But it's not for want of talent, so never say die; maybe this generation will break out. Dear punters, seek for Molly Brown, Liz Williams, Stephanie Swainston (and excuse me for any names I've missed): find out what's happening. Justina Robson is almost a veteran now, with two nominations for the Arthur C. Clarke award, for her near-future *Silver Screen* and *Mappa Mundi*. Her latest novel is a departure into deep space and esoteric hard science, leavened by acerbic humor and left-wing politics; it's one of the big UK sf books of the year 2003 and an optimistic conclusion for my top ten.

Three Best Men

Neuromancer: William Gibson

In 1984 there was a revolution in science fiction, involving a book called *Neuromancer*. The rocketship fantasies of the fifties were finally dead, the galactic empires played out. From here on the only true science fiction was to be about *the future of now;* its hallmarks would be close extrapolation from the present, contemporary referents, political and emotional realism. Times change, and now everyone's writing space opera again, but this book was a revelation and a liberation to me; it has shaped my whole attitude to writing sf.

Lord of Light: Roger Zelazny

Far away places, with strange sounding names… Science fiction is a genre for people who love to travel in the realm of ideas, but also a treasure house of exotic locations and romantic reworkings of real-world human cultures. In *Lord of Light*, humans have become the gods of the Hindu Pantheon, on a distant planet. The story's glorious pulp, but the use of vivid local color is artistry. Classic treatment of an alien locale.

The Gods Themselves: Isaac Asimov

This is a departure for Isaac Asimov, not just a fascinating science-procedural but a real novel of character. It's about a "pump," whereby free energy can be transferred from another universe (what a great scam). The weird aliens in the other universe are remarkable: as convincing as Tiptree's "Tyree fliers."

Imagination Space

An acceptance speech delivered by proxy, at the SFRA conference 2008, Lawrence, Kansas.

Dear People,

First, let me say how sorry I am that I can't be with you in the home of the Apocalypse (as Mark Bould reminded me, temptingly); and that I'm missing my only chance—on the return trip—to use one of my favorite iconic sayings in its original context. I'm not in Kansas, and it's a real shame, but I've given up flying, until further notice—and it'd be a sad thing, after my rash, intransigent pilgrimage through sf criticism, if I dumped a rash, quixotic vow to come and collect the Pilgrim Award.

I'm honored, I'm astonished, I'm very proud to be a recipient of the Pilgrim Award. Despite Adam's kind protestations (I think I initially responded to his phone call by saying, *are you sure this isn't a joke?*), I still feel bemused. What did I do to deserve this? Caused a little trouble, maybe, occasionally, once upon a time (which seems, according to previous Pilgrims' accounts of themselves, to be something of a trend…). But I'm both glad, and sorry, to feel that this is an honor for a particular, *awkward* kind of sf feminism. Not the "girls get to be guys" type of feminism. Nor the equally anodyne "women are morally superior" variety—but the deeply offensive contention that our whole global culture (and specifically, the *future* of our culture) could stand to be a little less masculine. Could stand a strong infusion of the values designated as "weak" and "feminine"—negotiation above conflict, empathy above self-interest, and all the rest of that repertoire. So, I'm glad I'm getting this award as a feminist, and I'm sorry—because I'd much rather that my ideas and opinions were *individual* but mainstream, and didn't merit a special label.

Reviewing books—unless you were an academic or a well-paid columnist—was an esoteric occupation for adults, before the internet created Amazon, but it's been an everyday activity for untold generations of school children. Even the most reluctant kid-critic has to produce a few book reports. I took a liking to the game, as I remember, in what you'd call Senior High School here—praising at length the "cinematic quality and wide-screen feel" of passages of Virgil's *Aeneid*. (My Latin teacher was impressed: a hip buzzword or so from another field does wonders for your credibility.) From there, I passed seamlessly to reviewing the random assortment of novels that arrived (who knows how?) in the offices of a Singapore glossy magazine called *Her World*. I was doing all kinds of freelance journalism, earning a pittance: but the reviewing was the most fun. I couldn't resist the *free gift included* aspect. It was in Singapore, in the seventies, that I reviewed Joanna Russ's *The Female Man*, my maiden foray into science fiction's sexual politics. Sadly, I have no idea what *Her World* readers made of the book—or of my review...

I'm not sure exactly when I got started in sf critical venues. I wrote a book called *Divine Endurance*. As soon as it was published I was *hailed*, by a community that I hadn't known existed. (I'd read a lot of sf, but never been to a convention, never been a "fan" in the technical sense of the term.) Someone must have sent me one of those alluring free gifts, and off I went, reviewing for *Vector*, for *Foundation*, having a troubled, on-and-off relationship with *Interzone*—and later, maybe most significantly, writing regularly for David Hartwell's *New York Review of Science Fiction*. Things became a little heated, from time to time. There was a correspondence with Brian Stableford, in *Foundation*, on the subject of Margaret Atwood's *The Handmaid's Tale*... I remember contacting the then-editor, Edward James, and asking him, is this Stableford chap okay in a scrap? He understands about play-fighting? I won't make him cry or anything? Edward duly assured me that I need have no fear. Mr Stableford was bulletproof.

What I chiefly recall about those gun-slinging years is that I never, or very rarely, chose the books that I reviewed. (The exceptions that spring to mind are Colin Greenland's *Take Back Plenty* and Rachel Pollack's *Unquenchable Fire*.) I would tell the reviews editor, don't worry, just send me whatever you like. I'm not primarily interested in giving people tips on what to buy, and I don't *want* to have advance guidance on what I'm supposed to think. It doesn't matter to me if the novel is obscure. I want to see what's happening in science fiction, I want to take books apart, find out how they work. How they relate to popular culture, sexual politics, global politics. How sf writers are using the constructive or destructive interferences between technology, science, human life… I didn't realize, way back then, that I had crossed the line: I was no longer *reviewing* books, I'd become a *critic*. I didn't even realize how different, in practice and in purpose, those two activities are—and that this blissful ignorance could get me into trouble. I remember the look of hurt astonishment in the eyes of a certain illustrious cyberpunk, when he'd read my review of Neal Stephenson's *Snow Crash*, in the *New York Review*. *But Bruce* (no, I didn't say this, but I thought it)—*surely you noticed that this book positively licks the boots of mindless violence? You're a decent human being, surely you were repelled by Hiro Protagonist's smug, shallow machismo…?*

Those were the days. I wouldn't dream of behaving in the same way now. For one thing, thanks to the internet explosion, it's become almost impossible *not to know* what the community thinks you should think, about any given sf novel… For another, I'm older and a little wiser. I no longer think it's such a great idea to stand alone and shoot the bad guy full of holes in the middle of Main Street. When I was young, I was convinced that writers who took a "bad" review personally were deluded, possibly a little deranged. You can't please everyone. You have to take the rough with the smooth if you put your stuff out there. The reviewers aren't attacking you, or your livelihood! They're engaging in the discourse, you just happen to provide the raw material. Today I understand that reviewing books is a *business*: a tightly woven network of what the Chinese call *guanxi*, sometimes known as "social capital." Friendships, alliances, cliques, "movements," call them what you will, these slightly shifty arrangements have been around forever, and it's up to the individual to decide where to draw the line. Would I silently expect a helpful review from a known friend of my cause? Probably. (And I'd be hurt and astonished if I found that my friend had written, instead, *don't bother with this one, it's only for bleeding-heart girlies…*) Would I accept, or solicit, a novel for review, having decided *before reading it* whether to praise or blame? I hope not; but that's always going to be a slippery slope. The publishers, and the hungry writers, are after one thing: selling the product—and if that means schmoozing reviewers and trashing the opposition a little, *c'est la guerre*. Who can blame them? The gateway that leads to success is very narrow. Reviews are part of the machinery of publishing and "getting noticed." Literary *criticism*, as an independent, disinterested, intellectual endeavor, lives in the chinks. It's up to us keep the game as honest as humanly possible, while accepting we'll never be pure as driven snow.

Science fiction scholarship is something else again, and I didn't know I'd crossed *that* line until the morning I picked up the phone and found I was getting a call from the President of the SFRA. So, well, if I *am* a scholar, an amateur scholar, how did that come about? I promise you I never did it on purpose. I have to thank the late George Hay, that kindly, wonderful eccentric, who pushed me into writing my first major sf article (called "Getting Rid Of The Brand Names," it was published in a US journal called *The World and I*, the year my son was born). Mark Bould, Andy Butler, and James Kneale for running the gaudy explosion of ideas that was the Academic Fantastic Fiction Network and letting me hitch a ride. My bulletproof sparring partner Brian Stableford, for including me in that zany affair in 1989, when he convinced British Telecom to allow a bunch of sci-fi writers into their corridors of power. They even paid us for the privilege—which was rather like the last fascinating secret tribe in the Amazonian Rainforest *paying* the anthropologists, but the anthropologists weren't complaining. Bruce Sterling, who—despite my dreadful betrayal of the Movement over *Snow Crash*—sent me along in his place to a UK conference on the "Governance of Cyberspace" in 1995. Darko Suvin, the renowned sf scholar who wrote to me praising my criticism, when (how can I put this?) I didn't know I existed. Nina Tyolahti, of the University of Oulu, Finland, who invited me, out of the blue, to speak at a marvelous multimedia conference about the Apocalypse (it seems Kansas doesn't have exclusive rights). Charles Brown, David Hartwell, Sherryl Vint, Sarah Lefanu, Andy Sawyer…

Enough names, I'm going to stop there: but you see how it was. I just wandered about at random, a fictioneer getting interested in things; writing "papers" so I could be a fly on the wall at futuristic conferences; finding in myself a long-buried love for academic research, for analysis, for concentrated *thought* about this sorely undervalued art form: the interface between *science* (the stories we tell ourselves about the world out there) and *fiction* (the stories we tell ourselves about the human heart).

For the last several years, I've been very interested in the concept of information space. It's related to information theory, and the Claude Shannon and Warren Weaver seminal work *The Mathematical Theory of Communication*, 1963, which first conceived of information as a measurable physical quantity, like density or mass, expressed in on/off yes/no "bits." Shannon and Weaver's immensely powerful insight was the foundation of our digital age. It offers those "bits," the 0s and the 1s, as the final, logical building blocks of everything, giving us a model of the state of all states that unites the material and the immaterial, mind and matter—neutrinos, zebras, dreams, artificial chromosomes—all made of the same *stuff.* There's a lot of fun in this for sf novelists—especially those who love to see wild fantasies creeping ever closer to the marketplace. But I also like to think of Science Fiction itself as a volume, a set (overlapping with many others), in the vast, contained yet unlimited ocean of information—furnished, with the icons of the genre: Spaceships, Aliens, The End of History, The Battle of the Sexes. Within *this* volume, every significant writer opens up a new Imagination Space, as if adding to a mansion in Second Life: William Gibson's polished future-surfaces, Sheri Tepper's apocalyptic visions, Gwyneth Jones's depiction of Otherness…

It used to worry me that science fiction tells the same story over and over. It used to worry me that *I* tell the same story over and over (until I hit on the idea that I was furnishing my own Imagination Space, with variations on the décor, the style, that belongs to me alone). But science fiction, the art form that takes as its subject, quintessentially, the preoccupations of the present day, can only reflect the state of the world out there. How can we help going round and round in circles? The Great Escape is taking a lot longer than we thought it might when we first dreamed of spaceships. My plan for reducing global levels of machismo is not in a good place either, right now. But we keep on circling, and maybe the horizon keeps moving, by imperceptible degrees. Probably we'll feel the same when there are colonies on Mars, and engineered post-gendered posthumans frolicking in the ice-capped methane seas of Triton. The project's stalled! We're doomed! When are we *ever* going to get out of this damn solar system???

Maybe the work of science fiction scholarship is not sterile taxonomy, nor yet to goad the genre into passing beyond its limits (How can we *progress?* The plan is always the same.), but to forge links, build complexity, refine the details; and to rescue the genuine novelty from each writer's *generic* contribution. Did Gibson's Sprawl books say anything new about AI? Was the king of cyberspace really interested in digital technology? I don't think so. What Gibson gave to sf, his proliferating legacy, was a vision of the future, any future, as, *always, already*, a place of decay: a cabinet of curiosities, a lovingly preserved, make-do improvised, jumble of antiques.

Closer to my own turf, Sheri Tepper, by far the most popular "feminist" writer after Ursula K. Le Guin, has *appalling* visions of the Battle of the Sexes, *horrific* ideas about where male-ordered civilization is headed—enforced and made palatable by the sheer beauty of her world-building. But I notice the details: like those conjoined twins in *Sideshow*—signifying the doomed partnership of male and female human beings, joined at the hip but incapable of working as a team. In her 2007 book, *The Margarets*, they turn up again, as a metaphor for the inseparable mix of good and evil in all humanity... I think that's progress, somehow. Changing hats for a moment (if I were up here in person I would have brought two hats, one for the fictioneer, one for the critic), Istvan Csicsery-Ronay once said that the term "Aleutians" in my "Aleutian Trilogy" must be a conscious or unconscious elision of "Alien." No, not quite. The Aleutians are an *illusion*. If you look closely, you'll see that Gwyneth Jones isn't really interested in "depicting Otherness." On the contrary, she's saying that the great bogey, "The Other," *is an illusion*. Women and men are not so different. You think that's a weird stranger coming towards you. Look again, you're facing a mirror—

Gibson, Tepper, Jones... What about all the rest? How do we choose our material? In *Count Zero*, which I'm not claiming is a great Gibson novel, there's one immensely arresting image. The story is about the mysterious appearance on the market of six *boxes*, very like the evocative collections of random objects created by real world artist Joseph Cornell. The young woman charged with finding the source finally locates the artist. In a semi-abandoned space station an emergent AI, hanging in the midst of the spinning fragments of a lost civilization, is picking out, apparently at random, "a yellowing kid glove, an armless doll, a fat, gold-fitted black fountain pen..." That's what we do. We snatch scraps from oblivion, and canonize them. Maybe our choices are arbitrary. My choices, as I've recounted, have always seemed arbitrary to me. It doesn't matter. It's all connected. Any part can be used to invoke the whole.

Enough of this rambling. Off with my hats, to the gathered SFRA. Thank you again, the Pilgrim award is a very great honor. Thank you for all the work you do, and again, I'm sorry I can't be with you.

Bibliography

A. D. G. *Je Suis un Roman Noir*. Carré noir, 468. Paris: Gallimard, 1983.

Asimov, Isaac. *The Bicentennial Man, and Other Stories*. London: Gollancz, 1977.

———. *The Gods Themselves*. Garden City, NY: Doubleday, 1972.

———. *The Rest of the Robots*. London: D. Dobson, 1964.

———. *I Robot*. Garden City, NY: Doubleday, 1950.

Barnes, John. *A Million Open Doors*. New York: Tom Doherty Associates, 1992.

Barthes, Roland, and Honoré de Balzac. *S/Z*. New York: Hill and Wang, 1974.

Baxter, Stephen. *Voyage*. New York: HarperPrism, 1997.

Bear, Greg. *Blood Music*. London: Legend, 1988. New York: Arbor House, 1985.

Benford, Gregory. *Timescape*. New York: Simon and Schuster, 1980.

Beswick, Norman. "Ideology and Dogma in the 'Ferocious' Sf novels of Sheri S. Tepper," *Foundation* 71 (1997): 32-44.

Bixby, Jerome. 1957. *It! The Terror from Beyond Space* (screenplay). [S.l: s.n.]. Dir. Edward L. Cahn, United Artists, 1958.

Boucher Anthony. "The Quest for St Aquin." In *The Complete Short Science Fiction and Fantasy of Anthony Boucher*. Ed. James A. Mann. Framingham, MA: NESFA Press, 1999.

Bradbury, Ray. "Dark They Were, And Golden-Eyed," In *Thrilling Wonder Stories*, August (1949).

Bujold, Lois McMaster. *Diplomatic Immunity*. Riverdale, NY: Baen Books, 2002.

———. *Paladin of Souls*. New York: HarperCollins, 2003.

———. *Shards of Honor*. New York: Baen Books, 1986. (London, Simon & Schuster, 1998.)

———. *The Warrior's Apprentice*. New York: Baen Books, 1986.

Burke, Edmund. *An Essay on the Sublime and Beautiful*. London: Cassell & Co., 1887.

Butler, Octavia E. *Bloodchild: Novellas and Stories*. New York: Four Walls Eight Windows, 1995.

———. *Dawn*. New York: Warner Books, 1997.

———. *Mind of My Mind*. Garden City, NY: Doubleday, 1977.

———. *Parable of the Sower*. New York: Four Walls Eight Windows, 1993.

———. *Parable of the Talents*. New York: Seven Stories Press, 1998.

———. *Survivor*. Garden City, NY: Doubleday, 1978.

———. *Xenogenesis*. New York: Warner Books, 1988.

Byron, George Gordon Byron. *The Giaour, a Fragment of a Turkish Tale*. London: Printed by T. Davison, for John Murray, (5th edition), 1813.

Cadigan, Pat. *Mindplayers*. New York: Bantam, 1987.

———. "The Power and the Passion" In *Patterns: Stories*. Kansas City, MO: Ursus Imprints, 1989.

———. *Synners*. London: HarperCollins, 1991.

Calder, Richard. *Dead Girls*. London: HarperCollins, 1992.

Capek, Karel, and Paul Selver. *R.U.R. (Rossun's Universal Robots); a Fantastic Melodrama*. Garden City, NY: Doubleday, Page, 1923. (London: Oxford University Press, 1930.)

Card, Orson Scott. *Children of the Mind*. New York: Tor, 1996.

————. *Ender's Game.* New York: Tor, 1985. (London, Arrow Books. Century Hutchinson Ltd, 1986).

————. *Speaker for the Dead.* New York: T. Doherty Associates, 1991.

————. *Xenocide.* New York: Tom Doherty Associates, 1992.

Carey, Jacqueline. Kushiel series.

————. *Kushiel's Dart.* New York: Tor, 2001.

————. *Kushiel's Chosen.* New York: Tor, 2002.

————. *Kushiel's Avatar.* New York: Tor, 2003.

————. *Kushiel's Justice.* New York: Warner Books, 2007.

Carter, Angela. "Company of Wolves." In *The Bloody Chamber.* London: Vintage, 1979.

————. *The Company of Wolves.* New York: Harper & Row (c 1979), 1981.

Carter, Raphael. "Congenital Agenesis of Gender Ideation." In *Starlight 2*, edited by Patrick Nielsen Hayden. New York: Tor Books, 1998.

Charnas, Suzy McKee. *The Vampire Tapestry.* New York: Simon and Schuster, 1980.

————. *Walk to the End of the World.* London: Hodder & Stoughton, 1981. (Original edition, 1974, New York: Ballantine Books.)

Cherryh, C. J. *Cyteen: The Vindication.* New York: Warner Books, 1988.

Clarke, Arthur C. *Childhood's End.* New York: Harcourt, Brace & World, 1953.

————. *Rendezvous with Rama.* New York: Harcourt Brace Jovanovich, 1973.

Clover, Carol J. *Men Women and Chainsaws: Gender in the Modern Horror Film.* London: BFI, 1992. (Princeton, NJ: Princeton University Press, 1992.)

Clute, John, and Peter Nicholls. *The Encyclopedia of Science Fiction.* New York: St. Martin's Press, 1993.

Couégnas, Daniel. *Introduction à la Paralittérature*. Paris: Editions du Seuil, 1992.

Cross, Janine. *Touched by Venom*. New York: ROC, 2005.

Delany, Samuel R. *Nova*. Garden City, NY: Doubleday, 1968.

Derrida, Jacques. *Writing and Difference*. Chicago, IL: University of Chicago Press, 1978.

Dick, Philip K. *Do Androids Dream of Electric Sheep?* Garden City, NY: Doubleday, 1968.

Donawerth, Jane, and Carol A. Kolmerten. *Utopian and Science Fiction by Women: Worlds of Difference*. Syracuse, NY: Syracuse University Press, 1994. (Liverpool, UK: Liverpool University Press, 1994.)

Dorsey, Candas Jane. *Machine Sex—And Other Stories*. Tesseract book. Victoria, BC: Porcépic Books, 1988. (London: Women's Press, 1990.)

Egan, Greg. *Distress: a Novel*. New York: HarperPrism, 1997.

———. *Permutation City*. London: Gollancz, 2008. (First edition, London: Millennium, 1994.)

———. *Schild's Ladder*. New York: EOS, 2002. (London: Gollancz, 2002.)

Elgin, Suzette Haden. *Native Tongue*. Daw Collectors' Book No. 589. New York: Daw Books, 1984.

Emshwiller, Carol. *Venus Rising*. Cambridge, MA: Edgewood Press, 1992.

Feintuch, David. *Challenger's Hope*. New York: Warner Books, 1995. (London: Orbit, 1996.)

Fowler, Karen Joy. *Sarah Canary*. New York: H. Holt, 1991.

Friday, Nancy. *My Secret Garden: Women's Sexual Fantasies*. New York: Pocket Books, 1973.

Gearhart, Sally Miller. *The Wanderground: Stories of the Hill Women*. Watertown, MA: Persephone Press, 1978.

Gibson, William. *Neuromancer*. New York: Ace Books, 1984.

Gomoll, Jeanne. "An Open Letter to Joanna Russ." *Fanthology 87*. (Reprinted from *Sixshooter*; http://www.geocities.com/Athens/8720/letter.htm.)

Goonan, Kathleen Ann. *Light Music*. New York: EOS, 2002.

———. *Queen City Jazz*. New York: TOR, 1994.

———. *In War Times*. New York: Tor, 2007.

Green, Jen, and Sarah Lefanu. *Despatches from the Frontiers of the Female Mind: An Anthology of Original Stories*. London: Women's Press, 1985.

Guevara, Ernesto, and Ann Wright. *The Motorcycle Diaries: A Journey Around South America*. Critical studies in Latin American and Iberian culture. London: Verso, 1995. (First English edition. London: Harper Perennial, 2004.)

Halam, Ann. *Don't Open Your Eyes*, London: Orion Children's Books, 2000.

Haldeman, Joe W. *The Forever War*. New York: Ballantine Books, 1974. (London: Futura Publications, 1977.)

Hall, Sandi. *The Godmothers*. London: Women's Press, 1982.

Haraway, Donna Jeanne. A Manifesto for Cyborgs: Science, Technology, and Socialist Feminism in the 1980s. *Socialist Review*, 80, 65-108 (1985). (In Haraway, Donna. *Simians Cyborgs and Women: The Reinvention of Nature*. London: Free Association Books, 1991, 1995.)

Heinlein, Robert A. *Starship Troopers*. New York: G.P. Putnam's Sons, 1959.

Helford, Elyce Rae. *Fantasy Girls: Gender in the New Universe of Science Fiction and Fantasy Television*. Lanham, MD: Rowman & Littlefield, 2000.

Herbert, Frank. *Dune*. New York: Putnam, 1984.

Home, Henry, and Peter Jones. *Elements of Criticism.* (Sixth edition) Natural law and enlightenment classics. Indianapolis, IN: Liberty Fund, 2005.

Hopkinson, Nalo. *Midnight Robber.* New York: Warner Books, 2000.

Jones, Gwyneth A. The Aleutian Trilogy, *White Queen.* New York: Tor Books, 1993.

———. The Aleutian Trilogy, *North Wind.* New York: Tor Books, 1996.

———. The Aleutian Trilogy, *Phoenix Café.* New York: Tor Books, 1998.

———. *Deconstructing the Starships: Science, Fiction and Reality.* Liverpool, UK: Liverpool University Press, 1999.

———. *Escape Plans.* London: Allen & Unwin, 1986.

———. "Getting Rid of the Brand Names," in *Deconstructing the Starships: Science, Fiction and Reality.* 1999. (First published in *The World and I*, New York: Washington Times Corp., Oct. 1987.)

———. *Life.* Seattle, WA: Aqueduct Press, 2004.

———. "Metempsychosis of the Machine: Science Fiction in the Halls of Karma," *Science Fiction Studies,* 24, 1, 1997.

———. *Seven Tales and a Fable.* Cambridge, MA: Edgewood Press, 1995.

Jordan, Neil, dir. *The Company of Wolves* (story by Angela Carter), 1984.

Kames, Henry Home. *Elements of Criticism.* New York: Johnson Reprint Corp., 1967.

Keller, Evelyn Fox. *A Feeling for the Organism: The Life and Work of Barbara McClintock.* San Francisco, CA: W.H. Freeman 1983.

Kress, Nancy. *Beggars in Spain.* New York: William Morrow, 1993.

———. *Beggars & Choosers.* New York: Tom Doherty Associates, 1994.

———. *Beggars Ride.* New York: Tor, 1996.

Kuhn, Thomas S. *The Structure of Scientific Revolutions.* Chicago, IL: University of Chicago Press, 1970.

Larbalestier, Justine. *Daughters of Earth: Feminist Science Fiction in the Twentieth Century.* Middletown, CT: Wesleyan University Press, 2006.

Le Fanu, Joseph Sheridan. *Carmilla.* Bruxelles: Ed. La Boétie, 1946. (French)

———.*Carmilla.* Prime classics library. Rockville, MD: Wildside Press, 2005. (English)

Le Guin, Ursula K. *The Dispossessed: An Ambiguous Utopia.* New York: Harper & Row, 1974.

———. *The Left Hand of Darkness.* New York: Walker & Co., 1969 (Ace, 1969).

Lefanu, Sarah. *In the Chinks of the World Machine: Feminism and Science Fiction.* London: Women's Press, 1988.

Livingstone, Margaret. *Vision and Art: The Biology of Seeing.* New York: Harry N. Abrams, 2002.

Lovecraft, H. P. "I Wore the Brassiere of Doom" In *The Nursery of Terror*, ed. By Stéphane Bourgoin (In French) Amiens: Inking Pulps, 1987.

———. "The Rats in the Walls." In S. T. Joshi (ed.). *The Dunwich Horror and Others* (9th corrected printing ed.). Sauk City, WI: Arkham House, 1984. (First published Weird Tales, 1924.) Available online at http://www.dagonbytes.com/thelibrary/lovecraft/theratsinthewalls.htm.

Machen, Arthur. *The Great God Pan.* London: Creation Books, 1993. (First published as a short story in 1984.) Available online at http://www.gutenberg.org/ebooks/389.

MacLeod, Ken. *Newton's Wake: A Space Opera.* New York: Tor, 2004.

Margulis, Lynn, and Dorion Sagan. *Acquiring Genomes: A Theory of the Origins of Species.* New York: Basic Books, 2003.

Marigny, Jean. *Le Vampire dans la Littérature du XXe Siècle.* Paris: Champion, 2003.

Matheson, Richard. *I Am Legend.* Garden City, NY: Nelson Doubleday, 1954.

McCrone, John. *Going Inside: A Tour Round a Single Moment of Consciousness.* London: Faber and Faber, 1999. (New York: Fromm International, 2001.)

McDavitt, Jack. *The Engines of God.* New York: Ace Books, 1994.

McHugh, Maureen F. *China Mountain Zhang.* New York: Tom Doherty Associates, 1992.

McIntyre, Vonda N. *Dreamsnake.* London: Gollancz, 1978.

———. "Of Mist, Grass and Sand." In *Fireflood and Other Stories.* Boston, MA: Houghton Mifflin, 1979.

Melzer, Patricia. *Alien Constructions: Science Fiction and Feminist Thought.* Austin, TX: University of Texas Press, 2006.

Merrick, Helen, and Tess Williams. *Women of Other Worlds: Excursions Through Science Fiction and Feminism.* Nedlands: University Of Western Australia Press, 1999.

Mitchison, Naomi. *Memoirs of a Spacewoman.* London: New English Library, 1964.

Moon, Elizabeth. *Once a Hero.* Riverdale, NY: Baen Books, 1997.

———. *Rules of Engagement.* Riverdale, NY: Baen Books, 1998. (Serrano legacy, 5. London: Orbit, 2000.)

———. *Speed of Dark.* London: Orbit, 2002. New York: Ballantine, 2002.

Perkins Gilman, Charlotte. *The Yellow Wallpaper and Other Stories.* Mineola, NY: Dover Publications Inc, 1998. ("The Yellow Wallpaper," first published 1892 in *New England Magazine.*)

Perrault, Charles, and Arthur Rackham. *La Belle au Bois Dormant.* Paris: Librairie Hachette, 1920. (Paris: Nathan, 1990.) (French)

Petrarch. *Sonnets,* translated by Thomas Wentworth Higginson. Boston, MA: Houghton Mifflin, 1903.

Piercy, Marge. *Woman on the Edge of Time*. New York: Knopf, 1976.

Pohl, Frederik. *Gateway*. New York: St. Martin's Press, 1977.

Polidori, John William, George Gordon Byron Byron, and Leopold Voss. *Der Vampyr*. Leipzig: Bei Leopold Voss, 1819.

Poole, Steven. *Trigger Happy: The Inner Life of Videogames*. London: Fourth Estate, 2000.

Pullman, Philip. *The Amber Spyglass*. New York: Alfred A. Knopf, 2000.

———. *The Golden Compass*. New York: Alfred A. Knopf, 1996.

———. *The Subtle Knife*. New York: Alfred A. Knopf, 1997.

Pynchon, Thomas. *Gravity's Rainbow*. New York: Viking Press, 1973.

Reid, Robin Ann. "'Momutes': Momentary Utopias. In Tepper's Trilogies," In *The Utopian Fantastic: Selected Essays From the Twentieth International Conference on the Fantastic in the Arts*, M. Batter (ed.). London: Praeger (pp. 101-109), 1999.

Renard, Christine. *La Mante au fil des Jours: Roman*. Bibliothèque Marabout/Fantastique, 621. Verviers, Belgium: Marabout, 1977.

Reynolds, Alastair. *Revelation Space*. London: VGSF, 2000.

Rice, Anne. *Interview with the Vampire: A Novel*. New York: Knopf, 1976.

Robinson, Kim Stanley. *Blue Mars*. New York: Bantam Books, 1996.

———. *Green Mars*. New York: Bantam Books, 1994.

———. *Red Mars*. New York: Bantam Books, 1993.

———. *The Years of Rice and Salt*. London: HarperCollins, 2002.

Robson, Justina. *Natural History*. London: Pan, 2004.

Russ, Joanna. *The Female Man*. New York: Bantam, 1975.

———. *The Two of Them*. Foreword by Sarah Lefanu. Middletown, CT: Wesleyan University Press, 2005.

———. "When It Changed." First published in *Again, Dangerous Visions*, edited by Harlan Ellison. New York: Doubleday, 1972. Text online at: http://www.scifi.com/scifiction/classics/classics_archive/russ/russ1.html.

Ryman, Geoff. *Air*. New York: St. Martin's Griffin, 2003.

———. *The Warrior Who Carried Life*. London: Unwin Paperbacks, 1985.

Saxton, Josephine. *The Power of Time*. London: Chatto & Windus, 1985.

Scott, Melissa. *Dreamships*. New York: TOR, 1992.

———. *Shadow Man*. New York: TOR, 1995.

Shannon, Claude & Weaver, Warren. *The Mathematical Theory of Communication*. Urbana, IL: University of Illinois Press, 1963. Available online at http://cm.bell-labs.com/cm/ms/what/shannonday/shannon1948.pdf.

Shelley, Mary Wollstonecraft. *Frankenstein, or, The Modern Prometheus*. First editions. London: Printed for Lackington, Hughes, Harding, Mayor & Jones, 1818. (New York: Dutton, 1818.)

Shelley, Percy Bysshe. *Prometheus Unbound. The Text and the Drafts*. New Haven, CT: Yale University Press, 1968.

Shelley, Percy Bysshe, and Lawrence John Zillman. *Prometheus Unbound, a Variorum Edition*. Seattle, WA: University of Washington Press, 1960.

Short, Roger V., and Evan Balaban. *The Differences Between the Sexes*. Cambridge, UK: Cambridge University Press, 1994.

Sinclair, May. "Where Their Fire Is Not Quenched," in *Uncanny Stories*. Ware: Wordsworth Editions, 2006. (First published in 1923, New York: Macmillan Co.)

Sinisalo, Johanna, and Herbert Lomas. *Not Before Sundown*. London: Peter Owen, 2003.

Slonczewski, Joan. *A Door into Ocean*. New York: Orb, 2000.

Spivak, Gayatri Chakravorty. "Can the subaltern speak?" In. *Marxism and the Interpretation of Culture*, Cary Nelson and Lawrence Grossberg (pp. 271-316), 1988.

Sterling, Bruce. "The Cyberpunk Manifesto." Preface to *Mirrorshades, the Cyberpunk Anthology*. London: HarperCollins, 1994.

———. *Schismatrix*. New York: Arbor House, 1985.

Stoker, Bram. *Dracula*. New York: St. Martin's Press, 1999. (First published in 1897, London: Rider and Co.; Westminster, Archibald Constable & Company 1897.)

Sturgeon, Theodore. *Some of Your Blood*. New York: Ballantine Books, 1961.

Tepper, Sheri S. *The Awakeners*. Garden City, NY: Nelson Doubleday, 1987.

———. *The Companions*. New York: EOS, 2003.

———. *The Enigma Score*. London: Corgi, 1989.

———. *The Gate to Women's Country*. New York: Foundation Books, 1988.

———. *Gibbon's Decline and Fall*. New York: Bantam, 1996.

———. *Grass*. New York: Doubleday, 1989.

———. *The Margarets*. New York: Eos, 2007.

———. *Raising the Stones*. New York: Doubleday, 1990.

———. *Shadow's End: a Novel*. New York: Bantam Books, 1994.

———. *Sideshow*. New York: Bantam Books, 1992.

———. *Singer from the Sea*. New York: Avon Eos, 1999.

———. *Six Moon Dance*. New York: Avon Eos, 1998.

Thompson, Hunter S. *Fear and Loathing in Las Vegas; A Savage Journey to the Heart of the American Dream*. New York: Random House, 1971.

Tiptree Jr, James. "The Girl Who Was Plugged In." In *Warm Worlds and Otherwise*. New York: Ballantine Books, 1975.

———. *Up the Walls of the World*. New York: Berkley Pub. Corp., 1978.

———. as Sheldon, Racoona. "The Screwfly Solution" in *Her Smoke Rose Up Forever*. New York: Science Fiction Book Club, 2004. (First published in *Analog Science Fiction/Science Fact*, June 1977.)

Tiptree Jr, James, and Robert Silverberg. *Warm Worlds and Otherwise*. New York: Ballantine Books, 1975.

Tuttle, Lisa. *A Spaceship Built of Stone and Other Stories*. London: Women's Press, 1987.

Viard, Henri, and Bernard Zacharias. *Le Mytheux*. Série noire, 1110. Paris: Gallimard, 1967. (French)

Weber, David. *On Basilisk Station*. Riverdale, NY: Baen Books, 1993.

———. *The Honor of the Queen*. Honor Harrington Series. New York: Baen Books, 1993. (London: Earthlight, 2000.)

Wells, H. G. *The War of the Worlds*. London: W. Heinmann, 1898.

Wilhelm, Kate. *Where Late the Sweet Birds Sang*. New York: Harper & Row, 1974.

Wise, Herbert Alvin, and Phyllis Cerf Wagner. *Great Tales of Terror and the Supernatural*. New York: Modern Library, 1944. (London: Hammond, 1957.)

Wittig, Monique. *Les Guérillères*. Paris: Éditions de Minuit, 1969. (French)

———. *Les Guerilleres*. New York: Vanguard Press (first English ed.), 1969.

Wolfe, Gene. *Calde of the Long Sun*. New York: Tor, 1994.

———. *Exodus from the Long Sun*. New York: Tor, 1996.

———. *Lake of the Long Sun*. New York: Tor, 1995.

———. *Nightside of the Long Sun*. New York: Tor, 1993.

———. *Return to the Whorl*. New York: Tor, 2001.

Yolen, Jane. *Briar Rose*. New York: T. Doherty Associates, 1992.

———. *Cards of Grief*. New York: Berkley Pub. Group, 1984.

———. *The Devil's Arithmetic*. New York: Puffin Books, 1990.

———. *Sword of the Rightful King: A Novel of King Arthur*. San Diego, CA: Harcourt, 2003.

Yolen, Jane, and John Schoenherr. *Owl Moon*. New York: Philomel Books, 1987.

Zelazny, Roger. *Lord of Light*. New York: Avon Books, 1969.

Index

Author Biography

Gwyneth Jones, writer and critic of science fiction and fantasy, is the author of many novels for teenagers, mostly using the name Ann Halam, and several genre novels for adults, often addressing feminist, popular culture and gender issues. Her critical essays and reviews are collected in *Deconstructing the Starships*, 1999. Recent honors include the P. K. Dick award for *Life*, published by The Aqueduct Press, and the Pilgrim award for science fiction criticism. She's done some extreme tourism in her time, and enjoys mountain walking, playing with her websites, and watching old movies. Her latest novel is *Spirit, or The Princess of Bois Dormant* (Gollancz UK). She lives in Brighton UK.

Other Gwyneth Jones books from Aqueduct

Life

Winner of the 2004
Philip K. Dick Award
Short-listed for the 2004
James Tiptree Jr Award

"[T]his is a rich, potent, challenging, and original novel which does exactly what we always demand of the very finest science fiction: it makes us think about ourselves, about our future and how we want to be."

~ Paul Kincaid, *Foundation*, Autumn 2005

"Jones's genius here…is in the many layers and textures of experience she gives us, her recognition that great discoveries, great science, great art—like great sorrow and tragedy—take place against the minutiae of our days."

~ James Sallis, *Magazine of Fantasy and Science Fiction*, December 2005

"Remarkably rich and sophisticated…*Life* [is] a bold but accurate title for a work that anchors itself in the commonest meaning of the term (the old 24/7) and subtly weaves its way toward the larger scientific and philosophical versions that we tend to give capital letters and a lot more respect."

~ *Locus*, November 2004

Conversation Pieces, Volume 25

The Buonarotti Quartet   Stories by Gwyneth Jones

In Gwyneth Jones's White Queen Trilogy, the reclusive female genius called Peenemunde Buonarotti invented the instantaneous transit device of the same name. In the four stories of *The Buonarotti Quartet*, Gwyneth Jones shows us humans traveling via the device to alien worlds and situations. Some are diplomats, some are extreme travelers, some are prisoners. All are in for a rough, wild ride.

Forthcoming from Aqueduct Press: 2010

The Secret Feminist Cabal: A Cultural History of SF Feminisms
by Helen Merrick

"…a terrific read. Here you'll find everything you always wanted to know about women in fandom, women in publishing, women as writers: why "James Tiptree Jr" was thrown out of the legendary Khatru symposium on gender; what really happened in the ancient UK scandal of Femizine, the "all female" fanzine that wasn't. . .with the added value that the snippets of tasty vintage gossip are woven into a rich fabric of discourse."

~ Gwyneth Jones

"An amazing book for cultural analysts of all kinds… This is a story-laden feminism, one that weaves together not only the historical contexts for women's presences in sf and the varieties of feminisms women did and did not espouse, but tells us HOW all this happened."

~ Katie King

Narrative Power: Encounters, Celebrations, Struggles
edited by L. Timmel Duchamp

Inspired by the WisCon 32 Narrative and Politics panel, which discussed how ideology infuses narrative and thus often blindsides writers, scholars, and intellectuals whose work expresses itself as narrative. In this volume, Samuel R. Delany, Lance Olsen, Andrea Hairston, Wendy Walker, Carolyn Ives Gilman, Eleanor Arnason, Rachel Swirsky, Claire Light, and other writers and scholars take a close look at narrative politics and the power of narrative.

The Universe of Things: Short Fiction
by Gwyneth Jones

The stories in the *Universe of Things* span Jones's career, from "The Eastern Succession," first published in 1988, to the just-published "Collision." Each opens a window into a richly depicted culture in which its intelligent, resourceful characters struggle to make sense of the mysteries of their world.